HF

Antarctica

ANTARCTICA

Exploring a Fragile Eden

Jonathan and Angela Scott

Illustrations by the authors and Mishi Bellamy

Collins
An imprint of HarperCollins Publishers
77–85 Fulham Palace Road
London W6 8JB
www.collins.co.uk

First published in 2007

10 9 8 7 6 5 4 3 2 1

ISBN-10 0-00-718345-3
ISBN-13 978-0-00-718345-6

Collins uses papers that are natural, renewable and recyclable
products made from wood grown in sustainable forests.
The manufacturing processes conform to the environmental
regulations of the country of origin.

Edited by Caroline Taggart
Design and layout by Emma Jern and Liz Sephton
Repro by Dot Gradations Limited
Printed and bound in Italy by L.E.G.O.

To Neil and Joyce Silverman
for their kindness and generosity
over many years

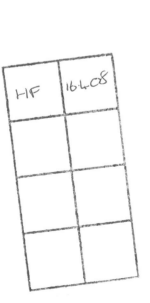

Mixed Sources
Product group from well-managed
forests and other controlled sources
www.fsc.org Cert no. SW-COC-1806
© 1996 Forest Stewardship Council
FSC

Contents

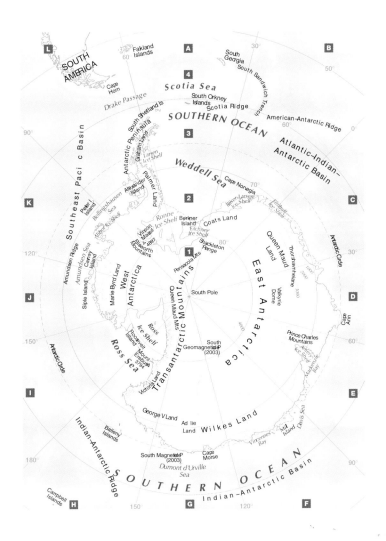

Maps

Scotia Sea

Ushuaia

Drake Passage

South Orkney Islands

Cumberland Bay
South Georgia

Elephant Island

Point Wild

South Shetland Islands

Deception Island

Paulet Island

Snow Hill Island

Robertson Island

Weddell Sea

Anvers Island

Palmer Station
Neumayer Channel
Torgersen Island
Gerlache Strait
Lemaire Channel

Antarctic Peninsula

Vashel Bay

SHACKLETON'S "ENDURANCE" TRIP

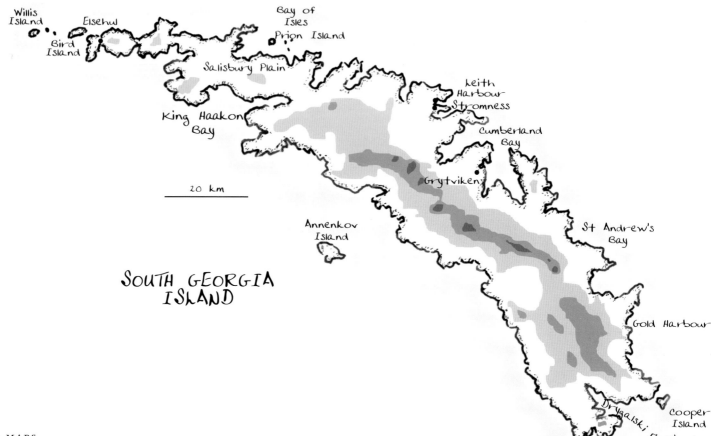

Willis Island

Elsehul

Bird Island

Bay of Isles

Prion Island

Salisbury Plain

Keith Harbour
Stromness

King Haakon Bay

Cumberland Bay

Grytviken

20 km

Annenkov Island

St Andrew's Bay

SOUTH GEORGIA ISLAND

Gold Harbour

Drygalski Fjord

Cooper Island

Jason Islands

Carcass Island

Keppel Island

Pebble Island

Saunders Island

Westpoint Island

Port San Carlos

Volunteer Point

Berkeley Sound

Teal Inlet

Stanley

Port Howard

No Mans Land

EAST FALKLAND ISLAND

Passage Island

WEST FALKLAND ISLAND

Falkland Sound

New Island

Goose Green

N

Weddell Island

Lafonia

Staats Island

Port Stephens

Tea Island

30 km

Bird Island

FALKLAND ISLANDS

Ross Ice Shelf

Scott's Hut at Hut Point

Scott's Hut at Cape Evans

Mt Terra Nova

Shackleton's Hut at Cape Royds

Cape Crozier

Mt Terror

Mt Erebus

10 km

Ross Sea

ROSS ISLAND

Introduction

Mention the word Antarctica to most people and they think of a massive expanse of ice at the bottom of the world, conjuring up visions of brave men in winter clothing and heavy beards festooned with icicles. This image owes much to the legacy of the 'heroic age' of explorers – such as Amundsen, Scott and Shackleton, expedition leaders who carved out a name for themselves in the first two decades of the twentieth century in their quest to be first to the South Pole. In his wonderfully understated way, the mountaineer Sir Edmund Hillary captures perfectly the stoicism that men like these had to call on to survive. Discussing the ill-fated expedition that left Shackleton's men marooned on ice floes in the Weddell Sea, he wrote:

'Danger is one thing, but danger plus extreme discomfort for long periods is quite another. Most people can put up with a bit of danger – it adds something to the challenge – but no one likes discomfort.'

Despite the pain and suffering experienced by the early explorers, many of them returned again and again to savour Antarctica's starkly beautiful landscape. Antarctica became a symbol of 'something other', of life distilled to the bare essentials. As the American novelist Thomas Pynchon put it, 'Everyone has an Antarctic' – that inner white space of clarity and reflection that you feel when you visit Antarctica.

Even today, the continent helps to instil a sense of wide-eyed wonder at our world: inhospitable yet alluring, bigger and more powerful than man and his inventions. It is not just the whiteness. The appeal of Antarctica is multi-faceted: the landscape, wildlife and history combine to make a journey there a unique experience. To visit is like turning the pages of a classic piece of literature, each day revealing a new layer of awe and complexity. Antarctica swamps the senses: the excitement of glimpsing your first towering iceberg, being stunned into silence by the raucous braying of a penguin colony, witnessing a pod of killer whales knifing through the water in pursuit of prey – and the chance to enter the world of the explorers as you step inside one of the historic huts.

My own interest in Antarctica was fuelled primarily by my love of wildlife. Having spent much of the past 30 years as a wildlife photographer in some of Africa's most spectacular wilderness areas, I saw Antarctica as the ultimate challenge, the all-pervading whiteness of snow and ice replacing the russet earth colours of wide open savannas, with animals and birds that spend much of their time at sea rather than on land: an abundance of penguins and seals to rival the sight of a million wildebeest and zebras on migration.

But over and above the lure of the wildlife, my fascination with the southern continent stretches back to my childhood. Born with a name like Scott, how could I fail to notice those other Scotts – the wildlife artist Sir Peter and his famous

Shackleton

Amundsen

Scott

Mawson

father, 'Scott of the Antarctic'. Both men achieved international acclaim in very different ways, with Peter making a name for himself as a conservationist and wildlife artist. Like him, I had lost my father when I was only two years old. An architect and a talented artist himself, my father loved Peter Scott's portrayal of the English countryside – and so did I; a signed print of one of his trademark wildfowl paintings hung on our dining-room wall.

When I was a child, Captain Scott's epic journey to the South Pole and his ill-fated trek home were still the stuff of comic-book heroes and I remember being enthralled by his story (which is discussed more fully in Chapter 9). But it was Peter Scott who inspired me to believe that I too could find a way of turning my passion for wild creatures into a career. By chance, when Angie and I were given the opportunity to travel to the Antarctic for the first time aboard the

Lindblad Explorer or 'little red ship', as she was fondly known, we discovered that this was the same ship in which Peter Scott had made so many journeys around the world as a naturalist and lecturer, including visits to the Antarctic. We were captivated the moment we set foot in Antarctica and have returned there more than a dozen times over the last 15 years.

· · · ● · · ·

The story of Antarctica is both ancient and modern, an island continent covered by ice. There are rocks buried beneath the surface of the icecap in Greater (East) Antarctica that are 3.8 billion years old, while those underlying much of Lesser (West) Antarctica are a mere 150–200 million years old. Yet this ancient continent wasn't even recorded as having been sighted until 1820 – less than 200 years ago – despite the fact that the ancient Greeks had prophesied the existence of a great southern continent some 3,000 years earlier.

Antarctica and its icecap measure 14 million sq. km (5 ½ million square miles), and if you were to film the region from space with a time-lapse camera it would appear to pulse with energy as the pack ice expanded and retreated, doubling the size of the continent in winter. But the wonder of Antarctica is defined as much by the Southern Ocean that surrounds it as it is by the ice. Virtually all the wildlife here gains sustenance from the ocean, coming ashore only during the brief Antarctic summer to breed. The handful of sub-Antarctic islands that fall within the Antarctic Convergence – the circular belt of water with a characteristic temperature and chemical composition, in which the cold southern waters meet the warmer Atlantic, Indian and Pacific waters – are biologically part

of what we know as Antarctica, offering a refuge and breeding site for many of the animals and birds that live in this region.

To tell the story of Antarctica I have used the journey that Angie and I have taken so often to reach the continent: there is a natural progression mapped out by the very process of travelling south, which also reflects the discovery of the lands leading to the frigid heart of Antarctica. The quickest and most direct route is to head for the Antarctic Peninsula from the tip of South America, a journey of nearly 1,000 km (600 miles). In this respect Ushuaia in Argentina – the southernmost city in the world – has for many become both the beginning and the end of an expeditionary cruise. Ushuaia has a charm all its own, a mosaic of colourful box-like wood-framed buildings crammed against the forested flanks of the surrounding mountains, a frontier town where the ambitions of travellers and adventurers meet at the edge of the great Southern Ocean and are best celebrated with a meal of fine seafood and a generous glass of blood-red Argentinian Malbeck. Monuments and propaganda mingle here and it is plain to see that Argentina is anxious to keep its claim to the Islas Malvinas (as the Falkland Islands are known in this part of the world) alive, along with its sovereign right to a slice of Antarctica itself.

Many of the trips we have undertaken have made a detour to include the Falklands – the first opportunity to see penguins and albatrosses – before heading to South Georgia and then onwards to the Antarctic Peninsula. In this way one can see how life has adapted to progressively colder climes, and how the early explorers must have struggled to make sense of what lay to the south of the pack ice that kept them at bay. Of that hardy breed of men, Captain James Cook stands out. He was the first person to circumnavigate Antarctica in 1775, discovering the island of South Georgia in the process. Indeed, it was he who gave the pack its name, remarking in 1794, 'We discovered field or pack ice…', wisely deciding that it was something to go round rather than force a way through, and that when weighed against the prize of being first to sight the fabled Southern Continent the risks it posed were too great. Cook must also take credit as the man who finally laid to rest the idea that a habitable and fertile southern continent was yet to be discovered. Rounding the southern tip of the 'Isle of Georgia' he found that his ambition of setting eyes on the continent itself had been thwarted. Nonetheless he must have felt a degree of satisfaction as he wrote in his journal:

'The intention of the voyage has in every respect been fully answered, the Southern Hemisphere sufficiently explored and the final end put to the searching after a Southern Continent.'

Though Cook was to be proved wrong, in as much as there was a southern continent, his intuition as to what it might be like was correct – it was a paradise for seabirds and other wild animals, not humans.

When Cook's charts and journals were published they galvanized people into action. Before long, explorers gave way to sealers and whalers who quickly plundered the region, particularly the seas around South Georgia, the South Orkneys and South Shetlands, slaughtering millions of seals first, then whales. In recent years the fur seal population has recovered, but the heyday of the great whales may be gone forever and the issue of whaling continues to inflame public sentiment.

South Georgia has been described as the Serengeti of the Southern Ocean and I well remember when we made our first trip to the Antarctic Peninsula being told time and again by people who should know, 'You must visit South Georgia if you want to see Antarctic wildlife at its most spectacular.' It is almost as if the ark of biblical times had washed up on the shore of this remote island and opened its doors one last time – here you find fur seals in their millions, hundreds of thousands of elephant seals, four species of penguins, nesting wandering albatrosses and a variety of whales. South Georgia may not have as much 'ice' as the Antarctic continent, but it certainly has the wildlife, as we will see in Chapters 3 and 4.

Some cruise vessels try to continue south as far as the Antarctic Circle – the parallel of 66°33'S on which for one 24-hour period in each year the sun remains above the horizon in summer and is hidden in winter (south of the circle it is dark 24 hours a day in winter) – considered by many to be symbolic of entry into Antarctic waters. If you are a birder, there are a whole array of 'lifers' to be recorded on your journey south, from the tiny Wilson's storm petrel that flits across the water's surface like a butterfly to the wandering albatross with its 3.5-m (11-ft) wingspan. This is a time, too, to reflect on the importance of the pack ice to the biology of the Southern Ocean, the way a seemingly lifeless entity provides sanctuary to some of the unseen denizens of the sea – the microscopic plants and animals that are at the heart of the ecosystem, nourishing the tiny shrimp-like krill on which many of the penguins, seals and whales feed.

Cook's ships HMS Resolution and HMS Adventure were the first vessels known to have crossed the Antarctic Circle, on 17 January 1773. Over 200 years later, it is still an extraordinary experience to be aboard a ship when it crunches its way through the pack ice until forced to turn tail or risk suffering the fate of the Titanic, a

reminder of just how unforgiving and powerful nature can be. It is at times like this that you feel humbled by the landscape, conscious that Antarctica is truly the last great wilderness and an alien environment for us human beings.

You can also approach Antarctica from the other side of the world, striking out from Australia or New Zealand (both about 2,500 km/ 1,500 miles away). This is sometimes referred to as the 'historic gateway' to Antarctica, as it was the route chosen by many of the early explorers. Both countries are keenly aware of their Antarctic

King penguin colony, St Andrew's Bay, South Georgia. Colonies are occupied throughout the year.

heritage and the significant role they must continue to play in helping to preserve the southern continent.

Visitors embarking from this side of the continent will have more days on the ocean, which may not suit everyone, but that is a small price to pay for the chance to visit the Ross Sea and a variety of sub-Antarctic islands such as Macquarie, Auckland and Campbell. Angie and I recently completed a semi-circumnavigation of Antarctica to explore the Ross Sea region. We were filled with excitement at the thought of landing at Ross Island and visiting the huts – preserved virtually untouched – that were used by Scott and Shackleton as their base of operations for their attempts to reach the South Pole. We were also able to pay homage to the emperor penguin, largest of the penguin tribe, which breeds on the fast ice at some 40 remote colonies scattered around the continent. These areas are inaccessible to all but the most intrepid – or those on board an icebreaker with a helicopter capable of landing on the ice.

The emperor's story is not only remarkable in the biological sense, but is inextricably linked to the fates and fortunes of Scott's 1911 expedition. In the dead of winter, three of Scott's men – Wilson, Cherry-Garrard and Bowers – set out to try to reach an emperor penguin colony at Cape Crozier, 107 km (67 miles) away to the east. The journey was to become a living nightmare: the three men man-hauled two sledges with food and equipment weighing 343 kg (750 lb) for five excruciating weeks, enduring temperatures of below –45°C (–49°F) in order, as it turned out, to collect a mere three penguin eggs. Miraculously, the men contrived to remain cheerful in the most miserable of conditions.

It seems the greatest irony that Scott's men should almost have lost their lives in the pursuit of a better understanding of the emperor penguin – a bird that is supremely adapted to survive conditions that humans are so plainly ill-equipped to endure. In the end the three hard-won eggs did not provide the breakthrough Wilson – the naturalist of the party – had hoped for, though the episode did yield one of the classic works of travel literature, Cherry-Garrard's The Worst Journey in the World. Both of Cherry's companions were destined to perish with Scott on their way back from the South Pole only eight months later.

Scott became larger in death than in life, while the charismatic Shackleton went on to earn a reputation as an outstanding leader. Recently there has been a massive revival in interest in polar travel, particularly where Antarctica and Shackleton are concerned, and this has helped us to recognize some of the unsung heroes of the era – men such as Frank Wild and Tom Crean, who served with both Scott and Shackleton, and New Zealander Frank Worsley, a brilliant navigator who saw Shackleton safely across the open sea to South Georgia.

Another name that has recently gained wider recognition is that of the Yorkshire-born Australian geologist and explorer Douglas Mawson, who was a member of Shackleton's 1907 expedition and continued to be a tireless advocate of Australia's Antarctic interests right up to the time of his death in 1958 – the last surviving leader of the 'heroic age', and an early campaigner for the need to adopt a conservative approach to Antarctica's resources.

Antarctica is defined by the exploits of men such as these. You can feel their presence out on the ice, and you shudder with respect and admiration at their achievements and their failures. Their stories have a sense of unreality to them – rather like the continent itself.

The challenge now is no longer exploration, but

Douglas Mawson

preservation. The only thing that lies between Antarctica and exploitation is the Antarctic Treaty, which was signed in 1959 by twelve states and seeks to have Antarctica preserved for peaceful purposes, with science and strictly controlled tourism the only industries. All territorial claims are held in abeyance – neither validated nor denied – in the hope that, given time, humankind will come to realize that Antarctica is of vital importance to the overall health of our planet, and that it is wiser to leave the slumbering white giant alone, rather than plunder its resources for short-term gain. The ice cover of Antarctica represents nearly a tenth of the Earth's surface and this is the place where most of the world's heat loss occurs, acting like a giant reflector. The extreme differences in temperature between the polar regions and the tropics cause enormous transfers of energy, providing the engine that drives the world's climate. It is only relatively recently that we have begun to realize this – Antarctica has seemed so remote and frigid for so long that this important role could hardly have been guessed at...

But when visiting Antarctica the thought of exploitation is never far from one's mind – the millions of seals and whales that were

slaughtered here are a stark reminder of how quickly a pristine wilderness can be turned into a wasteland. Walking around the abandoned whaling stations of South Georgia you stumble over whale vertebrae the size of truck tyres. These are mournful places that echo with the sounds of human greed.

With the price of crude oil reaching record highs and other non-renewable resources in ever-diminishing supply, there can be no certainty that Antarctica will remain a wilderness for ever. Hopefully our photographs and drawings will help to evoke something of the magic of this unforgettable land, because there is no doubt that a disturbing trend is emerging. Pristine Antarctica is beginning to seem unexpectedly vulnerable.

This far south it is easy to be lulled into a comfortable sense that all is well with the world; that the only worry is to ensure you don't get caught out in the chill with nowhere to hide. When you travel within these regions, whether on an expedition overland or by cruise ship, the overriding impression is of a place distanced from any possibility of human impact, a land of such austere and frigid intensity that it appears at first glance to be indestructible. Yet this is a seductive illusion, Antarctica's beguiling beauty shielding the harsh realities of the changes that are being wrought – often unseen but now increasingly noticed – in the ocean, beneath the ice and in the air. We can no longer deny that this is so – nor that it would be both unforgivable and inconceivable to allow this icy world to melt away through our negligence.

Jonathan and Angie Scott
February 2007

**Katabatic winds blowing up a storm
along a glacier at Neko Harbour,
Antarctic Peninsula.**

CHAPTER I

Discovering Antarctica

Antarctica is the most remote and hostile of continents, an icy waste of which 80 per cent is still unexplored. The bulk of the continent is so cold, so waterless, so impoverished in soil and nutrients that only two flowering plants – the Antarctic hairgrass and the Antarctic pearlwort – grow here, and even they are confined to the shores of the western side of the Antarctic Peninsula, where conditions are less extreme. Apart from this the flora is restricted to small or microscopic plants that do not produce seeds – mainly lichens and mosses, as well as a number of fungi and liverworts that eke out a Spartan existence on the dry surfaces of bare rock (just 0.4 per cent of the continent) with the green and reddish tint of algae in places colouring the snow. Many of these tiny plants flourish close to bird colonies where droppings or 'guano' provide them with much-needed nutrients.

Animal life fares little better: the largest terrestrial predator is a wingless midge, and the mosses and algae provide ideal living quarters for other tiny invertebrates. The only creatures of any size that make Antarctica their home during the icy darkness of winter are emperor penguins that breed here and the Weddell and Ross seals that sometimes haul their streamlined bodies from the oceans to rest on the ice.

In many ways, then, Antarctica resembles an alien planet, life pared down to the bare essentials required to survive in an ice age – no indigenous people was ever hardy enough to conquer its frozen wastes; there are no artefacts or ancient history to embellish its austere beauty. The closest human populations to Antarctica live along the fringes of South America and New Zealand, and though the Alacaluf of Tierra del Fuego and the Maori of New Zealand may have tried at some point to venture this far south – or been blown off course – they would not have been

able to survive the extremes of climate for long. Little wonder, therefore, that Antarctica was the last of the seven continents to be discovered and the Southern Ocean the final ocean to be explored. It is only within the past hundred years that people have begun to see beyond Antarctica's frigid façade and to understand the unique role the continent plays in regulating our world's climate and weather systems and its status as a world heritage site.

But Antarctica hasn't always been trapped in the grip of a perpetual ice age at the bottom of the world. If you look carefully at an atlas, you can imagine the continents as parts of a gigantic jigsaw floating among the world's oceans. If you were to cut them out and move them around you would find that the edges of some of these landmasses (particularly if you use the continental shelf as the boundary) fit together almost perfectly. As early as 1596 cartographers noted that Africa and South America had once been joined together, but it wasn't until 1885 that Edward Suess, an Austrian geologist, named this supercontinent Gondwana, meaning land of the Gonds. The Gonds were an aboriginal tribe living in central India, where fossils that are common to all the southern-hemisphere continents have been discovered, indicating that they were once part of the same landmass. At the time no one knew the mechanism by which the continents move over the Earth's molten core: that they float like giant rafts on eight or nine large continental plates, which sometimes separate, sometimes converge, dividing the ocean floor and creating a volatile boundaries where volcanoes and earthquakes abound. This process has been going on for 4 billion years, gradually moving the continents and oceans to their present positions.

Antarctica was the keystone of Gondwana around which South America, Africa, India,

Australia and New Zealand fitted. When the supercontinent began to break apart 150 to 210 million years ago (mya), Antarctica lay at a more equatorial latitude and enjoyed more temperate conditions. In fact it was teeming with life, a green land dotted with plains, rivers, lakes and marshes surrounded by lush vegetation of palms, ferns and conifers where dinosaurs roamed. The first continents to separate were Africa and South America, followed by India (the Himalayas were formed when India 'hit' Asia). Gradually Antarctica itself broke free and moved

Taylor Valley, Victoria Land. Antarctica's dry valleys are a mosaic of rock, gravel and ice covering an area of around 3,000 sq. km (1,1600 square miles), deserts where for at least 2 million years no rain has fallen.

south, with a deep seaway forming between it and India around 100 mya. Australia and New Zealand then broke away around 40 mya; by 35 mya Antarctica was settling into its current position over the South Pole and soon ice-sheet formation was underway. The final step was the separation of the Antarctic Peninsula from South America, which occurred about 23 mya, opening the dreaded Drake Passage – 900 km (600 miles) of open water which during rough weather can ensure two days of misery for those prone to seasickness, though more often than not in summer it is as calm as a lake.

With Antarctica freed from the other continents, the deep-water, circumpolar current or west wind drift evolved, propelled by air masses driven clockwise by the Earth's rotation, isolating it from the warmer ocean water and more temperate weather to the north. The big chill had begun, smothering the southern continent beneath an ice sheet that is 2.8 km (1 ¾ miles) thick at the Pole. Cycles of dark and light became more seasonal, with only the hardiest, most cold-adapted species able to survive as Antarctica slipped into an ice age that has lasted for 40 million years. Today fossils of a 10 m (33 ft) crested dinosaur that once lived here – in Australia, too, and probably South America – are reminders of those times, along with the remains of the 200-million-year-old hippopotamus-like reptile Lystrosaurus, a marsupial, Polydops, and the ferns Dicroidium and Notophagus.

Though the Antarctic continent appears to be a single lump of rock covered by ice, geologically it can be divided into two main areas – west and east – joined by the more than 3,200 km (2,000 miles) long Transantarctic Mountains. West or Lesser Antarctica is the younger of the two, with a bedrock composed of five fragments of rocks of different geological ages, stretching from the age of dinosaurs to the age of mammals. Though it has mountain ranges of Himalayan dimensions, the weight of ice keeps them buried as much as 2,500 m (8,200 ft) beneath the ocean. East or Greater Antarctica is much older and mainly above sea level, with a single type of geological rock known as the Precambrian Shield that formed long before there were any signs of life on the planet. Greater Antarctica makes up about two-thirds of the continent and is home to the high polar plateau where from out of the whiteness of the interior fierce katabatic winds of dry super-cooled air pour downhill, hurtling towards the coast at speeds of up to 300 kph (180 mph). The plateau rises to about 3,000 m (10,000 ft) near the South Pole, making the climate here much colder than in West Antarctica – as the explorers found to their cost. It has been estimated that if the ice sheet covering Antarctica were to melt – at its thickest it is 4,776 m (15,670 ft) with bedrock at 2,341 m (7,678 ft) below sea level – West Antarctica would rise by 500 m (1,500 ft) and break down into a number of islands East Antarctica would rise by 1,000 m (3,300 ft), and sea levels the world over by 60 m (200 ft), sufficient to devastate vast regions of the planet.

The World of the Ancients

Today there is still a sense of mystery and otherworldliness to Antarctica, a continent that began to crystallize in the imagination of the ancient Greeks some 3,000 years ago, long before anyone had any idea what form it might take. In those days the hub of European civilization was the Mediterranean, where ancient soothsayers and sages relied on the star-

Magellan

filled sky for inspiration. They were mesmerized by the most conspicuous of the northern constellations, the one that never set, naming it Arktos, 'the bear', and christening the point around which it seemed constantly to revolve the Arctic Pole. At this time people still envisaged the world as a flat disc and assumed that a similar fixed point or Antarctic Pole must lie beneath the Earth at the heart of a region of darkness and terror – the Hell conceived of by Christians more than a thousand years later.

In the sixth century BC the Greek philosopher and mathematician Pythagoras was one of the first scholars to conceive of the Earth as a sphere around which the sun, planets and stars revolved, and the Greeks' passion for symmetry was reflected in the views of men like Parmenides, another philosopher, who believed that the northern and southern hemispheres were virtual mirror images of one another, each divided into a series of similar climatic zones. According to this theory, the areas furthest to the north and south were uninhabited and inaccessible frigid zones, giving way to more temperate regions (including the known Mediterranean world) and separated from one another along the equator by

a torrid zone too hostile for people to live in. Some two centuries after Pythagoras, Plato – who with his teacher Socrates and his pupil Aristotle is considered to be the father of western philosophy – supported the idea that the Earth was spherical, and it was Aristotle – tutor of Alexander the Great – who proved this by drawing attention to the Earth's ability to cast a circular shadow on the moon during an eclipse. In all probability Aristotle was also the person responsible for the earliest notions of a great southern land as a counterpoint to those in the north, an *Anti Arktos*.

The Egyptian geographer Ptolemy (writing around 150 AD) and certain medieval geographers took the idea of a *Terra Australis Incognita* – or unknown southern land – one step further, filling the southern hemisphere with a vast continent. Contrary to the views espoused by classical Greek philosophy, Ptolemy believed that this southern land was not so much frigid as fertile and inhabited. Enticing as this thought might have been to early explorers, it was tempered by the conviction that any such land, inhabited or not, was cut off from the known world by the torrid zone that Parmenides had favoured, a place of boiling seas, fire and terrifying monsters – a view that helped ensure that it would be more than a thousand years before people ventured in search of this *Terra Incognita*.

The enlightened and imaginative thinking of the ancient philosophers was now obliterated by the stifling intellectual repression of the Middle Ages, buried beneath the powerful forces of religious dogma. If Adam were indeed the progenitor of the human race, then how were the early Christian Fathers to account for these unknown people supposedly living beyond the fiery gulf of the equator – implying a whole region of the Earth cut off from the

Drake

teachings of the Gospel? The solution was simple: the idea that the world was round and that inhabited regions lay waiting to be discovered to the south was denounced as heretical and punishable by excommunication. The 'flat earth' theory gained new credence, conveniently dispensing with the need for a southern hemisphere and a *Terra Incognita*.

Fortunately Ptolemy's ideas were preserved by the Arabs and in the tenth century they made their way north again with the advance of the Moors into Spain. When these and other ancient texts were translated into Latin and French, it heralded the onset of a new era of enlightenment – the period we call the Renaissance – reigniting debate about the shape of the Earth, reviving the theory that it was round not flat and that other lands must surely lie to the south of the known world. In 1475 Ptolemy's *Geography* was published, containing his charts of the Earth and sky, which showed a *Terra Incognita* joined to Africa and accounting for a third of the southern hemisphere, and for

the next 200 years these ideas found favour with Renaissance scholars, stimulating the quest for new lands. By now the Church had been forced to acknowledge that the Earth was a globe and Pope Alexander VI himself began to encourage maritime exploration. Ships eagerly probed coasts, bays and inlets, intuitively recognizing that the world's oceans were interconnected. At the prompting of the Pope, Portugal and Spain signed the Treaty of Tordesillas in 1494, dividing the world in half along the forty-sixth meridian (370 leagues west of the Cape Verde Islands). The Portuguese were to explore the regions to the east of this line with the Spanish holding sway to the west. Today, both Chile and Argentina evidence this treaty and their Hispanic heritage to bolster their claims to sovereignty over portions of Antarctica.

The Age of Exploration

Spain and Portugal were well positioned to lead the race to discover routes to the southern hemisphere, each boasting men with a tradition of fine seamanship and a willingness to take risks. They favoured small vessels known as caravels, which combined the best of European and Arab design features, with two masts and triangular lateen sails. Caravels weighed 50–60 tonnes, measured around 20 m (70 ft) in length and were crewed by up to 30 men. It didn't take long for these intrepid sailors to discover inhabited land – not boiling seas or monsters – casting doubts on Ptolemy's ideas of torrid zones, and for a time the wisdom of the ancients was discredited.

More than anything, the expeditions of explorers such as Columbus and Magellan proved that the Earth was a globe of almost unimaginable size, prompting further exploration to reveal the

true nature of the continents and oceans. A number of other explorers made a name for themselves during this period. In 1487 Bartolomeu Dias ventured further along the southern coast of Africa than anyone had been before and was the first to round the Cape of Good Hope from the west; ten years later Vasco da Gama followed the same route and sailed onward to India, proving that the Indian Ocean was not an enclosed sea. But the prospect of discovering the southern continent continued to intrigue. Having circumnavigated the southern hemisphere in 1520, Ferdinand Magellan discovered the passage – now named after him – that separates the South American continent from the island of Tierra del Fuego, and believed he had found the northern edge of the great southern continent. But when Sir Francis Drake passed through the Strait of Magellan in 1577 he met 'an intolerable tempest' and was blown far enough south of Cape Horn – the tip of Tierra del Fuego – to find himself tossed about like a cork in the turbulent waters where Atlantic and Pacific Oceans meet, quashing the notion that any part of South America was connected to land further south. Mapmakers were not so easily convinced and the first modern atlases published around this time still show Terra Incognita as an enormous chunk of land incorporating what we now know to be Australia, New Zealand, Antarctica – and Tierra del Fuego.

It is hard to imagine the reality of life aboard the wooden ships of those days. Many of the crew were drawn from the lowest echelons of society and suffered all manner of privation. Exposed to the elements out on deck, life consisted of an endless rota of four-hour watches, of setting sails, swabbing decks and clambering among the rigging – often soaked to the skin with a gale blowing in your ears. In Magellan's day living space was at best cramped and sparse, with the

crew forced to bed down on the decks – no mattresses or hammocks; only officers had cabins and bunks. Wooden cages suspended over the rails served as latrines, and when conditions were too dangerous for that the men used the bilges as a toilet. Food, water and wine were stored in wooden casks and quickly spoiled; after a few days at sea fresh water was in short supply. One hot meal a day was the best you could hope for, cooked over a fire kindled in a box on the open deck. And the food was often barely edible, sapping the men's strength as surely as boredom dulled their spirits. Ships' rations consisted of salt beef or pork (a lump of cheese, some beans and onions too if you were lucky) which rotted as the voyage lengthened, and the black bread and ship's biscuits soon became mouldy and infested with cockroaches, weevils and maggots. The only living things that flourished were the ever-present rats or mice which were auctioned off when food became scarce. The biggest killer at sea in those days was scurvy, a disease caused by a lack of vitamin C, as fresh fruit and vegetables were rarely available. Before long the tell-tale signs appeared – gums would blacken and swell, teeth would fall out and joints weaken until it was impossible to stand. Those who died were thrown into the sea. Not until 1795 were British seamen ordered to drink a daily ration of lime juice to combat scurvy – hence the nickname 'Limey'.

Musical instruments such as drums and tambourines were provided as a diversion for the crew, along with the staple diet of shared tales of past adventures. Life at sea was not for the faint-hearted, and it was hard to maintain discipline among men subjected to the terrors of unknown seas, uncertain destination and grave discomfort. Captains often preferred to employ new men to create a balance with the more experienced seamen who would try to second-guess the captain's orders, increasing the risk of mutiny. Deterrents were brutal in their simplicity – being dragged on ropes beneath the hull (keel-hauled) or flogged with the 'cat o' nine tails' were common forms of punishment, and just one step away from execution. Sometimes the men were away from home for two or three years at a time and many did not survive to see their families again. Those who did often sought solace in beer and rum. But life was little better for the unskilled worker on land, and for the seaman there was always the dream of adventure and a share of the booty – if you survived long enough to enjoy it.

The prime objective of these early explorers and buccaneers was to seek trade for their countries, so they were often reluctant to reveal the exact location of where they had seen land, making life difficult for geographers and mapmakers. It was not until the middle of the eighteenth century that the chronometer was invented and accurate charts could be produced. Many was the time when the true position and nature of the great southern land was thought to have been discovered, with the South Pacific providing most of the 'sightings'. Intermittent landings made by seafarers were initially thought to indicate the position of peninsulas jutting out from *Terra Australis*, and the Solomon Islands, New Hebrides, New Guinea, Tasmania and parts of New Zealand were each in turn believed to be extensions of the 'southern land'. People were still expecting to find a tropical paradise, a land of gold and honey, a New Europe – a continent like America, only better.

By now most maritime nations were losing interest in pursuing what still remained a mere idea – a figment of the imagination perhaps, a costly enterprise that had so far reaped few tangible rewards. Consequently many discoveries of new land came about by chance, often as a

Captain Cook

result of vessels being blown off course in the stormy oceans. In 1592, the English seafarer John Davis was forced off the coast of Patagonia and on 18 August came upon the Falkland Islands, and in 1675 a London merchant, Antonio de la Roche, was blown off course while rounding the tip of South America during stormy weather, eventually anchoring at a latitude of 55°S in what is now known as Drygalski Fjord on the island of South Georgia. But it is the Frenchman Jean Bouvet de Lozier who is often credited with being the first to make a determined effort to find the southern continent. In 1739 he discovered the sub-Antarctic Bouvetøya, which he thought was a cape of *Terra Australis*, and he was certainly the first person to describe tabular icebergs, as well as reporting the occurrence of seals and penguins, proof enough of the proximity of land.

With both land and animal life now known to exist this far south, there was a revival of the dream that a great southern land might yet offer a great reward for those brave enough to seek it.

The First Antarctic Hero

One man stands out in the search for the southern land, a man who elevated exploration to a science, refusing to be blinded by myth and wishful thinking. This is the man who was destined to discover more of the Earth's surface than anyone else past or present, visiting all seven continents and crossing both the Arctic and Antarctic Circles before being stabbed to death in Hawaii on 14 February 1779. James Cook was the son of a Yorkshire farm labourer, the second of eleven children. In 1746, at the age of 18, he went to sea, earning a meagre living as a deck hand on the colliers that plied the stormy English coast between Whitby and London, steadfastly working his way up to the position of mate before joining the Royal Navy in 1755. Within five weeks of enlisting he earned his rating as master's mate and from then on he was marked out for success. Cook was extraordinarily able, as well as being brave and truly adventurous. He was a brilliant navigator, using the newly invented chronometer to accurately reckon positions of longitude, and his skills as a chart-maker are unequalled – his charts are still usable to this day. Throughout his career he lived by the pledge to go 'farther than any man has before me but only as far as I think possible....'

Cook's determination and innovative nature helped him overcome nearly every disaster. When his ship HMS *Endeavour* ran aground in 1770 on Australia's Great Barrier Reef, he beached and fixed it within a month, then waited another month for favourable winds to set sail again. Above all else Cook was an exceptional leader who understood his men. He had experience of doing the most menial work, knew the dangers inherent in a seafarer's life and made every effort to see that his men had sufficient food and drink and as healthy a diet as possible under difficult circumstances. On his first journey south (1768–71) the crew had suffered terribly from scurvy, which was still poorly understood. Subsequently, Cook insisted that his crew ate plenty of fruit and vegetables (mainly sauerkraut), taking on board an ample supply of citrus fruits when wintering in New Zealand and the Pacific Islands, and helping to ensure that none of his men suffered scurvy again.

By the time of Cook's first expedition, glimpses of mainland Australia, Tasmania and New Zealand by various Dutch and Spanish explorers had aroused speculation that the southern continent might be a combination of all three landmasses or that an even vaster land lay further south, centring perhaps on the Pole. Many people still clung to the belief that the much-dreamed-of southern land might yet prove to be a fertile Garden of Eden, inhabited by friendly people with whom trade could be established. Cook carried with him geographers, naturalists and artists who produced detailed records of the landscape and wildlife, and during this first expedition he methodically investigated the remaining coasts of the Pacific, circumnavigating and mapping New Zealand, thereby proving that it at least was not part of a southern continent. Australia too would succumb to Cook's scrutiny and prove to be unconnected to a *Terra Australis*, in the process inheriting part of the old name.

A year after he returned to England, the British Admiralty sent Cook – now elevated to the position of Commander – on his second voyage of discovery (1772–75), with the specific intention of finally proving or disproving the existence of a southern continent. He was ordered to keep to as high a latitude as possible in pursuit of his goal and claim whatever he might find for his king. For transport Cook favoured the flat-bottomed

ABOVE

Ice fingers, Antarctic Peninsula. The sharp features of newly calved icebergs gradually erode into more rounded weathered forms, with an average life of perhaps four years, as they migrate to warmer seas.

colliers he was familiar with from his youth: ships with ample space for provisions, shallow draught and capable of being beached in case of repair, with the added advantage that they were less prone to rock around. He choose a pair of Whitby-built vessels refitted as naval sloops, naming his flagship HMS *Resolution* and her sister ship, captained by Tobias Furneaux, HMS *Adventure*. *Resolution* was just 33.7 m (110 ft) long and 10.8 m (35 ft) across the beam with a hold 4 m (13 ft) deep; *Adventure* was even smaller. Cook employed a crew of 110 seaworthy men, many of

whom had sailed with him before, with a further 80 for *Adventure*. He provisioned the vessels for a two-year voyage, making elaborate preparations for fresh food and insisting on a measure of hygiene in the crew's quarters. The two ships sailed from Plymouth Sound in July 1772, and five months later met their first iceberg along with fierce storms, high seas and thick fog. But Cook was undeterred by the elements, intent only on fulfilling his mission.

For three years Cook circumnavigated the Earth in latitudes generally south of 60°, finding

Fur seal colony on Prion Island, Bay of Isles. During the breeding season fur seals gather along every available stretch of beach and in the olden days proved easy targets for the sealers.

sea where others had imagined there to be land, chipping away at the speculative work of the mapmakers. One can only imagine the sense of longing he and his men must have experienced: 'We were almost perpetually wrapped in thick fog,' he wrote, 'beaten with showers of rain, sleet, hail and snow, surrounded by innumerable islands of ice, against which we daily ran the risk of being shipwrecked, and forced to live on salt provisions, which concurred with the cold and wet to infect the mass of our blood.' Ice clung to the masts and rigging, sails were like sheets of metal, the boat buffeted by bergie bits and growlers – as the fragments from the gradual break-up of icebergs are known in increasing order of size – yet still Cook and his men stuck to their tasks and not one man was lost to the sea.

Though Cook was destined neither to set foot on land nor even to glimpse the coast of Antarctica (despite unknowingly sailing within 200 km/125 miles of it), he succeeded in circumnavigating the Southern Ocean and crossing the Antarctic Circle. To avoid the perils of winter he was forced to head north to New Zealand until conditions became more amenable to travel. Determined as ever, he set sail again the following spring, crossing the Antarctic Circle due south of New Zealand and sailing on an easterly course, probing and penetrating the pack ice whenever possible in the search for land. His tiny ship was constantly dwarfed by towering icebergs and battered by the unforgiving seas but, despite all the obstacles, on 30 January 1774 he eventually reached a latitude of 71°17'S at a point near Marie Byrd Land, within touching distance of what is now known as the Amundsen Sea. He had travelled further south than anyone had ever been before, and it would be half a century before his achievement was surpassed. (In 1823 James Weddell reached 74°15'S during exceptionally

warm weather, a record that would stand for the next 90 years.) Unable to venture further, Cook could only record that 'it was indeed my opinion that this ice extends quite to the Pole, or perhaps joins to some land to which it has been fixed since creation', rightly believing that the huge tabular icebergs they encountered were evidence of a continent further south. Gone were any lingering dreams of a fertile, inhabited land of untold wealth – an idea that Cook had always questioned. Once more he headed north to avoid being trapped among the pack ice during winter.

On 11 November 1774, Cook set sail from New Zealand again, heading for Cape Horn at a latitude of 54–55°S, with the object of proving that no continent lay in that part of the Pacific. He sighted land on 14 January 1775, but the joy of discovery was short-lived. The desolate snow-covered place he and his men had stumbled upon proved to be an island – the Isle of Georgia, as Cook named it 'in His Majesty's name' – and on rounding its southern tip (christened Cape Disappointment) he realized for certain that this was not after all part of the great southern continent. It was a historic moment nonetheless, marked by the firing of muskets and raising of the flag – the first claim to sovereignty made in the Antarctic. Cook named the place where they landed Possession Bay.

South Georgia is wild country, with inlets blocked by giant icebergs calved from its many glaciers, snow-covered mountain summits often concealed by the clouds, and not a tree in sight. Not surprisingly Cook's disappointment was tempered by the nature of what he had seen: 'For to judge of the bulk by the sample it would not be worth the discovery.' Nevertheless he explored the eastern coast of the island, charting the bays that would 135 years later become the sites of the great whaling stations. He made one last attempt to find land further south, but the pack ice was so thick that he was forced to the northeast, in the process discovering the South Sandwich Islands. By the time he reached England again on 30 July 1775, he and his companions aboard *Resolution* had travelled more than 97,000 km (60,000 miles) on a journey that had lasted three years and eight days.

Having ourselves just travelled over 8,000 km (5,000 miles) in considerable comfort during a month's journey across the Southern Ocean, the immensity of Cook's achievements are hard to overestimate, particularly when you consider the remoteness of the places he and his men visited, the equipment they had available to them and the enormous distances they travelled in pursuit of their goals. Stories of those days only add to the allure of the white continent and its surrounding ocean, an environment that continues to test human resolve and ingenuity to the limits.

It is an irony that Cook's greatest achievements of discovery were in proving what did not exist – in defining the precise extent of coasts rather than in finding new lands. Nonetheless he ended the last of his southern journeys convinced that there was 'not the least room for the possibility of there being a continent, unless near the Pole and out of the reach of navigation…'. As far as Cook was concerned there was no way to enter the ice and no reason to attempt it: if there were indeed a southern continent, then it was an uninhabited wasteland bounded by an ocean of treacherous ice. He had finally swept aside the last remnants of the myths created by the ancients, whittling away at the *Terra Australis Incognita* that had virtually filled the southern half of the globe in the minds of the early mapmakers, reducing it to a semblance of its true magnitude within the vastness of the torrid Southern Ocean. But it would be another 50 years before anyone set foot on the continent itself.

Unknown to Cook, at the time of his travels the Earth was nearing the end of the 'little ice age', a period that began in the mid-1600s and reached its peak around 1700. Across the globe the weather was rarely fine or clear, winters were severe, summers short and it is likely that the pack ice was more extensive than today. With the milder conditions Angie and I have often been blessed with on our journeys south, Cook would undoubtedly have achieved his ambition and been first to sight the continent. But the fact that he didn't should take nothing away from his accomplishments. His journeys across the Pacific Ocean between the tropics and the temperate zone led to the discovery of new islands, new species of birds and plants and 'above all, for friends of humanity new races with unknown living customs'. Amundsen described Cook as 'the greatest sea hero of his century', adding that 'few people nowadays have a proper understanding of this act of heroism, only a few grasp what courage and contempt for death was necessary in order to take on themselves such a great risk. With two heavily manoeuvrable ships – by today's notions veritable boxes – these people travelled into the heart of the pack-ice and with that did something which, by the unanimous declarations of all earlier polar travellers, meant certain ruin.'

The description Cook's journals provided of South Georgia and the South Sandwich Islands left little doubt as to their inhospitable nature: 'Lands doomed by Nature to perpetual frigidness: never to feel the warmth of the sun's rays; whose horrible and savage aspects I have not words to describe.' But his reports of large numbers of fur seals hauled out on the rugged beaches of South Georgia had caught the attention of the owners of the sealing fleets of Europe and America – to them rough seas and hardship were daily fare.

With the stocks of both seals and whales diminishing in more northerly regions, it suddenly seemed that a handsome living was to be made for those prepared to risk their lives in heading further south.

The Age of Exploitation

Up until now the focus of the attention of the sealers had been the more accessible northerly regions and for as long as supplies lasted the sea otters and fur seals of the North Pacific were easier fare than the seals and whales of the Southern Ocean. But stocks there had already begun to dwindle. Mineral oils were still unknown, and whale oil and seal blubber were in great demand to provide lighting and as protection for ships' ropes, sails and timbers. As the eighteenth century drew to a close the world was experiencing rapid change as the industrial revolution transformed first Britain, then other Western European countries and North America into industrial nations. The demand for high-quality oils to lubricate machine parts intensified, and with increased prosperity fur coats made from sealskins became highly fashionable.

With the charts and descriptions of the explorers and navigators such as Cook to guide them, sealers made their way south along the shores of South America towards South Georgia; others beat a different path along the coasts of Australia and New Zealand and their sub-Antarctic islands, quickly decimating the seal population. A million fur seal skins were taken around the island of Masafuera off the coast of Chile in 1798 alone, and with some 1,800 men and 14 ships working the island three million seals were slaughtered in seven years.

Sealing vessels were also the first to explore south as far as the Antarctic Peninsula, but their skippers were secretive about their operations and few if any scientists accompanied them. Consequently much of what was seen and charted remained hidden for fear of losing ground to rivals in the quest for skins. In 1819 renewed interest in Antarctica was prompted by the chance discovery of the South Shetland Islands by the British merchant captain William Smith, whose ship was blown off course in a storm while headed for Chile. Word of the abundant fur seal population spread quickly and the islands – which are only 120 km (75 miles) from the Antarctic Peninsula – were soon swarming with British and American vessels; 320,000 skins were taken in just two years. South Georgia fared little better, with the slaughter of an estimated 1.2 million seals within a period of 50 years leading to the near extinction of an entire species.

The year 1820 is a pivotal one in the history of Antarctic exploration. The net had been tightening around *Terra Incognita* ever since Cook's day and the discovery of the South Shetlands helped stoke the fires of ambition.

sealers

With possible commercial interests at stake, Britain dispatched a naval expedition under the command of Edward Bransfield, the senior British officer at Valparaiso, accompanied by William Smith as pilot, to lay claim to the South Shetlands, take soundings, survey the coastline and report on the natural resources. Bransfield was also instructed to ascertain the character and customs of the indigenous people, highlighting the fact that the hope of finding inhabitable land this far south had been slow to die. He continued south into the gloom only to find his ship beset by reefs and icebergs, and shrouded in fog. As conditions improved Trinity Island was sighted to the southwest, and behind it snow-covered mountains extending to the south. As the fog lifted, the coastline of the Antarctic Peninsula appeared, separated from Trinity Island by a narrow strait. The date was 30 January 1820.

Sealing vessels from America had also gathered in the vicinity of the South Shetlands, including fleets sent south by the merchants of Stonington, Connecticut. On 16 November 1820 the Stonington flotilla numbering five ships entered the narrow channel providing access to the flooded caldera known as Deception Island, offering a harbour sheltered from the elements. On landing Captain Benjamin Pendleton climbed a high ridge from where he thought he spied land to the south. Pendleton then dispatched Nathanial Palmer – commander of the 45-tonne sloop Hero – to investigate. Unaware of Bransfield's earlier voyage, Palmer was deemed by the Americans to have found the coastline of the fabled southern continent.

But these two powerful nations were not alone in their quest to discover as yet unknown land, whether for science or commerce. Russia's Tsar Alexander I had sent Fabian Gottlieb von Bellingshausen on an extended voyage of discovery with the aim of finding southern anchorages for the imperial fleet, sailing as close to the South Pole as possible 'and only abandoning the undertaking in the face of insurmountable obstacles'. Bellingshausen was a great admirer of Cook and had interviewed men who had worked with him, as a result refining his equipment and providing his men with good supplies of pickles and fruit. Although he did not know it at the time, he was the first man to navigate and chart the Antarctic continent, sighting its ice-encrusted edge at about 69°35'S off Dronning Maud Land on 27 January 1820, just days before Bransfield, though he made no claims.

The existence of the last continent had finally been proved and the seal population brought to the point of extinction. The whales would follow a century later as men scrambled to capitalize on whatever was there for the taking, following the familiar pattern that now clouds our future and the wellbeing of our planet – exploration and discovery leading inevitably to exploitation, a vicious cycle that we have yet to break. Scientific expeditions were next to make an appearance on the white continent, opening the door to the 'heroic' age of polar exploration when men would risk their lives for the honour of being first to the South Pole.

Our journey, though, starts with a visit to the windswept Falkland Islands, which – while not biologically part of Antarctica – have played a pivotal role in the history of the exploration of the more southerly regions and, furthermore, hint at the glory of Antarctic wildlife to be encountered further south.

Adélie penguin displaying, Cape Adare. This is the site of a huge Adélie breeding colony, with more than 280,000 pairs estimated to breed here. No other bird breeds further south than the Adélie penguin. They are migratory and after breeding do not return to their colonies until the following spring.

CHAPTER 2

The Falkland Islands

In 1690 the English sloop *Welfare*, captained by John Strong, was blown off course while heading for what is now Argentina, landing instead at Bold Cove on the remote Sebald Islands in the South Atlantic. Sailing between the two main islands of the archipelago, Strong named the passage the Falkland Channel (now Falkland Sound) after the fifth Viscount Falkland, who had been responsible for financing the expedition on behalf of the Admiralty and later became First Lord of the Admiralty. Although discovery of the Falkland Islands is generally credited to the Elizabethan navigator John Davis in 1592, it was in this way that they gained their name.

The Falklands – or the Islas Malvinas as they are known in Argentina – are a composite of 700 scattered islands and islets lying 490 km (300 miles) east of Patagonia, clustered like the jagged pieces of a jigsaw around two main islands, known as West and East Falkland. In total they cover 12,173 sq. km (4,700 square miles), an area roughly the size of Wales or Connecticut, and are one of the world's most isolated dependent territories, home to around 3,000 people. Some 70 per cent of these are of British descent, mainly Scots and Ulster Scots. Most of the remainder trace their ancestry to French, Portuguese and Scandinavian settlers and some to whalers who reached the islands during the last two centuries; then there is a small minority of South Americans, mainly of Chilean origin, and in more recent times people from St Helena have come to work here.

The character of the landscape mirrors its isolation – stark, with gently rolling hills and craggy uplands marked by bare peat and scree slopes, a pattern that is repeated again and again – kelp-fringed islands with a belt of dense tussock grass (a giant species of *Poa* that flourishes on many Falkland islets) giving way to a windswept treeless interior scored by narrow streams that meander towards the sea through peat-forming heaths and bogs. From the air everything looks sparse and brown, reminiscent of the western isles of Scotland, with West Falkland being the more rugged and mountainous of the two main islands, the kind of tough, hearty, outdoor place that schoolchildren might have been dispatched to for an adventure survival course in days gone by. Though lying north of the Antarctic Convergence and therefore not strictly qualifying as sub-Antarctic, the Falklands' climate is influenced by cold surface currents flowing north from the Southern Ocean, with blustery westerly winds wafting sea smells of kelp and seals and seabird colonies. It snows around 50 days a year. No wonder that the first British governor, Richard Moody, wrote in his dispatches in 1842 that 'the settlers best adapted to colonize these islands would be from among the industrious population of the Orkneys and the Shetlands, accustomed to a hardy life and as much seamen as landmen…'.

In 1982 Britain and Argentina went to war over possession of the islands. While the war, like the Falklands themselves, was quickly forgotten by the rest of the world, it is impossible for residents who lived through that time to banish the memory. An estimated 18,000 unexploded Argentine mines lie scattered across the islands, fenced off from the public (with a £1,000 fine for those foolish enough to ignore the signs marked 'Danger'), while the wreckage of downed aircraft is a more visible reminder of the 655 Argentines, 255 British and three Falklanders who perished. Despite its losses – with Britain's and the islanders' refusal to negotiate on sovereignty – Argentina still does not accept that the islanders prefer the Falklands to remain British territory. A posting here can be a tough assignment for British servicemen and women. Being 12,000 km

Magellanic penguins, Volunteer Point, East Falklands. Magellanics are closely related to the African, Humboldt and Galapagos species, which breed further north and in much warmer climates than other penguins.

(8,000 miles) from home is no picnic, and loneliness and a sense of alienation from the local community only heighten the problems. Most stay for four to six months, which isn't so bad if it coincides with spring and summer, but the winter months can be long and bleak.

Ironically for many of the islanders, the war helped to transform this remote British outpost from an archaic colonial backwater into a prosperous, forward-looking society. Prior to this the population had been declining, with a moribund economy based primarily on the price of wool – this, after all, is the tight-knit community whose coat of arms boasts a fine Falklands sheep, and there are still more than 670,000 sheep on these islands, but very few sheep farmers. At the start of 1982, absentee landlords still owned much of the land, helping to perpetuate an almost feudal system of tenure. After the war – having

successfully defended its claim to control the Falklands indefinitely – Britain had no choice but to invest heavily to allow the islands to become economically viable, something that it had been reluctant to do in the past. A land-reform programme has helped to put an end to the bane of absentee landlords, whose vast farm holdings have been divided and sold to local people.

Disputes over the sovereignty of the Falklands date back to their discovery some 400 years ago, with France, Britain, Spain and Argentina all at various times claiming possession. The islands were uninhabited when Europeans discovered them, but the presence of the Falkland Island fox or warrah (*Canis antarcticus*) – and arrowheads and the remains of a canoe – is thought by some to be proof of earlier visitors, though the foxy canine may have arrived via a landbridge during the last ice age. Several British and Spanish historians

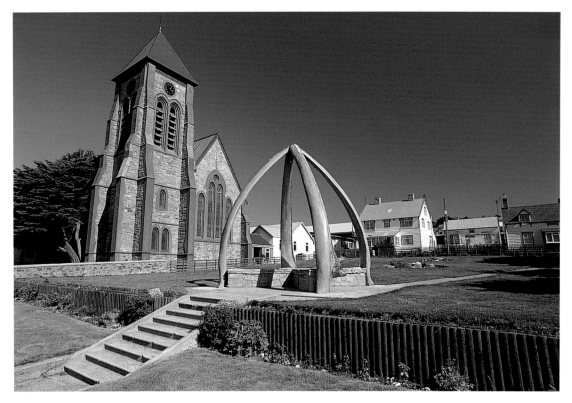

LEFT
Christ Church Cathedral, Port Stanley, featuring the centennial memorial constructed from the jaw bones of blue whales. The cathedral is one of the dominant features of the skyline as you approach the Falklands by sea and was consecrated in 1892.

support claims for their own explorers being the first to arrive, and in 1600 a Dutch expedition commanded by Sebald de Weert sighted three small islands in the region and named them the Sebald de Weert Islands (they are today known as the Jason Islands). From that time Dutch mapmakers used the name the Sebald Islands for what we now call the Falklands.

Although various ships – including HMS *Welfare* – made landfall in the islands over the next 150 years, the first settlement, established in 1764 at Port Louis on Berkeley Sound, East Falkland, was French. And thus began a legacy of claims and counter-claims by acquisitive nations, a pattern that casts a shadow of uncertainty over the islands to this day. A year after the French had made their mark, the British captain John Byron, unaware of the French settlement, claimed Saunders Island in West Falkland for Britain,

naming the harbour of Port Egmont, and claiming other islands he sailed past for his king, George III. A few months later Britain dispatched an expeditionary force of three ships under the command of Captain John McBride to reinforce her claims. McBride established a British settlement at Port Egmont in 1766 – the same year that Spain acquired the French colony at Port Louis, renamed it Port Soledad and placed it under a governor answerable to Buenos Aires.

Spain then tried to expand its control by attacking Port Egmont in 1770 and forcing the British to withdraw. They returned the following year, but withdrew again in 1774, though not before leaving a plaque asserting their claims. The Spanish maintained a settlement until 1811 and then – just as the British had done – departed, leaving a plaque. When Argentina declared independence from Spain in 1816 she too laid claim to the uninhabited islands and in 1820 sent representatives of the new government to take possession again. In the interim the islands had become a haven for sealers and whalers and in 1831 the United States destroyed the settlement at Port Soledad during a dispute over sealing rights. Two years later the British returned, removing the last vestiges of the Spanish settlement and populating the islands with their own citizens. Despite ongoing Argentine claims, the Falklands have remained in British hands ever since.

Life in the Falklands

Stanley is home to nearly 2,000 people and has been the capital since 1845, when the seat of government was moved from Port Soledad to provide a secure and accessible anchorage for the Royal Navy. At first glance it resembles a quaint toy-town with its white-walled, box-like houses with neat, grassy green gardens; a mosaic of multi-coloured roofs all blues, reds and yellows set among a grid of steeply inclined roads running down to the harbour. There is a strong sense of British village life, with the supermarket and pub focal points for a chat or a pint of ale, and *empanadas* – tasty triangles of meat-filled pastry best eaten hot – about the only hint of the islands' proximity to South America. Signs of life are muted except for the odd horse or sheep plodding round the gardens, and residents cruise the streets in noisy diesel Land Rovers that hint at unpredictable weather and a more rugged existence beyond the city limits. As you explore you may discover one man's shrine to the great leviathans, featuring various bits of whale anatomy, some of it varnished and displayed in extraordinary fashion with a couple of Falkland sheep wandering around the walled garden

adding a touch of life – an eccentric individual's private epitaph to the whale.

In fact, placards demanding 'Save the Whale' are prominently positioned in the windows of a number of houses (alongside the occasional 'Hands Off' message to the Argentine government), testimony to the times when the Falklands were a centre for whaling and sealing vessels, and it is impossible to miss Christ Church Cathedral overlooking the harbour with its magnificent whalebone arches erected in 1933 from the jaws of two blue whales, a fitting memorial to the largest animal that has ever lived. Christ Church was consecrated in 1892, making it one of the oldest buildings in Stanley and the world's southernmost cathedral. The series of registers begun by Chaplain James Moody, brother of Richard, the first governor, help to paint a vivid portrait of an evolving Falklands community with representatives from every echelon of society – soldier, gaucho, shepherd, bricklayer, merchant, convicted felon, schoolmaster, harbourmaster, naval surgeon, publican and gentleman, all of whom brought their children to be baptized here.

A picnic taken along the waterfront with kelp gulls and skuas as your companions allows you to see the charm of this incongruous outpost and to take time to reflect. In summer, rainbows arch across the darkening skies, their rippling façade reflecting crystal-clear in the water. Kelp gulls, the southern equivalent of the adaptable black-backed gulls found in more northerly climes, paddle about in the shallows, duck-diving for brightly coloured starfish as the light intensifies – primary colours of red, yellow and green; but it is always the purple edge to the rainbow that catches the imagination, as if you had never before seen such vivid colours, a surreal moment hinting at the mysteries that lie to the south for travellers to Antarctica.

Stanley certainly no longer deserves to be described as 'the most miserable bog hole' in the islands, as one eighteenth-century visitor put it. During the California Gold Rush of the 1850s the port prospered as a repair depot for ships attempting to round Cape Horn, and later it found fortune as a base for commercial whaling and sealing, where the men could get supplies of fresh produce such as pork, beef, mutton and upland goose. These industries in turn gave way to wool production, with the scattered farms providing the Falklands' wealth, ensuring Stanley's continued growth until the invention of cheap synthetic fibres knocked the bottom out of the wool market in the early 1950s.

Everywhere outside Stanley is referred to as the Camp, from the Spanish *campo* meaning countryside, and 25 years ago 40 per cent of the population lived out in the nearly trackless interior. Settlements were so isolated that visiting your neighbours might entail a day or more's journey by horse, with a three-day ride for some

ABOVE
The kelp gull is the only gull regularly found in the Antarctic, where it feeds mainly on limpets whose shells are regurgitated after the flesh has been digested. Breeding sites are characterized by middens of these regurgitated shells.

on their annual visit to Stanley. Today fewer than 450 people live in the Camp, which embraces the small and medium-sized farms scattered across the islands, with most settlements numbering two to ten residents, and Port Howard on the east coast of West Falkland, which has 30 inhabitants, a store, small school and even a war museum. On East Falkland the largest settlement after Stanley is North Arm, population 31. You still occasionally hear country folk referred to as 'kelpers', a reminder of the vast beds of kelp, commonly hundreds of metres in extent, found around the islands. Attempts to harvest the kelp in the late 1970s proved uneconomic due to its low concentration of alginate, the gelatinous-forming salt that makes seaweed useful to the food, textile, cosmetic and pharmaceutical industries. Today the Camp relies on a fleet of Islander light aircraft to ferry letters, food, money and gossip from one bumpy airstrip to another, with the pilot keeping a sharp lookout for Magellanic penguin burrows.

Despite the fall in demand, wool production is still the main occupation outside Stanley and is subsidized by the government, which is also keen to support the growing tourist industry based around the islands' plentiful wildlife, old-fashioned home-stays, excellent trout fishing – and for some the chance to visit the battlefields of the Falklands War such as Mounts Longdon, Kent and Fitzroy. While land-based tourism accounts for just a thousand visitors annually, the use of the islands as a departure point or port of call for some 80 cruise ships attracts 40,000 visitors travelling to or from South America, South Georgia and the Antarctic every year.

Much has been made in recent times of rich offshore oil reserves that are thought to lie beneath the ocean floor, prompting scientists, oil experts, politicians and market speculators to take a renewed interest in the islands. Not so long ago The Times of London referred to the Falklands as 'the new Kuwait'; geologists were talking of reserves of up to 2.5 billion barrels and a potential oilfield half as big again as that in the North Sea, which if true would make the Falklands the richest islands in the world. While there have been no commercial discoveries yet, six wells drilled in 1998 proved the presence of very rich organic rock with a potential yield of up to 60 million barrels, and with seven separate areas licensed for exploration more drilling is scheduled for 2007. One thing is certain: the discovery of oil can only heighten political tension over sovereignty, ensuring a continued British military presence.

Most islanders see the prospect of oil as a mixed blessing. They are wary of the changes it would undoubtedly bring to their way of life: other places that have struck oil have witnessed the disintegration of traditional local communities. There are also concerns about the possible damage it might cause to an otherwise unpolluted landscape teeming with 500,000 pairs of penguins, the world's largest colony of black-browed albatrosses and numerous seals. On the other hand they would welcome the added financial security

female kelp goose

Rockhopper penguin breeding colony, New Island.
Colonies are typically on rocky slopes and among
tussock grass, with a small nest made of tussock, peat
and pebbles. In recent years rockhopper populations
have declined substantially over most of their range.

that it promises, and greater ease of access to the outside world. For a while now the options have been limited to 18-hour TriStar flights to the UK via Ascension Island, operated six times a month by the Royal Air Force, and a single commercial flight each week from Santiago in Chile. Argentina and Chile have their own quarrels over their common border and Argentina still refuses Chile permission to overfly its air space en route to the Falklands. Attempts by the Argentine government to limit opportunities for economic development in the islands by maintaining a stranglehold on external communications have been dubbed 'economic terrorism', and most people would prefer to see joint issues concerning the environment and protection of wildlife topping the agenda now.

And so it continues, with Argentina's current president, Nestor Kirchner, insisting in a speech given in 2004 on the occasion of the twenty-second anniversary of the war that the islands would once again be part of Argentina. If oil is found then of course it will give Britain more reason to honour its pledge not to negotiate with Argentina on this subject. One thing that Britain's political parties currently agree on is that there should be no change in sovereignty without the agreement of the islanders. Meanwhile the Falklands remain a self-governing overseas territory.

rockhopper

Wildlife

While a visit to these islands offers tourists a unique cultural and historical experience, many people come for the wildlife – and in particular the birds. Apart from the 63 species that nest here (17 of which are regarded as Falkland races or endemics), there are a further 84 non-breeding visitors and vagrants, offering the chance of spotting something a little more exotic: in recent times black-necked swans and plumbeous rails have been among the rarities swept within reach of the islands on strong westerly winds. There is quite a narrow range of habitat here in the Falklands – inland grass, coastal cliff, tussock, seashore – limiting the diversity of species, but that is of little consequence if you have never seen a wild penguin or albatross before. In fact the Falklands are home to five species of penguins: in descending order of size, the king, gentoo, macaroni, Magellanic and rockhopper. The islands are at the edge of the global range of king penguins, which were said to be quite common when the Falklands were first settled, but had been exterminated by 1870. Today there are 400–500 breeding pairs, a healthy increase on the 38 pairs recorded in the 1980s. The majority can be found at Volunteer Point on East Falkland, looking somewhat incongruous marooned in the open on a grassy rise with sheep wandering past. Even so they have a majesty that is hard to deny.

Surely nothing could be more different than an albatross and a penguin, though we now know for certain that penguins shared a common flying ancestor and did not evolve from flightless birds – if ever there was a case for being cautious in deducing the relationship between different bird species from their looking similar and having similar adaptations to life, then this is it. Molecular biology is now able to help clarify how closely different species are by examining their DNA, and along with morphological clues points to loons (or divers as they are known in Europe), petrels, albatrosses and some families of frigatebirds as the penguins' closest relatives. These groups probably originated from waterbirds living in the Jurassic and early Cretaceous periods, with some experts favouring the loons and petrels, and others the albatross. The earliest fossil records for penguins date back 55 million years.

Whatever their origins, and regardless of species, penguins are unmistakable in their design, with webbed feet for paddling; short, stumpy wings acting as muscular flippers for diving and rapid swimming underwater; a layer of fat or blubber beneath the skin to help insulate them against the cold. The blubber layer is thinner than in whales or seals, because penguins rely more on a special suit of feathers to keep their core temperature at optimum levels. Their feathers are three to four times the density of flying birds', and are short (3–4 cm/1–1 ½ in), stiff and lance-like, with a long after-feather of downy filaments designed to trap air. The stiff, coarse tips of the feathers mesh together like waterproof Velcro, helping to resist compression when the bird dives and trapping the air next to the skin. It is not uncommon to see penguins preening, maintaining the waterproofing of their feathers by smearing them with oily secretions from the uropygeal gland at the base of the tail.

With penguins generally congregating in large colonies during the breeding season, finding sufficient food to sustain themselves and their chicks while confined to land (or the fast ice in the case of the emperor) is one of their greatest challenges. While the Antarctic penguins fall into three groups in terms of relatedness – kings and emperors (genus *Aptenodytes*); gentoos, chinstraps

OPPOSITE

King penguins displaying. Breeding displays involve a number of elements, with males initially singing with lowered heads. When the females arrive a pair stands face-to-face, followed by mutual sky-pointing and duetting. The two then perform in a distinctive swaggering, waddling gait, usually led by the male. The final act in this nuptial display is bowing followed by copulation.

and Adélies (Pygoscelis); and rockhoppers and macaronis (Eudyptes) – as far as procuring food is concerned they can be divided into two groups, depending on how far they must travel to find prey. Those that have a good supply of food close to their breeding sites (within 50 km (30 miles) during incubation) are known as inshore foragers – the gentoo is one of these – while those that must travel further afield are called offshore foragers and must fast for longer periods while tending their eggs. Kings, emperors, chinstraps, Adélies, rockhoppers and macaronis are all offshore foragers, and as such tend to be migratory, returning to their breeding colonies only to rear their young and perhaps to moult.

Kings are slightly different due to their extended breeding cycle – at 14–16 months it is the longest of any bird – and you will always find some birds in a king penguin colony at any time of the year, regardless of location.

The commonest penguin seen along the sandy shorelines of East Falkland is the burrow-nesting Magellanic, sometimes referred to as the jackass penguin due to its braying call. This species occurs at over 90 locations on the Falklands, making this one of the most important breeding sites in the world with around 100,000 pairs. Magellanics number 1.3 million pairs globally and are also found in southern Chile and Argentina, with the occasional vagrant recorded

LEFT

Antarctic shag, also known as the blue-eyed cormorant. It is closely related to the imperial shag or king cormorant that occurs in the Falklands and the opinion differs as to whether they should be considered a subspecies or a single species.

Gentoo regurgitating
food for its chick.
Gentoos breeding in the
Falklands and other more
northerly regions are up
to 50 per cent larger than
those breeding on islands
nearer the Antarctic.
Adults generally form
long-lasting pair bonds
and are faithful to the
previous year's nest.

on South Georgia; at Palmer Station, an American base near the Antarctic Peninsula; and as far afield as Australia and New Zealand. Their burrows are from 1.2 to 2 m (4–6 ft) deep and you have to be careful to tread lightly as you move about inland or through the tussock islands so as not to disturb them – or twist an ankle for that matter; and it is also not uncommon to find them nesting under bushes at suitable locations. It is a joy to see these stocky, lumpy-headed birds with their tell-tale double black chest band scurrying along these rugged, windswept beaches rather than as an exotic exhibit in some alien land. But globally there are concerns for their future, with some 20,000 adults and a similar number of juveniles killed along the Argentine coast each

ABOVE

Carcass Island, West Falkland. A popular landing site for cruise vessels, whose passengers come to enjoy the island's wildlife. The presence of algae and kelp colours the shore yellow and brown.

year due to disturbance, oil pollution and birds becoming entangled in fishing nets – factors that are a threat to many seabirds.

While nothing like as numerous as the Magellanics, the gentoos – with a distinctive white headband behind the eye (the name gentoo is an archaic word for Hindu, because early seamen apparently associated the white head markings with a turban) – are versatile in their habits and will construct their nest from mud and vegetation where available or resort to building with pebbles, as they must when breeding along the Antarctic Peninsula, where vegetation isn't an option. The gentoos seem quite prepared to hike cross-country to reach the most favourable nesting sites and some of their rookeries are up to 5 km (3 miles) inland. The Falklands are a major breeding centre for this species, whose presence here has increased recently to reach 113,000 pairs – over a third of the world's population.

One of the most popular places to enjoy the wildlife and glimpse your first penguin is Carcass Island, a tiny, privately owned area of

1,600 hectares (4,250 acres), one of a chain of islands embracing the northern approaches to the West Falklands. Many of the cruise ships headed for Antarctica stop off here for a half-day tour. The owners – almost uniquely among the islands – have managed to keep their farm free from rodents, cats and rabbits, the bane of indigenous wildlife elsewhere.

With the tide half out at Carcass Island, long parallel slabs of rock emerge from the sea, stippled a vivid mustard yellow with a coating of algae. The exposed shore is cobbled with pebbles, smoothed and honed by the ocean waves, shades of pinks, greens and black, or white and speckled, like an enormous collection of birds' eggs. There is a strong smell of seaweed, and there are places in the Falklands where the kelp stretches shiny and swollen for as far as the eye can see.

Kelp gulls stand facing into the wind on huge chunks of driftwood held fast close to shore. Among their specialities are the limpets which graze on algae in these regions. The gulls swallow the limpets whole, later regurgitating the shells intact. During the summer pairs of pied oystercatchers, handsomely attired in striking black and white plumage with long down-curved bills and bright yellow eyes, take it in turns to incubate a clutch of two creamy white eggs nestled in shallow depressions on the sandy rises. Though confiding in habits outside the breeding season, these noisy plover-like birds scurry away if people draw too close, with one of the pair immediately performing an elaborate display, feigning a broken wing to draw onlookers away from its nest. Once hatched, the tiny chicks will stay with their parents until they are five weeks old, following the adults as they probe and prod among the kelp and water vegetation. The adults constantly quarter the shoreline, dipping in and out of the

BELOW

Magellanic oystercatcher displaying. It is common to see these birds along the shore at Carcass Island, and they breed here during the summer.

shallow rock pools with their long, vertically flattened bills, as versatile as any Swiss Army knife, deftly cleaving open the mussels and scooping out the contents, prising open the shells of oysters and clams, chiselling limpets off rocks, spearing small crabs and probing for worms in the mud. Every so often one of the adults utters its characteristic shrill whistle, opening its bill and fluffing up the creamy white feathers beneath its tail, creating a stark contrast with its black underparts, to impress its mate. Though less common than its pied relative, the all-black Magellanic oystercatcher inhabits similar locations.

Parties of Magellanic flightless steamer ducks can often be seen sunning themselves among the kelp along the water's edge. These are heavy-set, quirky characters with large heads and yellow bills; being flightless, they storm away across the surface of the shallows when alarmed, flailing their stubby wings with rapid paddling motions. It is not uncommon to see males squabbling over a female, pounding at each other with their shorn-off wings, each blow reinforced by the large bony knob on the carpal joint at the bend of the wing, the avian equivalent of a knuckle-duster. For her part the female seems quite unmoved by the combatants' efforts. But once calm prevails the victorious male paddles off, mate in tow, diving among the kelp for mussels and crabs, leaving the vanquished male dabbling in the shallows. Amorous parties of Patagonian crested ducks are also found here, their startling wine-red eyes in marked contrast to their drab plumage. When not consumed with their courtship displays, they busy themselves quietly preening and drinking at a point where a stream of sparkling fresh water enters the sea.

Another birding highlight on Carcass Island is the striated or Forster's caracara – or Johnny Rook, as it is known locally. This distinctive raptor is one of the world's rarest birds, with fewer than 500 breeding pairs globally. The Falklands are home to 75 per cent of these, with the remainder located in the extreme southern regions of Chile and Argentina. Larger than a kite but not quite an eagle, the caracara is most commonly seen on the more remote of the offshore islands, where it nests under the tussock grass on the edge of craggy rocky places and lines its nest with sheep's wool. Historically the reason for its low numbers is conflict with sheep farmers, though its near-threatened status now warrants a fine of £3,000 for shooting one. Breeding birds prey primarily on colonial seabirds such as the burrow-nesting thin-billed prion, though they can sometimes be seen scavenging for scraps around settlements and are known to take geese and weak or sickly sheep and lambs. It is also not uncommon to see them loitering around the penguin colonies, pirating chicks and eggs when the opportunity arises.

Visitors heading back to their ship in inflatable zodiacs may be lucky enough to be entertained by a party of Peale's dolphins, chubby grey and white shapes porpoising through the water, exuberantly shepherding the visitors along. This species is confined to the coastal water of South America, and you sometimes also see small groups of Commerson's dolphins, strikingly patterned in black and white, mostly found close to the coast of Patagonia, but occasionally venturing out into the Drake Passage. They too are remarkably fearless, following the ships for a while, riding the pressure wave off the bow before vanishing beneath the surface of the ocean. Sadly they sometimes pay a heavy price for their boldness: Commerson's dolphin is the cetacean most commonly tangled and killed in fishing nets.

OPPOSITE
Black-browed albatross stretching its wings prior to lift-off, New Island, West Falkland. This species is the most abundant and widespread of all albatrosses. They have a much shorter breeding season than the great albatrosses and comfortably breed annually.

New Island

Some 70 km (42 miles) southeast of Carcass Island, New Island is another haven for wildlife. During the 1800s, while stocks of sperm whales and in particular southern right whales lasted, New Island was a popular harbour for American whaling vessels, whose men supplemented their diet with albatross and penguin eggs collected from the islands. But by the early 1900s whales had become scarce in these regions and attention switched to South Georgia and the Antarctic, allowing the wildlife of New Island a chance to recover.

New Island is home to wildlife artists and naturalists Tony Chatter and Ian Strange. Ian knows the Falklands as well as any man alive and was one of the pivotal figures in establishing the Falkland Islands Conservation Foundation, now Falklands Conservation, set up in January 1979, with Sir Peter Scott acting as the catalyst in trying to ensure that 'progress' didn't diminish the abundant wildlife or destroy the other features which make the Falklands so special. The initiative was prompted by the deteriorating wildlife habitat on New Island, caused in part by the increasing sheep, cattle and particularly rabbit

BELOW
Male kelp goose with goslings. While the male is primarily white, the female is predominantly dark with a white eye ring. Usually seen in pairs and never far from the sea, kelp geese feed on seaweed exposed at low tide.

populations, resulting in considerable loss in tussock and erosion that threatened the nesting colonies of rockhopper and macaroni penguins. Peter Scott envisaged something far grander in design than simply resuscitating the islands' ecology and safeguarding the bird colonies. Falklands Conservation covers wildlife, historic areas, building and wrecks, and encourages wise management of conservation areas on the basis that farming, tourism and wildlife can complement one another. With tourism beginning to prove itself a valuable source of income to the islands – and the current rapid increase in economic and human activity – the promotion of sound conservation practices was both timely and imperative.

New Island now boasts the smallest sheep farm in the Falklands – in the 1970s there were 3,300 sheep, but by 1993 the number was down to 300 in an attempt to reduce the adverse effects of livestock on the environment, with the northern part of the island set aside as a private nature preserve. A favourite spot for visitors, it is typical of the island's beautifully wild exterior, where years of pounding by heavy seas have smashed a deep cleft into the rugged shore, sculpting a steep-sided amphitheatre fringed by thick clumps of tussock grass that fan out at the top into a perfect nesting site for a variety of seabirds: black-browed albatrosses, blue-eyed shags and rockhopper penguins. There is even the occasional pair of orange-plumed macaronis tucked in among the rockhoppers, with several records of the two species interbreeding. Each species seems to know its place, reflecting subtle differences in their needs as well as loyalty to a particular spot, communities within a community. Blustery cliff-tops are ideal launch pads for the albatrosses, which hardly have to move, opening wide their massive wings and

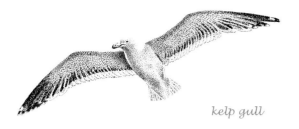

kelp gull

lifting off from their nests as they catch the updraughts. At other times they flip-flop through the colony to a high point and stand facing into the wind like surfers waiting to catch the right wave before committing themselves. There is little squabbling among the different species, who save their energies for battles with the predatory skuas that nest among the tussock at the edge of the colonies, where they can be assured of plenty of food for their growing chicks.

It is little wonder that the Falklands are so attractive to seabirds. The islands are scattered along the shallow water's edge of the Patagonian shelf, impeding the flow of the Falkland Current. This has the effect of squeezing the sea between the islands and forcing it up over the underwater ridges that link the island chain, helping to maintain one of the richest marine faunas in the world: where the current's flow is strongest, bottom-dwelling species from the deeper water are forced to the surface and, along with pelagic species, provide a rich harvest for surface feeders such as the black-browed albatrosses – and on occasion for wandering and grey-headed albatrosses, which are regular non-breeding visitors to the Falklands.

The birds here seem totally unafraid of human visitors, interested only in brooding their eggs and rearing their young. Activity at the colonies is frenetic, with a succession of rockhoppers emerging from the maze of pathways among the tussock. Far below wave after wave of penguins battle the surf as they attempt to reach land, popping out of the foaming white water like corks exploding from bottles of champagne, flinging themselves up onto the rocks and desperately trying to gain a foothold with their sharp claws. Hundreds more are already hopping and clambering their way upwards on the exhausting 100-m (100-yard) journey back to the rookeries.

Rockhoppers are short, stumpy characters – smallest and most aggressive of the polar penguins, weighing only 2.5 kg (5 ½lb) and the most abundant of those on the Falkland Islands, with an estimated 300,000 breeding pairs (the global population is around 2 million pairs). With their spiky hairdos and jaunty yellow head plumes, a rockhopper colony has the air of a gathering of punk rockers, their manic blood-red eyes shining like rubies in the sunlight, a vivid touch of colour in their coal-black faces. At first glance each individual looks the same, but in fact the males are larger, with heavier bills. They return from the sea in October to reclaim their nest sites, the females arriving about a week later. The majority of birds mate in early November and incubate their two white eggs for 33 days. Like most seabirds, penguins are forced to share the

rockhoppers

responsibilities of incubating and raising their young: it would be impossible for a female to lay eggs and brood chicks without the help of her mate, and in the case of the rockhoppers both sexes share incubation duties for the first twelve days, after which the male heads to sea to forage for food. When he returns he remains at the nest until the end of incubation. He will fast for the next 25 days, allowing his partner to forage further afield.

The crested penguins (rockhopper and macaroni – and four species found beyond Antarctica) are unusual among birds in that the first egg of a clutch is considerably smaller than the second, which is laid some four days later: in rockhoppers it is often barely half the size of the second. The most obvious explanation for this is that the smaller egg acts as a safety net in the event that the second and larger egg is lost or is infertile. This is the reverse of what happens with birds of prey, for instance, which lay two eggs and immediately begin to incubate the first. The first chick is therefore destined to be born a few days before its nest mate, with all the advantages that this implies – the second survives only if there is plenty of food. But in the rockhoppers' case the

first egg hatches second – if it hatches at all – and the chick rarely survives more than a few days.

In most rockhopper and almost all macaroni nests the two eggs do not remain in the nest together long enough for the first egg to provide any kind of insurance value: trying to incubate two such disparate-sized eggs on rocky terrain with such sparse nesting material is no easy matter. The female appears to respond to the greater stimulation of the large, bright-white second egg by pushing it into the most secure and comfortable posterior position in her brood pouch – a patch of bare skin with a rich supply of blood that acts as a safe, warm hideaway for penguin eggs and chicks. She then attempts to draw the small, greenish, somewhat dirty first egg into the anterior position, making for an uncomfortable fit and prompting her to constantly stand to try to adjust the eggs. As she turns around in the nest it is not uncommon for her inadvertently to dislodge the smaller egg from under her, leaving an easy meal for the ever-watchful predators.

If there are two chicks, not only does the smaller one have to compete with its larger, stronger sibling for food brought by its parents, but it is generally simply too difficult for the adults to defend two chicks and find sufficient food close enough to home to sustain them both. Some researchers have suggested that this may be a transitory step towards laying just one egg, as is the case with king and emperor penguins, which must forage widely to feed their offspring. Others postulate that the arrival of the first egg helps to prime the development of the brood patch. This takes a number of days and by the time the second egg is laid incubation can begin in earnest. The truth still remains a mystery.

When the first chick emerges it is the larger, male parent who does most of the guarding, and it may be up to a week before the female returns with

LEFT

Macaroni penguin. Distinguished from other crested penguins by having orange rather than yellow head plumes, macaronis are also slightly larger and generally found further south. Probably the most numerous of all penguins with a total population of around 10 million pairs (including a million royal penguins that breed on Macquarie Island and are considered a subspecies of the macaroni). Nevertheless, numbers have fallen substantially since the mid-1970s.

food, during which time the chick must rely on the highly nutritious yolk reserves that sustained it in the egg. The skuas are a constant threat to eggs and chicks, dark, sharp-eyed pirate birds wheeling overhead, searching for opportunities to bully and intimidate the penguins into revealing their brood. Members of a pair of skuas work in tandem – as one causes confusion overhead the other swoops in low with a noisy whoosh of its wings, landing in the middle of the colony, wings flared in a belligerent display of force, keening forward with bill agape, forcing a rockhopper to back up and reveal its egg. In an instant the skua snatches the egg away and is joined by its partner. If pecking at the shell fails to crack it open, one of the skuas grasps the egg in its bill and rises into the air, dropping the egg onto the rocks, scrambling the contents and quickly devouring them.

Skuas are not the only predators working the rookeries. Striated caracaras, kelp and dolphin gulls all sometimes prey on penguin eggs and chicks. But by clumping together in such dense breeding colonies the penguins help to reduce the effects of predators. By the time the rockhopper chicks are around three weeks old they join a crèche of similar-aged young, allowing both parents to share in the search for the shrimp-like krill, which they take it in turns to regurgitate for their chick. At ten weeks the chicks reach their adult weight, fledge and are ready to embark on their first sea outing. Their parents will already have begun to replenish their energy reserves, feeding mainly on krill, amphipods, small fish and squid, returning to the colony in healthy enough condition to spend a further four or five weeks ashore while they moult their old feathers. By April and May it is winter and, freed from the need to stay ashore, the adult penguins head back to sea and resume their migratory way of life in the environment to which they are most suited.

Black-Browed Albatrosses

The Falklands not only provide a wonderful introduction to the penguin family, they are also home to large numbers of black-browed albatrosses, the most widespread and numerous of the nine albatross species found in the southern hemisphere, and as we will see later a species that has been hard hit by the long-line fishing industry. They span the globe between latitudes 25° and 60°S, breeding on islands near New Zealand and in the Indian Ocean as well as here in the South Atlantic. When not raising young, black-brows wander widely, flying vast distances during their winter migrations in search of food – many birds banded in the Falklands have been recovered from the coasts of

LEFT

Black-browed albatross preening, part of their courtship display. Black-brows nest in dense colonies, often in the company of other albatrosses, penguins and cormorants. Juveniles remain at sea for two to five years, often returning to breed at around 10 years of age, close to the nest where they were born. They feed on fish, krill and squid as well as scavenging – particularly for scraps thrown out from fishing vessels.

Brazil, Uruguay and Argentina, suggesting that they are following the Falkland Current and its rich source of nutrients. Others have been found along the coasts of South Africa and Angola.

Standing atop the towering cliffs on New Island with the wind almost blowing you off your feet you can watch the albatrosses wheeling overhead, riding the blustery updraughts before turning into the wind to land, or belly-flopping in an untidy heap onto one of the table-top slabs of rock at the windward edge of the colony. Black-brows are handsome birds, resembling gigantic black-backed gulls. Their bills are beautifully sculpted, head plumage the most creamy of whites, dark eyes set beneath a prominent black brow like a smudge of mascara that some people think helps cut down the glare when feeding at the water's surface. On land they look ungainly, with their outlandish goose-like feet, but sailing aloft on their 2 m (6 ft 6 in) span they are all grace and elegance.

Black-brows begin breeding when they are six to twelve years old and return to the Falklands in September, during the southern spring, remaining faithful to the same nest site and partner for up to 20 years out of a lifespan of 30–40 years. The male arrives first and immediately sets about renovating the nest, a mud cone resembling an upended rough-hewn clay pot. He uses his broad spatula-like bill to replaster the walls with mud, guano, tussock grass and seaweed, with some nests reaching a height of 60 cm (2 ft), testimony to years of construction and repair. His mate arrives a week later. As with all members of the albatross family, their courtship is beautifully choreographed. Nest-building is part of the ritual, accompanied by much mutual preening (known as allo-preening), bill-stretching, nibbling, tail-fanning and wing-spreading. Prior to mating the pair gently preen each other, and

these long bouts of courtship help to reinforce the pair bond and to ensure successful breeding. The female lays a single large white egg, which is incubated for about 68–69 days.

In 1797 Captain Edmund Fanning, an American sealer, wrote in his journal that the black-browed albatrosses laid their eggs on New Island on 10 October, and two hundred years later Ian Strange can testify to the fact that the peak egg-laying date for that same colony is still 10 October. Timing is everything and is closely related to food supply, as we will see later. The parents brood their young for the first three weeks, making sure not to expose it unnecessarily to the attentions of the skuas. At this point the chick, covered in a coat of grey down, is large enough to sit unprotected on its mud throne – all fluffy feathers and large black beak. In April, towards the end of the autumn, the young albatross is ready to leave its nest, having been fed by its parents for the past four months. Now it must forage for itself out at sea, scavenging at times in the wake of the boats for as long as the Loligo squid fishing season continues. It will be five or six years before it returns to the colony of its birth and a further two to three before it breeds successfully. Most of the rest of its life will be spent on the wing.

The Squid Industry

Conservationists such as Ian Strange and Tony Chatter have long been concerned about the impact of the fishing industry on the millions of seabirds attracted to these islands. Fishing has been good to the Falklands, earning millions of pounds for the local government since the 200 nautical mile exclusive fishing zone was imposed around the islands and licences issued, something

brown skuas

that continues to be a source of disagreement with Argentina. But overfishing threatens not only the sustainability of the industry and the economy, but also the wellbeing of the wildlife – and by default the tourist industry that has grown up around it. Some 75 per cent of the fishermen's catch is squid, in particular the short-finned squid *Illex* (a delicacy with wide appeal in Eastern Asia) and the Patagonian squid *Loligo* (a fast-growing species that is served as *calamares* in Spain) – the same prey favoured by black-browed albatrosses, penguins and seals. In this respect the decline in rockhopper numbers is staggering – in 1984 the Falklands population was estimated at 2.5 million breeding pairs; in 2000 the figure was 272,000, and in colonies such as those at New Island, Ian Strange reckons the population may be as little as 5–10 per cent of previous estimates, primarily due to the effects of overfishing.

All vessels operating in Falkland waters are now required to log their positions and record the size of their catch and the species taken on a daily basis, allowing scientists to chart more accurately the distribution and movement of marine resources. Tellingly, perhaps, the revenue from fishing licences, which used to be fairly constant at around £20–25 million annually, has declined over the past few years to £12–15 million due to several poor *Illex* seasons.

The amount of food required by a big seabird colony is enormous and is usually dependent on the close proximity of rich fishing grounds. In 1989 Ian Strange calculated that Beauchêne Island, a small outlier on the southeast side of the Falklands archipelago, which at that time had a population of 1.5 million rockhopper penguins and black-browed albatrosses, required in the region of 60,000 tonnes of food annually. It is significant that enormous numbers of *Loligo* are found off Beauchêne, though little is known about the causes of fluctuations in their numbers. At that time 20 or more trawlers equipped with processing plants aboard gathered along the edge of the Patagonian shelf to capitalize on the *Loligo* swarms, and the albatrosses assembled in their thousands to feast on the tonnes of offal pumped back into the sea as the catch was processed – something of an irony when they could in fact have been feasting on the proceeds of the demise of their own food supply.

Strange also discovered that individual colonies of both black-browed albatrosses and rockhopper penguins breed at slightly different times according to their location, corresponding to food availability. The birds at Beauchêne, for example, lay their eggs ten to twelve days earlier than those on New Island. In the early stages of chick-rearing the adult rockhoppers forage predominantly for krill. Later in the season an abrupt dietary change takes place, prompted by the migration of squid into the bird's foraging range.

The best breeding sites in the Falklands are home to tens of thousands of seabirds, providing an unrivalled spectacle for visitors. Though wind conditions, adequate nesting material and precipitation are all important for the maintenance of a successful colony, an abundant source of food is the main priority: squid, fish and in some cases also lobster krill. The last of

Pair of black-browed albatross displaying, New Island. All albatrosses have elaborate courtship displays consisting of well-defined movements, including the 'rapier action' shown here, accompanied by tail-fanning and barely audible throbbing sounds.

these food items concentrates in 'food fields' borne along by currents, tides and upwellings, which help to provide rich feeding sites for seabirds, fur seals and penguins. The emergence of these food fields close to the seabird colonies during the nesting season plays a vital role – as do the swarms of Loligo squid – in ensuring successful breeding.

In 2001 the IUCN revised the status of the rockhopper penguin to globally threatened and recommended the exclusion of large-scale commercial fishing from within 50 km (30 miles)

of penguin breeding sites in the Falkland Islands. So far the government has refused. While the success of the sale of fishing licences and the prospect of oil offer huge potential benefits to the economy of the Falklands, it is essential that neither is allowed to compromise the future of their unique wildlife resource, which must be nurtured and protected according to the vision of men such as Ian Strange and Sir Peter Scott.

CHAPTER 3

South Georgia

The Falkland Islands are just a distant smudge on the horizon as the ship turns its bow southeast towards the windswept island of South Georgia some 1,360 km (850 miles) away. The sea reaches out in a wide arc of inky blue water, a gentle swell lapping against the sides of the vessel. Thin bands of clouds glow a deep, resonant orange as the sun completes its leisurely descent to the horizon and a party of black-browed albatrosses appears out of nowhere, floating effortlessly above the ocean. Suddenly they are gone again, perhaps heading back to their breeding colonies in the Falklands. Now everything ahead is water and all is quiet except for the drone of the ship's engines.

People who travel south of Cape Horn often bemoan the sea days, impatient to be among the ice that embodies most people's idea of Antarctica. But biologically Antarctica begins in the water, with the bounty of the Southern Ocean unsurpassed anywhere else on Earth. In fact of the two-thirds of our Earth's surface that is covered by water, 10 per cent is encompassed by the Southern Ocean, which spans the globe, connecting the Atlantic, Pacific and Indian Oceans, a giant watery glove encircling and isolating the Antarctic continent. These enormous bodies of water play a vital role in regulating the world's climate, storing and transporting vast amounts of heat and carbon dioxide. Heat from one region is absorbed and carried thousand of kilometres to new locations before being released into the atmosphere, bringing about large-scale, slowly evolving oscillations in temperature and rainfall. In this respect the polar regions act as 'heat sinks', absorbing heat from more temperate lands that then sinks to the ground at the South Pole, depositing a vast ice sheet 2.3 km (just under 1 ½ miles) deep on average that smothers the underlying rock. At the North Pole there is no land and large expanses of sea ice of around 1 m (3 ft) thick accumulate.

Here the strident winds and currents combine to cause water to well up from the ocean bottom, carrying nutrients that feed the simple plant organisms known as phytoplankton. These free-floating algae drift in the upper 200 m (650 ft) of water, using sunlight to trap energy in the form of simple carbon compounds, which in turn provide sustenance for the zooplankton – tiny animals such as krill, the primary food source of the majority of the ocean's inhabitants, from the great baleen whales who scoop it up by the tonne, to the squids, seals and penguins whose faeces are stained pink by its pigment. In spring and summer there is a surge of activity in the sea as the phytoplankton blooms, covering thousands of square kilometres of ocean with a greenish tinge and in places painting the ice floes a rusty red. This is the vital first link in the chain, food for the zooplankton which reaches its highest concentrations off the northern and western Antarctic Peninsula and Scotia Arc, within range of the breeding grounds of many of the birds and animals that inhabit the region.

Over millions of years the marine animals and plants have adapted to the ocean's own particular rhythm. While there are fewer niches for them to exploit in the sea than on land – for instance there are only 300 seabirds in the world, compared with 8,300 land birds – those that do occur are often found in astonishing numbers. By contrast the clear blue waters of tropical oceans hold little life – the waters are too calm to bring life-building nutrients within reach of the phytoplankton and with less food available birdlife is sparse except around islands.

After Antarctica split from South American 23 million years ago, there were no major

Crabeater seals are circumpolar in their distribution, sometimes reaching as far north as South Georgia. Perhaps the most abundant mammals on Earth after humans, crabeaters are creatures of the pack ice. They are great wanderers, rarely seen ashore. Despite their name, 90 per cent of their diet consists of krill, supplemented by small amounts of fish and squid.

landmasses to impede the flow of water around the globe, hence the Southern Ocean's reputation as one of the most unpredictable and tempestuous waters on Earth. Bounded to the north by the subtropical front and to the south by the icy continent, the Southern Ocean is prone to howling winds and mountainous waves, home to the 'Roaring Forties', 'Filthy Fifties' and 'Screaming Sixties'. Here at the bottom of the world a unique brew of ocean, atmosphere and sea ice generates ocean currents that – like the ocean itself – have a profound influence on the Earth's climate and the animals and birds that live here.

The Southern Ocean is dominated by the influence of two circumpolar currents – the inshore Antarctic Coastal Current that flows counter-clockwise in an easterly direction at around 65°S, and the Antarctic Circumpolar Current that flows clockwise in a westerly direction at around 53°S. The point at which this Circumpolar Current meets the waters of the other oceans forms one of nature's longest and most significant natural boundaries, the Antarctic Convergence. Here, cold, northward-flowing Antarctic surface waters meet and sink beneath the relatively warmer, southerly flowing waters of the other oceans.

Crossing the Convergence is of little significance for passengers lying snug under their blankets and duvets as the ship slips quietly

cape petrel

through the night, the temperature in their cabins warmly regulated by the air-conditioning vent in the ceiling above them. But according to the ship's log, at 5.30 a.m. the sea temperature drops a notch or two to 4°C (39°F) and out on deck you can actually feel the icy grip of the Southern Ocean taking hold – and so could the early sailors. For the explorers, whalers and sealers it meant battening down the hatches and bracing themselves for stormy, windswept seas and an icy welcome. The boundary of the Convergence is never exact but always apparent: it rarely strays more than half a degree of latitude from its mean position (around 59°S), except where it kinks up to embrace South Georgia at around 49°S, with the Falklands well to the north. Not only does the surface temperature of the sea drop dramatically as you hit the Convergence, but the mixing of the two bodies of water – one warmer and more salty, the other colder and less saline – produces a more dense appearance at the point where they converge.

Averaging 32–48 km (20–30 miles) across, but sometimes extending to 100 km (60 miles) and stretching for more than 20,000 km (12,500 miles) around Antarctica, the Convergence forms a barrier to the dispersal of birds and fish – and crucially to plankton that cannot survive in the warmer waters further north. The sea water here is cold, and much of it freezes during the winter months. By September the sea ice is at its maximum extent, covering an area of 19 million sq. km (7.3 million square miles), double the size of the continent, but with the onset of summer the sun sets for only a few hours each day and by February the sea ice shrinks to 3.8 million sq. km (1.5 million square miles). With the sunlight once again able to penetrate below the surface day and night, there is an explosion in the phytoplankton, heralding a time of plenty for all the birds, mammals, fish and other animals higher up the food chain. Being situated 350km (220 miles) south of the Convergence qualifies South Georgia biologically as part of Antarctica and, bleak and remote as it may appear, if you are interested in wildlife then this is a place you have to visit.

Approaching South Georgia

The wake of a passing ship is like a magnet to seabirds, creating updraughts that provide them with a free ride for as long as they wish to follow. The most conspicuous of these wandering seafarers are flocks of Cape petrels (also known as Cape pigeons or pintado petrels), dainty black and white birds whose mottled plumage creates abstract patterns against the foamy white crests of the waves. The petrels are mesmerizing in their passage across the wake, at times flying so close that you feel you could reach out and touch them, and you can certainly see every detail: the soft denseness of their plumage, their dark eyes so alive and enquiring.

Not to be outdone, a pair of snow petrels – unmistakable in their whiteness – add a touch of

ABOVE

Cape petrels riding the waves of the Southern Ocean.
Also known as the pintado – meaning 'painted' – petrel
due to its distinctive black-and-white markings. Often
in gregarious flocks around vessels in the hope of
scavenging scraps of food.

Bull elephant seal, South Georgia. The southern elephant seal is the largest seal in the world, with males weighing up to 4,000 kg (8,800 lb) and measuring 4.5 m (15 ft). They may live up to 20 years. Neither males nor females feed while ashore during the breeding season, with males fasting for up to 90 days and females for 30 days.

theatre, the brilliance of their plumage thrown into sharp relief against the inky black water. They twist and tease, matching one another turn for turn, lifting higher, one with mouth ajar, twittering and pirouetting in what appears to be some feverish dance of passion played out against the tawny sky. There is something ghostly about these birds: paper cut-outs for Christmas decorations, angelic figurines with dancing flight, a glimmer of light pinpointing the coal-black eye and sparkling outer edge of their short black bill. It is a rare treat to find snow petrels this far north – they rarely stray beyond 55°S. Icebergs and the pack are their chosen landscape, hence their startling whiteness; against the ice they all but disappear, their cryptic colouration making them less likely to fall victim to predatory birds such as skuas, and helping them to ambush their prey – fish and crustaceans as well as carrion – more easily.

Each spring the snow petrels fly up to 350 km (215 miles) inland from the ice edge, seeking the granite nunataks – patches of exposed rock which mark the place where isolated mountain peaks pierce the ice sheet, providing the crevices and hollows these birds need to nest. When they first arrive they may be forced to burrow 1 m (3 ft) through the snow to find solid ground, and at one favoured location called Smarthvaren they gather in their hundreds along with half a million Antarctic petrels. Southern polar skuas sometimes pluck the snow petrels out of the air, as well as taking eggs and chicks during the breeding season. But an even greater danger is posed by the extremes of weather the petrels must conquer to breed this far south.

The antics of the birds help while away the hours until the desolate crescent shape of South Georgia appears, a craggy speck in the vastness of the ocean. Some 170 km (105 miles) long by 2–40 km (1 ¼–25 miles) wide, its rugged façade has been shaped by the effects of intense glacial activity. From the air it looks like shark's teeth, curved and jagged-edged, with the mountain ranges of Allardyce and Salvesen forming a sharp central spine. There are eleven peaks of over 2,000 m (6,500 ft) and in winter the island lies under a blanket of snow that reaches to the sea.

The first people to really explore the treacherous coasts of the island were sealers from Europe, quickly followed by the Americans. These were hardy folk, with gangs of men often left to fend for themselves until their ship returned, a form of marooning heightened by the fear that the mother ship might meet with some mishap and never return or be delayed for months or years. It was tough and bloody work and killing was a crude affair – the big male fur seals were speared, the smaller animals clubbed, a brutally effective way of dispatching soft-skulled animals and far cheaper than using rounds of ammunition. The men clambered about on wind- and wave-swept rocks, killing as many seals as possible before they could escape to sea, stashing and curing the hides while their ship continued the search for new breeding colonies, eager to denude every last hiding place. At worst the men were left with virtually no provisions, forced to subsist on whatever they could kill, taking birds, seals and eggs; at best they lived long enough to earn a handsome wage. In those days the skin of the southern fur seal commanded premium prices in China: the Chinese had invented a method of removing the stiff guard hairs (which otherwise made it scratchy and uncomfortable). The fur from the softened skin could be used to make felt and the profits used to buy tea, silk and ceramics. There was good money to be earned by anyone prepared to hire a ship and brave the stormy southern seas, with an experienced sealer capable of killing and skinning 60 fur seals an hour.

The giant elephant seals (there are two species, northern and southern) proved an easy target too for the sealers, yielding over 20,000 tonnes of oil on the London market alone, the copious blubber rendered down in large cauldrons known as tripots, some of which can still been seen scattered along the shores, a visible reminder of those callous days. In the span of a hundred years 750,000 northern elephant seals were slaughtered for their oil, and in 1778 alone, English sealers were responsible for taking 2,800 tonnes of elephant seal oil, valued at £40,000, and 40,000 fur seal skins; by 1791 there were dozens of vessels scouring the Southern Ocean for seals. In 1800 an American vessel captained by Edmund Fanning took a record 57,000 fur seal skins from South Georgia and shipped them to China, where they fetched five or six dollars apiece. The following year 122,000 fur seals were killed around the island. But plunder of this magnitude could not continue indefinitely and by 1810 fur seals had been virtually exterminated here, later recovering sufficiently to yield good profits around 1820 and again in the 1870s. By the mid-1930s there were thought to be fewer than 50 pairs of fur seals along the north coast of the island, but as we shall see their recovery is one of South Georgia's success stories.

The Southern Elephant Seal

The sealers and whalers left a scar on South Georgia and the surrounding ocean that has had major repercussions for the whole ecosystem, but like visitors of today they must have marvelled at the scenes that greeted them on arrival at this remote outpost, for the abundance of wildlife stuns the senses. While the Falklands are more diverse and temperate, with 63 species of breeding birds compared with South Georgia's 31, South Georgia is seasonally far more productive and densely populated with wildlife, boasting 100 million breeding birds to the Falklands' 5 million. Vast king penguin colonies dominate the landscape, wedged between towering mountain ranges and pebble-encrusted beaches, often close to where meltwater gushes from glaciers.

It matters little which of the landing sites you step ashore at when visiting South Georgia, you always pray for good weather – although the scene before you is generally so outrageously spectacular that it seems almost greedy to ask for sunshine as well; come snow or rain it will leave an indelible mark. Most tourist ships visit in the southern summer, between November and March, but even so the weather may be so foul, the sea so rough, that you are not even able to set foot on the island. If you land early in the day it is not uncommon to be met by a light fog that closes out the sky to within a metre or so (a few feet) of the water. But so fickle is the weather here that an hour or so later it may well have cleared enough to reveal a patchwork of blue sky ribboned with white. Stepping ashore is no easy matter, with hundreds of penguins and dozens of elephant seals crowded along the shoreline, completely unfazed by their human visitors. Although it is always wise to keep a sharp look-out for fur seals guarding the beach.

At Gold Harbour, for instance, the beach is wide and long, composed of a fine grey powder where ancient rocks have been pummelled to dust by the effect of glaciation and crashing waves, leaving grains the size of a pinhead that smother cameras and lenses in dust. If you leave a rucksack unattended it will shortly be commandeered by an elephant seal pup looking for a comfortable and comforting substitute for its mother, who by now has abandoned it to its own devices. But better a

Bull elephant seal, Gold Harbour, South Georgia. A bull's inflatable trunk-like proboscis is fully developed by eight years of age, helping to amplify the intimidating roar of a dominant bull.

pup than one of the bulls that stand out from the crowd by virtue of their sheer size. The sea rarely freezes around South Georgia, which is why it is so vital to the wildlife of the region: half the world's 600,000 southern elephant seals – the largest seal in the world – come here each year to breed and in late spring the beach at the mouth of St Andrew's Bay, further north along the coast,

hosts from 6,000 to 8,000 seals. The bulls are immense – up to 4.5 m (15 ft) long and weighing 3–4 tonnes, with females around a quarter of this weight – and continue to grow throughout their lives, with the largest reaching nearly 5 tonnes.

It is a blessing that elephant seals aren't as feisty as fur seals; if they were it would be impossible to land along these beaches. Fortunately elephant seals are true seals and cannot produce the turn of speed that characterizes the fur seal and other 'eared' seals, whose hind flippers are highly manoeuvrable and can twist forward, allowing it to charge across the beach at an alarming rate of knots. But you certainly need to tread carefully around an elephant seal wallow, where these huge creatures bide their time while moulting and keeping cool, churning the mud into a foul-smelling pit-latrine accompanied by a noise factory of unmentionable sounds.

Adorned with an elephantine proboscis that acts like a blubbery foghorn to amplify the bubbling roars and snorts by which they announce their presence and intimidate rivals, the bulls haul out onto traditional beaches in early to mid-September. Bulls are sexually mature at six to seven years old, but due to fierce competition for breeding rights at the larger colonies they may not start breeding until they are ten. They do not defend a territory – they defend a group of females or harem – and when two mature bulls fight it is a battle of the Titans. Each of them rears up as much as 2.5 m (8 ft) above the ground, pushing and shoving, tearing and ripping with his thumb-sized canines, gouging the nose and neck of his opponent until one of them breaks free, bloodied and defeated, and lumbers off through the colony of cows and pups to nurse his wounds in the safety of the sea. Male elephant seals have a thickened 'breast plate' to help protect them from serious damage, but that doesn't stop them sometimes having half their proboscis torn off or losing an eye. For the victor the prize is a harem of up to 100 females (though 30–50 is more usual), but being a 'beachmaster' exacts a heavy toll – many bulls only manage a single year of breeding, though on Marion Island southeast of South Africa (where more than 10,000 animals have been tagged and monitored in the past 23 years) one is on record as breeding for seven consecutive years.

The females arrive at their traditional breeding sites between the end of September and mid-October, and pups are born a few days later. The moment of birth is marked by a scrum of skuas and giant petrels eager to feast on the afterbirth, and if the mother isn't vigilant or her offspring is sickly they will kill it. By this time the strongest and fittest of the males – the beachmasters – have asserted their dominance and over the course of the next few weeks they mate with the females as they come in to oestrus. This means that the beachmasters must go without food for two months in their quest to mate with as many females as possible before the females head back to sea.

Pups weigh around 40–50 kg (90–110 lb) at birth and are covered in thick black fur; they suckle for about three weeks, doubling their weight in the first two days and thereafter putting on up to 9 kg (20 lb) a day courtesy of their mother's copious flow of milk. She meanwhile remains on the beach without feeding, shrinking like a punctured balloon and losing up to 350 kg (800 lb) – nearly 40 per cent of her body mass – during the month it takes to wean her pup. Elephant seal pups are everyone's favourites, with their big, round, liquid eyes and engaging personalities, and once weaned they can often be seen at the water's edge frolicking and splashing about with their age-mates away from areas where the adults are mating, the bull pups already beginning to rear up and joust with one another. Having weaned her pup, the mother then returns to the sea to regain condition, hauling ashore again two months later to moult for around 40 days. Moulting is important for diving animals, keeping their streamlined skin in good condition and replacing the pelage, which wears out just as birds' feathers do, but during this

BELOW
Beachmaster attempting to mate with cow elephant seal (note the extraordinary difference in size between the sexes). Beachmasters breed with up to 80 cows a season, but most bulls are able to maintain their status for only around two years.

period the elephant seals cannot enter the water, so they must build up food reserves in advance.

Cumbersome as they may look on land, elephant seals are perfectly adapted to life at sea, where they spend the vast majority of their lives beneath the surface, a layer of insulating blubber up to 15 cm (6 in) thick providing them with the perfect wetsuit. To study this part of their existence, scientists at sub-Antarctic islands such as Macquarie and Marion have fitted satellite time depth recording (STDR)

instruments, using epoxy resin to glue them securely in place on top of each study animal's head. In this way they can monitor the elephant seals' location, movements, dive behaviour and body temperature. At times elephant seals roam the turbulent waters formed by the canyons and ridges of submerged mountain ranges that provide ideal feeding conditions for their primary prey – squid and fish. Squid makes up 75 per cent of an elephant seal's diet and the retinas of the seal's large eyes are very sensitive

to whatever light is available in the darkened world of the ocean depths, detecting the luminescence emitted by the swift-moving prey.

These mighty creatures can slow their heart rate to just eight beats a minute, dive to depths of 1.5 km (1 mile) in sub-zero temperatures – though most dives are more like 200–400 m (650–1,300 ft) – and remain beneath the water for up to two hours, having spent only a few brief minutes at the surface: feats that only the sperm whale can rival. Meanwhile their human observers sit in the comfort of a laboratory allowing their study

animals to reveal an alien world. To achieve this, elephant seals have evolved some remarkable physiological adaptations: they have no sinus cavities, can collapse their lungs and ribcage, and have a body density that is almost equal to that of water – all of which enables them to withstand the phenomenal pressure deep in the ocean. They also possess high concentrations of a protein called myoglobin in their muscle fibres, which allows them to soak up oxygen as they breathe it in, and a high tolerance for lactic acid, which builds up in their system when oxygen is in short supply.

Young elephant seals – 'weaners' – resting, Gold Harbour. Once weaned the pups are abandoned by their mother and then fast for a month before making their way to the water, where they must learn to find food for themselves. A cow may produce up to seven pups during an average lifespan of 12 years.

Many of the adult elephant seals that breed in South Georgia disperse as far south as the Antarctic Peninsula, spending the winter feeding under the pack ice, while others head north, covering huge distances. In fact, by six months a pup may have travelled 5,000 km (3,000 miles) from where it was born, and one two-and-a-half-year-old male that was being monitored travelled 10,500 km (6,500 miles) in eight months.

But for all their remarkable adaptations to life in the oceans elephant seals are under threat, their numbers having declined by 50 per cent during the last 60 years – and on Marion Island numbers are down 83 per cent since 1951. Nobody is sure exactly why this is and there may be a number of reasons, though food availability is likely to be the most significant one. As we saw in the previous chapter, fisheries take large quantities of squid, Patagonian toothfish and krill, and the effect of global warming and shifts in both current patterns and climate may also be influencing the distribution and abundance of the elephant seal's prey.

Some people question the need to manhandle wildlife in the name of science, but the elephant seal is a top predator in the Southern Ocean and acts as an indicator of the health of the whole ecosystem – as do penguins. It is vital that we have access to information such as this. The STDR device does not appear to interfere with the elephant seal's normal movements and is discarded when it comes ashore to moult, when it can be relocated and recycled – highly cost-effective at US$5,000 a unit. One thing is certain, as you travel around these remote lands it soon becomes apparent that a worrying trend is emerging, with the populations of a variety of species – including penguins, albatrosses and elephant seals – undergoing an indisputable decline in numbers.

Fur Seals

Ironically while the elephant seals are showing cause for concern, the recovery of the fur seal population throughout South Georgia has been of staggering proportions. By 1900 they were virtually extinct, with around a hundred discovered in the 1930s on Bird Island, a small island off South Georgia's western tip. From this nucleus the population had recovered to 360,000 in 1976, and by the 1980s it had reached one million with an increase of 20–30 per cent in some years. It may now be close to three million, causing profound changes to the landscape of places like Bird Island, where about half of the tussock grass has been eroded, causing problems for the wandering albatrosses, on whose nesting areas they have encroached.

On Bird Island, Prion Island in the Bay of Islands and suitable beaches all around South Georgia, by the height of the breeding season in November or December the fur seal beachmasters have sectioned off every available scrap of beach, which they guard tenaciously from other bulls – and people. Their breeding strategy is simple – herd as many females as possible on to their patch. As with the elephant seals, the females are so much smaller than the males that at first glance they could be mistaken for young animals – a phenomenon known as sexual dimorphism, with males built to fight and weighing on average 136 kg (300 lb) at maturity, by which time they will be ten years or older. Females reach maturity earlier, at five years old, but weigh only 38 kg (84 lb). Colour-wise there is no mistaking them – the males are clad in a dense salt and pepper coat, with females wearing a brownish-beige smudged rusty-red in places.

Sexual dimorphism is common wherever males compete for breeding rights with a

ABOVE

Fur seal scratching. The fur seal's coat consists of two layers: an outer layer of stiff guard hairs and an inner layer of very fine fibres which trap air to provide thermal insulation – fur seals do not have as well developed a layer of blubber as other seal species. They can regulate their body temperature through the exposed skin of their flippers, either radiating heat from them or conserving heat by tucking them under their body.

number of females – a polygynous mating system. Again like elephant seals, mature bulls arrive first on the beaches; the females haul out two or three weeks later and give birth to a single jet-black pup a day or so after that. By the time the first cruise ships arrive in mid-November the beaches are seething with life, and within a week of giving birth the females are ready to breed again – hence the males' frantic attempts to corral them until mating has been completed successfully. The gestation period is nine months, but – like bears, to whom fur seals are related – they employ an ingenious physiological strategy known as delayed implantation to ensure that the fertilized egg implants only if the female is in sufficiently good condition to endure the rigours of pregnancy and that pups are born at the appropriate time of the year. Mother and young stay together for about 140 days, with the pup quickly gaining weight on a rich diet of milk that comprises 28 per cent fat and 20 per cent protein (if you consider that an upmarket brand of ice cream is around 15 per cent fat, you get some idea of just how luxurious this is). Every six days or so the female must return to the sea to replenish her energy. The pup, left to fend for itself, finds a sheltered corner to hide in while its mother is away, greeting her noisily on her return with dog-like barking and whimpering.

A mother seal and her pup imprint on one another at birth and recognize each other by sound and scent. It is all too easy for tiny pups (which are only 6 kg (13 lb) and 30 cm (1 ft) long at birth) to become separated – or squashed – in the mayhem that surrounds a breeding colony, so 'voice' is a vital way of communicating their whereabouts. Perhaps the black natal coat makes the pups easier to find, as well as keeping them warm by absorbing the sun's rays. At low-density breeding sites losses may be as little as 3 per cent, but where seals gather at high densities as many as 30 per cent of the pups may die.

While ashore, seals spend much of their time resting, sprawled comfortably on their side or tummy. But the beachmasters cannot afford such luxuries. They advertise their presence by sitting upright, noses pointed to the sky in the manner of a dog waiting obediently to be rewarded for its patience: impressive-looking animals, distinguished from the younger males by a cape of thick fur around their shoulders – 160–180 kg (350–400 lb) of muscle and blubber, armed with razor-sharp canines stained a tobacco brown and emitting a pungent smell. The moment another bull approaches, or a female tries to leave, the beachmaster lumbers forward to cut them off, huffing and puffing over the shingles, uttering cries and wheezes of protest, bristling with aggression. Any animal hoping to gain access to the sea or higher ground must run the gauntlet of the territory holders. There is a lot of posturing and bluff to these aggressive displays, designed to intimidate rivals. But sometimes the stakes are high enough to provoke a potentially damaging fight – possession of a breeding female or the arrival of a new male prepared to mount a serious challenge for a territory. In these cases both males launch themselves across the beach, snapping at one another with a succession of well-aimed bites to face, neck and flippers, twisting and ripping, at times leaving an adversary with gaping wounds.

The best advice for humans is to give fur seals as wide a berth as possible, and the closest you are likely to get to them is when landing at places like Prion Island to visit the breeding grounds of the wandering albatross. The routine is for staff members to gingerly negotiate a

Female fur seal with
young pup. The otarids –
the fur seals and sealions
– have a visible earflap,
and use all their limbs for
locomotion on land. By
turning their hind limbs
forward beneath their
bodies and balancing
their weight on their very
large fore-flippers they are
able to walk or even gallop,
making them surprisingly
nimble on land.

Fur seal mothers remain with their pups for eight days, suckling at six-hourly intervals. They mate again before going to sea for three to six days to feed and synthesize more milk, then return to suckle their offspring for a further three days. This pattern is repeated for up to 115 days.

pathway across the beach, marking a narrow walkway with bamboo poles and streamers for visitors to follow. This is not always that easy, as some of the more aggressive beachmasters take exception to the intrusion. The crew then have to employ long wooden poles or paddles to keep the seals at a safe distance until they settle down, which they normally do quite quickly, though at particularly crowded and active beaches it is sometimes impossible to land. Beyond the beaches lies a muddy trail washed by meltwater from the higher, snow-covered ground and the cumulative passage of fur seals,

a number of which have usually taken up positions close to the path. For the younger males this is a chance to keep out of trouble, and for the vanquished to lick their wounds and recover from the energy-sapping rituals being fought out below. From up here they can monitor what is happening on the beach, snoozing comfortably in the tussock, stirring once in a while to raise their pointed heads skywards, grunting and protesting as the column of human visitors cautiously make their way past on their pilgrimage to the wanderers, which we will meet in the next chapter.

King Penguins

While the elephant and fur seals dominate proceedings by their size and presence, the glory of South Georgia is surely its king penguins. Seeing kings is like enjoying the company of emperor penguins without the hardship – you don't have to suffer bitter cold and katabatic winds to appreciate them.

King penguins are sleeker than their somewhat larger cousins – no need for such fulsome plumage or quite so much blubber in milder climes. But some of their colonies are vast – a broad band of grey, white and brown, an abstract canvas stippling the tussock-green hillsides. To fully appreciate what you are witnessing you need the benefit of elevation, and to achieve that you must clamber through the tussock, splashing knee-deep along runnels of mud and mire and guano. With each step – if you don't end up on your backside – the scene broadens out a notch, revealing yet another

King penguins displaying – raising the flipper and stretching the neck out signals the intent to attack. During the early stages of courtship and pair bonding, groups of four to eight birds may alternate pecking and flipper beating with sexual displays.

thousand penguins organized with military precision to allow them space to breed. Adults – the grey and white ones – are intermingled with clumps of fluffy brown: the juveniles, or oakum boys, as they were christened by the early sealers, who likened their feather suits to the teased-out hemp used for caulking ships. These youngsters appear so different from the adults that you might think they were a separate species. Emerging at the top of the tussock-cloaked hill you are forced to sit down – not just to catch your breath from the exertion of lugging tripods and rucksacks filled with cameras this far up, but because this is one of the great sights in nature, 10,000 birds at a glance, their vibrant calls echoing all around you. In fact at St Andrew's Bay an estimated 100,000 kings gather to breed, creating a living landscape of breathtaking scale.

The sheer size of kings and emperors marks them out from other penguins, and while kings stand nearly 1 m (3 ft) tall – waist high to a human and just 15 cm (6 in) shorter than emperors – at 12 kg (25 lb) they are only a third of the weight. The two species share a number of other characteristics: neither builds a nest, instead incubating a single egg on their feet; in the case of kings both partners take their turn incubating the egg over the course of two months. The divorce rate is higher among kings and emperors than the smaller species of penguin, with only 15 per cent of emperors and 19 per cent of kings reuniting the following year. This is hardly surprising when you consider that both are offshore foragers and that emperors are migratory and kings partially migratory, returning to their rookeries only during the breeding season and lacking a fixed nest site as a reliable meeting place. When one partner relieves the other at the nest site it prompts an outburst of raucous calling, with both birds raising their

beaks to the sky and calling – an activity often fittingly referred to as the ecstatic display, a form of behaviour seen in all species of penguins. This helps strengthen the pair bond that is so important in cementing successful courtship and breeding. Maintaining the pair bond may be easier for the species that forage close to shore and are non-migratory, as they have the benefit of more frequent changeovers and mutual displays.

The kings lay their eggs in spring, starting in late November with a peak around mid-December. This means that growing chicks can benefit from the plentiful supply of food available to them during the autumn in these more northerly waters. Even though they do not construct a nest kings still defend a nesting territory, and when incubating they stand rooted

to the ground at a flipper's length from the next penguin, the tell-tale bulge of an egg nestled within the brood pouch and concealed beneath their plumage. Males take the first incubation shift of two weeks, females the next two weeks, after which they alternate shifts of three or four days at a time. At six weeks the chick is half the size and weight of its parents and has moulted into a thick fluffy brown feather down, reminding one of an Edwardian grandmother in an old fur coat. These are penguins at their most comical, with throngs of young birds forming into crèches and crowding along the shoreline, all inquisitive innocence as they bide their time while their parents search for food. Kings feed predominantly on small myctophid fish that live in dense

King penguins emerging from the ocean, Gold Harbour. Kings dive to depths of up to 300 m (1,000 ft) during foraging trips which last from five to seven days.

schools and perform daily vertical migrations, but when fish are scarce they target squid, even though they gain less sustenance from them.

By April most chicks are almost adult size and must endure the winter with little or no nourishment, burning up the bountiful store of fat accumulated from food provided by their parents earlier in the season. This enforced fast can last for up to five months while the adults search for food, and by the end of winter chicks may be malnourished and prone to starvation. But if they survive, they quickly fatten up again and some time in November or December moult into their juvenile plumage before fledging and going to sea. At best kings are able to produce two young every three years, though they usually breed every two years and may attempt to do so annually. So to the inexperienced eye king penguin colonies – which are occupied year round – are a confusing mix of adults incubating eggs or tending babies alongside crèches of twelve-month-old chicks.

It is not just the urge to breed that impels penguins to come ashore at certain times of the year – feathers wear out and lose their insulating properties, and their waterproof aerodynamic suit must be replaced. This is simply not possible at sea, as all the feathers are replaced at one time, so the penguins must either come to land or haul out on the ice. Either way it is a huge drain on their resources, for once ashore they must rely on their fat reserves to sustain them for a fast of two to five weeks. It is quite common to see a penguin standing alone, head drooped against its shoulder and bill tucked under its wing, rooted to the ground in a state of semi-torpor, conserving every iota of energy while it moults, and it is imperative not to disturb a bird during this stressful time. Most penguins moult after breeding when they are already drained of energy from rearing their young, but kings, with their protracted breeding cycle, may moult either before or after mating. Whenever they do it, it is vital that the adults are capable of providing sufficient food to ensure their chicks the best start in life, as well as building up sufficient energy reserves to sustain themselves through the moult. This is particularly important for the Antarctic penguins, whose breeding season is linked to a strictly limited period when food is abundant.

Subcutaneous fat fuels the moulting process and penguins are capable of laying down fat reserves at a prodigious rate – a necessity when you consider that some lose almost half their body mass during moulting. During their pre-moulting foraging trip, kings gain over 5 kg (11 lb), increasing their body weight by nearly 50 per cent.

The new set of feathers is developed beneath the skin while the penguins are still foraging at sea and in the case of kings, rockhoppers and macaronis new feathers appear after four or five days ashore. At this stage they are about half their final length and they continue to develop for the first three weeks or so of the fast. Kings shed their old feathers from about day twelve and have lost them completely at three weeks – so for about nine days the birds are by their standards semi-naked. Some 30 days after the onset of the moult the kings are ready to re-enter their ocean home in a sparkling new suit of feathers.

Pausing amid the colour and noise of a king penguin colony to try to comprehend the complex physical and behavioural adaptations that allow these extraordinary flightless birds to survive such extremes, it seems only natural to turn one's attention skywards, to where a very different kind of Antarctic bird soars on blustery winds, as at home in the air as the penguin is underwater, inextricably linked by the seafarers of old to the winds and the weather on which their lives depended.

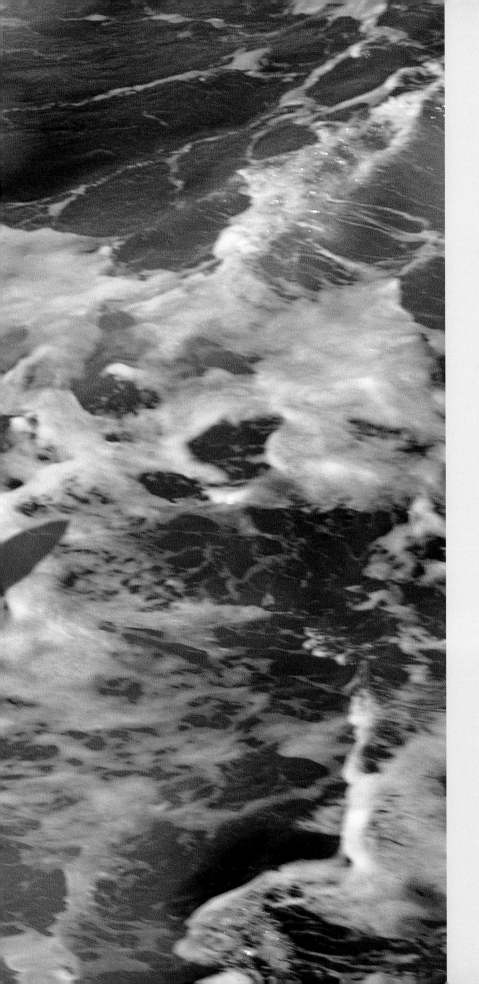

CHAPTER 4

Ocean Wanderers

The sea-going world of the wandering albatross is remote and mysterious, the majority of their lives spent flying great distances across the oceans to track their abundant but patchy food. Hour after hour they wheel across the sky, gliding within centimetres of the water's surface to capitalize on the energy of the wind. These largest of all seabirds are supremely adapted to the marine environment, having wings that are 18 times longer than they are wide (the largest aspect ratio of any bird), minimizing drag by spilling it off the pointed wing-tip. This design makes them supremely energy efficient – it only takes 20 per cent more energy for them to fly than to sit on their nest.

The albatross earned its name from fifteenth-century Portuguese mariners who first encountered long-winged black and white seabirds as they ventured down the coast of Africa into the windswept South Atlantic. They named these stout-bodied creatures *alcatraz* – derived from the Arabic *al-cadous*, used to describe the more familiar pelicans found in Mediterranean waters – and before long English sailors had corrupted *alcatraz* to *albatross*. Perhaps the Greeks had the albatross in mind when immortalizing great warriors who at death were believed to be reincarnated as large seabirds: hence the name *Diomedia* for the genus embracing the seven great albatrosses – Diomedes having been the King of Argos who fought heroically with the Greeks at Troy.

Standing on deck during sea days you long for the albatrosses to fly closer – and on many occasions the black-browed of their kind do. But the wanderers often appear shy and wary, keeping their distance, like dignified and important guests waiting to be introduced, peeling off in a languorous figure-of-eight just when you feel sure they will wander within reach, receding into the distance until they are no more than a tiny black and white speck.

Viewing these birds from a passing ship barely hints at their true size. You need to come face to face with a wandering albatross to appreciate how enormous it really is, and in a corner of the beautifully maintained museum on South Georgia you can do just that. Here a preserved wanderer hangs from the ceiling, a great lifeless bird suspended forever in time and motion, each wing equivalent in size to a man with his arms flung wide and the total wingspan averaging around 3 m (10 ft). One very old male caught 40 years ago in the Tasman Sea had a wingspan of 3.63 m (11 ft 11 in) and with so few birds ever having been measured it is likely that somewhere in the vastness of the Southern Ocean soars an even larger specimen – unconfirmed reports of birds up to 4.22 m (13 ft 10 in) may well prove to be true. Enormous they may be, but albatrosses need to fly light, with air-filled bones – they tip the scales at a mere 10–11 kg (22–24 lb).

Albatrosses are found throughout the oceans bar the North Atlantic and the frozen Arctic, with 24 different species divided into four genera – eleven mollymawks, two sooty albatrosses, seven great albatrosses and four Pacific albatrosses, with even the smallest having a wingspan of 2 m (6 ft 6 in). The heart of albatross country spans the southern seas between the Tropic of Capricorn and the Antarctic Circle, with the six Southern Ocean species all plying their trade among the great west winds and torrid waters of the Roaring Forties and Furious Fifties. Here winds of 10–50 knots (5–25 metres/second) blow continuously from west to east between the southern tips of the continents and the Antarctic ice. The weather is constantly changing, the winds forever shifting, transforming a crystal-clear sky into a blanket of cloud, enveloping the landscape. By harnessing a 10-knot (5 m/s) wind an albatross can travel 400 km (250 miles) a day, circling the

globe in a lot fewer than 80 days, a journey of 30,000 km (19,000 miles) at 40°S that four species – the wandering, black-browed and two sooty albatrosses – all undertake. How the early explorers must have envied these mysterious birds their freedom as they rode the ocean waves alongside their ships, at home in the roughest seas, independent of land for months – years even – at a time, free to explore the remotest parts of the southern oceans. If any creature truly 'knows' Antarctica and all its nuances it is these indefatigable wanderers.

Sometimes an albatross will track the movement of a vessel day after day, hoping perhaps for the wake to spit out a squid or the galley to offload garbage, occasionally landing on the water to feed. But when it chooses to, an albatross can outdistance a ship without even flapping its enormous wings, harnessing the energy of the prevailing westerlies. Albatrosses cannot fly efficiently by flapping – they are too big – and depend for their existence on moving air. When becalmed, they can be seen sitting or resting on the water.

They rest on the water at night, too: though some birds such as swifts can sleep on the wing by closing down one side of their brain like dolphins, albatrosses are probably unable to do this for fear of snagging a giant wing on the water.

It is hardly surprising that the albatross became a mystical bird to the sailors of old. Seafarers are superstitious folk, always looking for indicators of fine weather or foul, constantly scanning the sky for signs of change. They thought of albatrosses as the spirits of dead companions swept to their deaths in gales – harbingers of winds, mist and fog. The Ancient Mariner in Samuel Taylor Coleridge's poem was roundly condemned for killing the bird 'that made the breeze to blow' to help his ship through

the fog, although when the skies cleared the same shipmates praised him for killing the bird 'that brought the fog and mist'. Without wind both albatross and ship are helpless, deprived of the power of movement. Little wonder, then, that seafarers associated the great birds with storms and wind, knowing that 'the harder she blows' the more albatrosses they would see.

Sailors had their own names for albatrosses, lumping them together by colour – white ones and dark ones. They were seen as rather stupid creatures – 'gooneys' and 'mollymawks', the word gooney coming from the Old English word for a stupid person, the source of the slang word 'goon'. Mollymawk originates from the Dutch 'mallemok', meaning stupid gull, and was used collectively by seafarers for the 'small albatrosses' – everything but the wanderers and royals – and since ancient times Japanese fishermen have known albatrosses as 'bakadori' or fool-birds. Part of the reason for these unflattering epithets is the albatrosses' lack of fear of ships and their helplessness when stranded aboard. In an instant the glorious flying machine is transformed into a large, lumbering creature, as clumsy on the ground as it is sublime on the wing. The unpleasant habit albatrosses and petrels have of vomiting copious streams of foul-smelling stomach oil when distressed or threatened no doubt added to this view. This nutritious oily fluid is derived directly from their fishy diet and stored in cells lining the stomach wall; under less stressful circumstances it is regurgitated as food for their young. When threatened, however, the birds eject their stomach oil so violently through their mouth and nostrils that they not only make themselves lighter for a more rapid escape, the fluid is also so smelly and sticky that it has a defensive function when squirted at approaching predators. There are records of fulmars, which are

King penguins harassing
a southern giant petrel at
their breeding colony.
Giant petrels are the
'vultures' of the Southern
Ocean and are often seen
feasting at penguin and
seal colonies, scavenging
from dead animals and
picking off weaklings and
afterbirth.

related to albatrosses, causing the death of falcons by oiling them so badly that their flying ability and plumage insulation are destroyed.

Albatrosses, shearwaters, storm petrels and diving petrels belong to four closely related families within the order Procellariiformes, and are often referred to by an older name, Tubinares – 'those with tube-noses'– because among their most distinctive physical features are the gun-barrel-shaped nostrils that extend along either side of the bill in tubes in the case of the albatrosses or are united on top of the upper bill or culmen in petrels. All seabirds have to be able to excrete excess salt ingested with their food courtesy of a gland above the eye, and this then drips from the nostrils down to the end of their beaks. In the case of the tube-noses the nostrils are expanded to house a complicated system of tubes, which provide the birds with an astonishingly acute sense of smell that is critical to their survival, helping them to locate food, nest sites and a mate. They also serve as pressure-

sensing devices, allowing the birds to detect upward air movements caused by the waves and judge how close they are to the water's surface.

Albatrosses and petrels are the most numerous and omnipresent birds found in these parts and range in size from the mighty wanderers to the butterfly-like Wilson's storm petrel that weighs no more than 55 g (2 oz). All of the tribe spend most of their time wandering the oceans in search of food, rarely visiting land except to nest. Though albatrosses nest in the open, most tube-noses seek the safety of an underground burrow, coming ashore at night to incubate their egg, in an attempt to avoid the predatory gulls and skuas. The tiny fairy prions and Antarctic prions feed on plankton, which is often more numerous on the surface of the sea at night.

Most albatrosses breed in colonies on offshore or oceanic islands. The wanderers generally choose remote windswept islands, favouring tussock grass on higher ground where they can launch themselves straight into the wind with minimal effort, either from a cliff-top or via a 'runway' squeezed into the gaps between nests. The largest population of wanderers is found among the Antipodes Islands of the New Zealand continental shelf, where more than 5,000 pairs were counted in the 1990s. Annenkov Island and the Bay of Isles, both off the coast of South Georgia, are also good breeding locations. South Georgia's main breeding ground is Bird Island, where scientists began studying the wanderers in the late 1950s. By 1986 over 7,300 adults and 13,000 fledglings had been ringed, providing invaluable information on breeding behaviour. Scientists fit transmitters onto the wing feathers, which fall off when the birds moult if they don't return. Bird Island has been a Specially Protected Area since 1977 and visitors wanting to see the albatrosses go to nearby Prion Island.

Not surprisingly, given the recent increase in fur seal population, wanderers generally prefer to come to their nest sites before the seals arrive. Nevertheless, adult fur seals can be seen sleeping alongside nesting albatrosses, with curious pups moving right up to sitting birds. It is not uncommon to witness the albatrosses threatening seals that approach too close, snapping their bills to force them to back off. Established breeding birds adapt to the situation, but sub-adults appear less resilient, generally avoiding areas with high densities of fur seals when they are ready to breed. With fewer young birds to offset natural mortality among older breeders in fur seal areas, the population seems destined for further decline.

Approaching from the beach you come upon the nesting sites with little warning: suddenly you are among them – huge goose-like birds sitting motionless, like marble figurines. It feels as if you have been summoned to an audience with some mystical being, for surely the albatross is one of nature's great miracles. The birds stare out into a clear blue sky, snow-capped mountains sculpting the shores of the mainland of South Georgia further out to sea. Some glide overhead, twisting and turning above the tussock like model aeroplanes, before lofting higher and heading for the ocean, searching for squid that normally live in the ocean depths but come to the surface after spawning, making them easier to catch. Rough seas, tail winds and cross winds help to keep the albatrosses aloft, with stormy weather stirring up the water and bringing plankton to the surface. One male that was tracked with a satellite device travelled 8,000 km (5,000 miles) in twelve days, eating on average once every 100 km (60 miles) and consuming several kilograms of food a day.

Adult wanderers are pure white with black wingtips and it takes several years for young birds

Prion Island. The huge rise in fur seal numbers since sealing ceased has had a significant impact. Seals destroy tussock

grass and may rest close to nesting wanderers, disturbing the birds when they are at their most vulnerable.

to attain adult plumage, morphing from their first year's coat of brownish-slate through a succession of moults, with many birds observed out at sea in pied intermediate plumages. The sexes may be distinguished by the males' larger

bills and almost pure white bodies. All albatrosses have elaborate and distinctive courtship displays, magnified in the case of the wanderers by their size. These primordial rituals combine an awkward dance with bowing, scraping, snapping of bills and duets consisting of prolonged nasal groans and purring sounds on the part of the mating pair, sometimes with a number of other birds joining in. It usually begins with the courting couple facing one another, fencing with bills outstretched, then lifting their heads and beak-clapping. The pair then point their bills skywards and call, braying and gurgling, bringing the display to its natural conclusion when one of the birds stretches forward while the other averts its gaze, preening its shoulder. The sequence ends with a bow indicating the position of the nest site. Over the next three weeks a courting couple mates repeatedly.

Every variety of behaviour was on display one memorable afternoon when we landed on Prion Island. Birds slept with heads tucked back over their shoulder or sat preening their immaculate snowy white feathers, sometimes gently nibbling at their partner's dense plumage. One bird pointed its bill to the sky in a dramatic salute, while others neck-rolled, vibrated, sky-called and head-flagged. There was flank-touching and head-swaying too. But nothing could rival the moment when the pair stood facing each other with their wings flung wide like giant fans – something the males do regularly to show off their size. Sometimes during the breeding season a frenzy of activity erupts involving a number of birds, with the younger ones taking the opportunity to practise the complex sequence of moves that determine successful pair formation, eager to participate in a communal dance that does not seem unduly to disturb the breeding female.

At the top of the hill one magnificent adult bird stood statuesque, profiled against the rich blue of the sky, side-lit, turning its head left then right with military precision, stretching its wings to almost maximum breadth, pumping its chest muscles, thrashing the air as it primed itself for flight, monitoring the weather like a pilot checking all systems were go before hurtling down the runway. Then, with wings spread wide, it took two or three floundering steps downhill before abruptly aborting its take-off and pitching forward onto its face and chest (with feet placed far back on the body albatrosses tend to be clumsy when landing). A few minutes later it tried again, into the wind, huge webbed feet paddling along the uneven ground, the promise of flight ending in disaster as the bird collapsed a second time onto its chest in an untidy heap among the forgiving tussock. Later still the same bird wandered back to where a large chocolate-brown chick sat on a nest. The chick clattered its bill, begging for food, but there was none to give. The adult then approached its mate, sitting close by, and the two birds briefly displayed.

Albatrosses mate for life – or at least for many years, usually until one of the pair dies: divorce is rare. The male wanderer arrives first at the nesting grounds, in November, then sits patiently until his partner appears, calling her down from the blue, a ritual that older birds may have followed with the same partner for 30 years. The nest is an impressive mound of mud 30–50 cm (12–20 in) high and 1 m (3 ft) broad at the base, tapering to an egg-cup-like depression on the top, fashioned in the style of an upturned clay pot. A shallow moat running around the base may help to drain the nest site, though this is not found in all wanderers' colonies, so may not be a design feature.

Once the single white egg has been laid, the pair share the rigours of incubation, alternating a sequence of ten-day shifts away from the nest. Each time one of the partners returns from feeding at sea they display and vocalize to one another, reaffirming their bond. The egg hatches

Wandering albatross displaying its extraordinary wingspan. Such huge birds need plenty of help when taking off, choosing high ground with downward-sloping 'runways' which enable them to gain enough lift to launch them into the air.

after 65 days in the smaller species and around 80 for wanderers and royal albatrosses; the parents then feed the chick with regurgitated food – a nutritious mix of partially digested squid, fish and stomach oil. It takes a year of intense parenting to ensure the survival of a single offspring: a month preparing to breed, two-and-a-half incubating and nine feeding the chick. In fact the wanderer holds the record for the longest known interval between hatching and flying, mirroring the lengthy breeding cycle of the king penguin and highlighting the difficulty of finding sufficient food to sustain the young of such large species. By contrast, cormorants and terns that can find plenty of food near their breeding colony may rear several chicks at a time each year. After the albatross chick hatches the

parents head for the sea, returning every few weeks with food, and by the end of winter the chick is almost adult size. Fledging takes nine months, after which the young bird also goes to sea. The adults then spend the following year on the wing, raising one chick every other year, faithfully returning to their nesting area at the allotted time – a miraculous feat of precision and loyalty.

Both albatrosses and petrels tend to return to the same nest or nesting area year after year, helping to cement the pair bond between individuals. The key factor in this process appears to be familiarity with a general area rather than the actual nest. Only a quarter of the birds use a nest they have occupied previously, with most building new nests just a few metres from their previous site. Young birds spend the first few

years of their lives wandering over the South Atlantic before returning to the place of their birth – a form of behaviour known as philopatry – at the age of about six. They usually make several visits before acquiring a mate and breeding,

during which time all the behaviour patterns and rituals that are so essential to successful courtship are practised and refined; both partners may be ten years old before they produce their first egg. The late sexual maturity, the laying of a single

ABOVE

Courting royal albatrosses on Campbell Island. The great albatrosses mate for life and can live 50–60

egg, low breeding success but high adult survival rates and long life expectancy – birds are known to have bred in their sixties – reflect the harsh but stable reality of the albatrosses' environment both at sea and on land, demanding that they spend most of their lives travelling the oceans to find sufficient food. It is an eerie feeling standing in the presence of these great birds, quietly celebrating their enduring nature when you know what their life entails.

Conservation

Those same characteristics make albatross populations exceptionally vulnerable to unnaturally high mortality rates, with recovery a painfully slow process. Watching albatrosses on Prion Island, so relaxed and unafraid in the presence of humans, it seems impossible that these wonderful birds should face an uncertain future. But this is in fact the case, with the global population of wanderers currently estimated to be just 8,500 breeding pairs – not so long ago the estimate was 37,000 pairs. In olden times the albatross may have been revered by sailors, but that didn't stop them from killing them – fresh meat regardless of flavour was a welcome addition to the monotonous diet of salt horse and hardtack, and ships that found large rookeries on isolated islands plundered them, taking both birds and eggs for their stores. Even so, prior to the nineteenth century human activity had little adverse effect on albatross numbers. That changed when a market developed for their plumage, with wings used in

years. Their nuptial dance is an elaborate affair involving bows, bill gestures and vocalizations.

millinery and body feathers sold as a comfortable substitute for swansdown mattress and pillow stuffing. But even this pales by comparison to the current decline in numbers brought about by the fishing industry.

Albatrosses capture their food on the surface of the sea or make shallow dives of just 1 m (3 ft) or so, using the powerful hook at the end of their bill to puncture and break up fish and squid. Probably as much as 80 per cent of their diet is scavenged – leftovers spilled into the ocean by ships or the remains of whales, penguins and squid killed by other predators. And therein lies the problem. Each day a long-line vessel employing 30-km (20-mile) lines to catch Patagonian toothfish and tuna may set 3,000–10,000 hooks and bait them with frozen chunks of fish. Such a ready supply of food is, of course, irresistible to albatrosses and petrels, which target fish scraps close to the surface, gulp the bait down along with the hook and are then dragged to their death under the water. It is estimated that one albatross is killed for every 3,000 hooks and, with perhaps 100 million hooks being baited oceanwide, that accounts for 40,000 albatrosses a year in the Southern Ocean.

Whereas the wanderers prefer to fish alone and only occasionally join groups, smaller species

black-browed albatross

such as the black-browed albatross feed communally, gathering in their hundreds in the wake of a ship offloading offal or setting long lines, making them particularly vulnerable. It is estimated that tuna fishing kills up to a thousand black-browed albatrosses each day in Antarctic waters, with long-lining off South Africa threatening the South Georgia population and operators off South America endangering those of the Falklands and Chile. In the Falklands, which hold 60–70 per cent of the world's population of black-brows, numbers have dropped from an estimated 458,000 breeding pairs in 1995 to 382,000 in 2000, with a loss of 41,200 breeding pairs at Steeple Jason alone, the second largest colony after Beauchêne Island. The problem is exacerbated by the number of vessels fishing illegally in the Southern Ocean, with an annual catch of 10,000 tonnes worth US$120 million.

In the case of the wanderers a disproportionate number of females and young birds are being lost because they favour the warmer subtropical waters around South Africa where there is a rich source of food – both for albatrosses and for long-liners. As we have seen, it takes years for a pair to perfect their glorious dance, and with fewer females available for breeding more males are competing for their attentions, disrupting the normal patterns of courtship.

The first signs of trouble in the Southern Ocean emerged in the late 1970s and '80s, with declines in the number of wandering albatrosses reported from breeding sites that were only later linked to the impact of the long-line fishing industry. Some sites, such as Macquarie Island, where wanderers, black-brows and grey-headed albatrosses all breed, are particularly vulnerable because the populations are small to begin with.

In 1998 the British authorities in South Georgia – the island is a British Overseas Territory administered from the Falklands – moved the fishing season from summer (when the albatrosses are breeding) to winter, a decision that has had a big influence on reducing seabird mortality. A massive campaign to sensitize the public – and the fishing industry – to the dramatic fall-off in albatross numbers is at last beginning to take effect. Guidelines for the most appropriate method of discharging offal have been developed, and some fishing vessels now run their long lines out via poles that help ensure the baited hooks sink to a depth where the shallow-diving albatrosses cannot reach them.

Seabirds are less active at night and an agreement has recently been signed in South Africa demanding that tuna fishermen set their long lines at night in waters south of latitude 30°S. Other initiatives include the use of 'Tori pole' or streamline devices to scare birds away, thawed baits that will sink more quickly, faster-sinking lines employing integrated weights, and perhaps most importantly the halting of fishing during the months when birds are breeding. Leafing through the IUCN's list of species causing concern makes sombre reading: wandering albatross 8,500 breeding pairs – vulnerable; black-browed albatross 680,000 breeding pairs (possibly fewer than this) – endangered; grey-headed albatross 92,300 breeding pairs – vulnerable; light-mantled sooty albatross 21,600 breeding pairs – near threatened; shy albatross 12,000 breeding pairs – near threatened. And warnings continue of a possible decline of up to 50 per cent in albatross numbers in the next ten years unless the guidelines are adhered to.

It isn't just the seabirds that are threatened by the fishing industry – it's the fish. Scientists have been examining a thousand years of fishing records from all oceans and data, revealing some startling trends. It would appear that the

OVERLEAF
Giant petrels aloft over the Southern Ocean. Sailors of old associated petrels and albatrosses with the onset of stormy weather, making them unwelcome visitors – harbingers of ill winds.

Wandering albatross. After spending the early part of their life at sea, wanderers return to their breeding colonies at three to eight years old, though they will not breed until they are at least six – and occasionally as much as 13 – years old.

combined effects of overfishing, pollution and climate change are destroying the oceans, with experts prophesying that fisheries could collapse worldwide and that every fish and shellfish currently eaten could vanish in the next 50 years. This could well be the last century in which people will enjoy wild seafood. A third of fish species targeted by fishermen since 1950 have either been destroyed or declined by 90 per cent. Limits on catches or on the time boats spend at sea are not working fast enough to stem the decline.

All this could have far greater repercussions on our lives than simply a change in eating habits. The loss in productivity and stability of the entire ocean ecosystem could damage its ability to break down sewage, promoting the growth of toxic algae and spreading disease. Adding to the problem is the dramatic drop in phytoplankton, whose populations shrink when the world's seas become warmer, as they inevitably do when the destabilizing effects of El Niño weather patterns or global warming are at work. The only way forward is to establish fishing quotas and ensure they are adhered to, designate more marine reserves, tackle pollution and resolve our part in causing global warming. Anything less will spell disaster, not just for places like Antarctica and the animals that depend on fish to sustain them – but for us too.

In 1992 the Cape Horn Memorial was inaugurated on a hilltop overlooking the ocean, erected to the memory of men of the sea of all nations who have lost their lives in the vicinity. Visitors can admire José Balcells' striking 7-m (23-ft) steel sculpture of an albatross, built to withstand the winds of up to 200 kph (125 mph) that characterize Cape Horn. The poem inscribed on the plinth captures something of the spirit of the albatross:

> I, the albatross that awaits at the end of the world…
> I am the forgotten soul of the sailors lost,
> rounding Cape Horn from all the seas of the world.
> But die they did not in the fierce waves,
> for today towards eternity, in my wings they soar,
> in the last crevice of the Antarctic winds.

Although the albatross is perhaps the ultimate emblem of the seas – an icon of the ocean wilderness – it is also far more than that: it is a visible measure of our impact on life in this remote corner of the globe. Its fate now lies in our hands. It is up to us all to ensure that albatrosses continue to soar on the Antarctic winds, for the delight and awe of generations to come.

CHAPTER 5

Shackleton

Antarctica is as much about the past as it is about the present and the future, brought alive by the stories of the men who braved the Southern Ocean in their quest for answers. Everyone who travels here finds themselves caught in the thrall of the explorers who made Antarctica famous a hundred years ago, with three names in particular capturing the imagination. One of them was Roald Amundsen, the ice-cool Norwegian who in 1911, with the support of four companions, was first to reach the South Pole. Then there was Captain Robert Falcon Scott of the Royal Navy, who reached the Pole nearly five weeks after Amundsen, but perished with his party before he could return to his ship. The third was Ernest Shackleton.

Even today you cannot visit South Georgia without hearing that name echoing from the sea and the ice. Destined to become Scott's great rival, both for sponsorship and for the attention of the public, Shackleton was a charismatic Anglo-Irishman who learned his craft as a mariner in the Merchant Marine. While

Shackleton

Amundsen and Scott reached the South Pole – and Shackleton didn't – Shackleton went on to earn himself a reputation as an outstanding leader, the solid bedrock on which an expedition could be built, someone you could rely on to get you home when all seemed lost.

Of all the places that 'the Boss', as he was affectionately known to his men, visited in his years of exploration, it is with South Georgia that he is most closely linked. Not only is he buried here, but in 1914 this was the starting and finishing point for perhaps his greatest triumph, one of the most extraordinary adventures of this age of discovery. Shackleton was already a hero with plenty of first-hand experience of the Antarctic: he had been part of Scott's 1901–04 *Discovery* expedition, during which he was chosen to accompany Scott and Dr Edward Wilson, Scott's chief scientist and mentor, in an attempt to trek south towards the Pole. The three men reached 82°17′S, 735 km (460 miles) north of the Pole, before being forced to turn back in the face of bitter cold and the debilitating effects of scurvy. The sledging dogs were done for, reduced to walking alongside them, then shot and fed to the survivors as they weakened, something Scott in particular found hard to stomach. Meanwhile the men hauled their own equipment – skis strapped impotently to their sledges rather than on their feet. Their food rations proved woefully inadequate and Shackleton, the heftiest of the three, suffered the most physically, coughing blood and eventually being reduced to riding on the sledge, adding to his companions' hardships. He was subsequently invalided home by Scott, a perceived slight that he never forgot.

Six years later the Boss was back, this time commanding his own ship, HMS *Nimrod*, with every intention of being first to reach the Pole. Though he had learned some valuable lessons,

ABOVE

Shackleton's Cape Royds' Hut on Ross Island, his base during the 1907–09 Nimrod expedition. The bare black rock offered some protection against storms, far less hazardous than attempting to winter on the treacherous ice of the Barrier.

Shackleton had gained little in the way of skiing ability and chose to take ten Manchurian ponies and just nine dogs, despite the fact that well-managed teams of dogs with men on skis had long since proved their value in the Arctic. Nonetheless, by sheer persistence and force of character Shackleton and three of his men – Adams, Marshall and Wild – struggled to 88°23'S, just 180 km (97 nautical miles) short of the Pole, planting the flag given to them by Queen Alexandra on 9 January 1909, before turning and heading back to their base at Cape Royds on the Ross Sea. It was the furthest south anyone had ever been.

It was the fact that Shackleton valued his and the lives of his men over all else that helped to make him such a revered figure. He knew that achieving the honour of reaching the Pole would have meant starving to death on the homeward journey. As he remarked to his wife on his return, 'I thought you'd rather have a live donkey than a dead lion' – something that ironically was to be

The Endurance beset by pack ice. She was frozen in by 19 January 1915, and Shackleton and his men were forced to abandon ship on 27 October. Almost a month later, on 21 November, the Endurance sank beneath the icy waters of the Weddell Sea.

Scott's ultimate fate. Meanwhile a second party from Nimrod comprising two Australians, Professor Edgeworth David and Douglas Mawson, and the Scottish surgeon Dr Alistair Mackay successfully located the South Magnetic Pole, sledging for three months across Victoria Land and covering 2,028 km (1,260 miles) – the longest unsupported sledge journey ever undertaken in the Antarctic until recent times. The discovery of the Magnetic Pole would prove invaluable for preparing navigation charts and was reason enough to plant a second flag, this one in the name of King Edward VII. There was much else to be proud of, too, as Antarctica revealed more of her secrets, including coal deposits, showing that the region had once been covered with forests; the confirmation of the hitherto

accepted but unproven belief that the South Pole lies on a high plateau instead of a polar sea, and that there is no such thing as polar calming – on the contrary, the nearer you get to the Pole the more violent air currents seem to be.

Shackleton's prize for his 'furthest south' was a knighthood from the king and honours and adulation around the world. But at the age of 40 he wasn't done with exploring yet. With Britain and Germany about to become embroiled in the First World War, Shackleton prepared to set off once again for Antarctica in a 44-m (144-ft) three-masted wooden ship with a coal-fired steam engine. He christened the ship Endurance in honour of his family motto, Fortitudine vincimus – 'By endurance we conquer' – determined to accomplish the last great expedition left on Earth:

the 2,880-km (1,800-mile) crossing of the continent on foot, with South Georgia acting as a gateway to the Antarctic via the Weddell Sea. The plan was for *Endurance* to pick her way carefully through the pack ice to Vahsel Bay on the Antarctic coast. Shackleton would then lead his men overland via the South Pole and link with a support party at the Beardmore Glacier on the Ross Sea side of the continent. Successfully completing the greatest polar journey ever attempted would put Britain firmly 'back on the front pages' after the Norwegian achievements three years earlier. There were some who questioned the propriety of undertaking such an expedition with a war in the offing, and Shackleton offered his ship and expedition members to the service of his country, but Winston Churchill, who was First Lord of the Admiralty, gave the order for them to proceed.

The *Endurance* Expedition

There was no shortage of volunteers: 5,000 people answered Shackleton's call for men willing to risk all in pursuit of his dream, and though no copy has ever been found of the advertisement said to have been placed in a newspaper of the time, the oft-quoted version of it captures the stark reality of what was required:

'Men wanted for Hazardous Journey. Small wages, bitter cold, long months of complete darkness, constant danger. Safe return doubtful. Honour and recognition in case of success.'

Shackleton selected 27 men, a mix of officers, scientists and seamen with the distinctions destined to be blurred to a far greater degree than if it had been a Royal Navy expedition. (Scott, as a naval officer, maintained divisions of class and rank, making for a less integrated and

harmonious team.) Shackleton had no hesitation in procuring the services of Frank Wild as his second in command: the two men had become firm friends when they travelled together on Scott's *Discovery* expedition. Wild was a tough little Yorkshireman who, like Shackleton, had first gone to sea at the age of 16, had served under both Scott and Mawson and was one of the most experienced explorers of his generation. He had a cool head and knew exactly what it took to survive the rigours of Antarctic travel; in fact he relished it. Another key figure was a tough and indomitable Irishman called Tom Crean, the kind of man who would give his all until he dropped, who didn't know when he was beaten. Essential to any expedition was a first-rate navigator and for this crucial role Shackleton chose the New Zealander Frank Worsley, appointing him captain of *Endurance*; this allowed Shackleton to oversee the whole operation unhindered by other distractions. Like Wild and Crean, Worsley was no newcomer to Antarctic expeditions; he revelled in adventure and, despite his rather erratic temperament with a tendency to high-spiritedness and a lack of discipline, nobody could doubt his ability as a sailor.

Shackleton would need a second ship, HMS *Aurora*, to land his support party of six men at his old base at Cape Royds to lay depots inland – stores of food and fuel to see the expedition safely through the latter part of their journey, allowing the men to travel more lightly than if they had to carry all they needed from the outset. This time Shackleton had heeded the advice of the Norwegians to take dogs – 69 Canadian sledging dogs to be precise – though none of the party had a true understanding of working dogs and only one knew how to ski, an advantage that the Norwegians had exploited to the full during the race to reach the South Pole.

While there is no doubt that Shackleton was a great leader, great explorers need to be able to plan, to pay attention to logistics and detail – by no means the Boss's strengths. When he left England in August 1914, his intention had been to travel to Buenos Aires to load stores, then to stop off again in the Falklands to take on last-minute provisions, but the outbreak of the war prevented that. Instead, he carried on to South Georgia, reaching the whaling station at Grytviken in November. For the past ten years South Georgia had been home to Norwegian whalers, a hardy

ABOVE

Late evening, Marguerite Bay, Antarctic Peninsula. As well as being a great leader, Shackleton was a lover of poetry who was inspired by the beauty

and majesty of the frozen south. He wrote: 'The ice and waves had a voice of menace that night but I heard it only in my dreams.'

breed of men drawn from the fringes of society – men who were prepared to work under the toughest conditions and who could look after themselves in a tight spot. South Georgia must have appeared bleak indeed in those days, not just because of the perpetually foul weather but also thanks to the stench of rotting flesh that pervaded the whaling stations. But Shackleton would have felt a natural empathy with the whalers – after all, he too had learned from an early age to fend for himself, had grown up at sea and trekked to within a few days' walk of the Pole. The Norwegians would have welcomed the Boss as one of their own.

Nevertheless, the signs did not bode well. Although this was theoretically the beginning of the southern summer, the weather in this part of the world doesn't always go according to plan. The whalers reported that the pack ice had extended further north than ever before and that conditions were the worst in living memory – so bad, in fact, that Shackleton was forced to delay his departure for a month. Ever the optimist, he saw the hiatus as time well spent, an opportunity for the men to work the dog teams and for the scientists to collect specimens. But the whalers knew the dangers posed by the ice better than anyone and cautioned Shackleton to wait until later in the summer. However, with debts to pay off and the war weighing on his mind, it was now or never; on 5 December Endurance sailed out of Cumberland Bay with the crew rested and eager to continue their adventure to the great white south – having added two live pigs to their stash of food.

The whalers had been right. The going was unbelievably tough as Endurance was warily plotted along a course through the pack ice, at times forced to build up a sufficient head of steam to ram a way through, with the men disembarking when necessary to work at the ice

with pick axes and crowbars – at one point even employing the services of a giant ice saw to try to cut a path to a 'lead' (a gap in the ice offering a channel to pass through) that opened 400 m (1,300 ft) from the ship. But there were good times, too – football on the ice, singsongs and theatrical skits played out in the warmth of the ship, special days celebrated with good food and wine. And nothing could stop the men from marvelling at the beauty of their surroundings: towering icebergs set against the vivid pinks and orange of the evening sky, parties of Adélie penguins and crabeater seals riding the floes, pressure ridges thrusting up a rubble of ice pierced by caverns of the most exquisite shades of blue – and, frustratingly, the blow of a whale effortlessly navigating its own path among the leads before submerging again to continue its journey.

By 18 January 1915 Endurance had become immobilized by the ice, trapped 'like an almond in a chocolate bar'. It was a miracle that the men got as far as they did, travelling 1,600 km (1,000 miles) through the pack and closing to within 125 km (80 miles) of their destination – a day's sail from Vahsel Bay – before their luck ran out. The wind picked up, the sea froze around them and agonizingly they drifted away from their longed-for landing site. On 24 February Shackleton declared the ship a winter station – they could go no further until the spring came round again – his dreams for the moment shattered by the ice. But it was at times like this that the Boss's understanding of his men proved crucial; he had selected them not just for their individual skills but for their attitude. Now he expected each and every one of them to measure up and repay his faith in them. They were nearly 2,000 km (1,200 miles) from the nearest outposts of civilization and nobody knew what had become of them; ironically the Argentines had

Summer in the Antarctic can be surprisingly sunny, with clear blue skies and stunning sunsets and sunrises divided by an interval of just an hour or so.

given Shackleton a wireless in Buenos Aires, but there had been insufficient funds to purchase a transmitting plant to allow it to send messages. Yet despite the precarious nature of their position and the doubts that he himself must have experienced at times, there was the Boss willing his men on: 'Don't worry, boys, have no fear, we'll get out in the spring,' he encouraged, refusing to countenance anything less. Such was his presence and single-mindedness that they believed him.

One thing Shackleton insisted on from the first day they became trapped in the ice was that the men ate fresh meat. To stave off the cold and boost morale they were issued with the winter clothing that had been allocated for the shore parties, including lightweight but virtually windproof Burberry tunics and trousers. Shackleton set a strict routine to help counter the psychological strain that the darkness and silence of an Antarctic winter can conjure up, encouraging the scientists to set to work on the many scientific investigations that he had promised his sponsors they would undertake. But the Weddell Sea is dominated by clockwise prevailing winds and currents that constantly moved the pack ice around, relentlessly marching their stricken vessel north. McNish – the carpenter, master craftsman and shipwright – who was quick to speak his mind and could be contrary, nonetheless worked marvels with his tools, fashioning rows of cubicles 1.5 x 1.8 m (5 x 6 ft) to house two men apiece in what was to become known as the Ritz, making life far warmer and cosier for the scientists and ship's officers whose cabins had been located on the deckhouse, where temperatures in March hovered between –12 and –30°C (+11 and –24°F). Meanwhile many of the birds and seals had already begun their retreat to warmer regions further north, signalling to the men that winter

was on its way; on 1 May the sun disappeared entirely and would remain hidden for the next four months.

By now the pack had begun to flex its muscles with terrifying certainty, causing great chunks of ice to ride up and smash against the hull of *Endurance*. The sound of the ice would have been a terrible bedmate to add to the winter darkness – the ship groaning and protesting under the pressure, nagging away at the psyche of even the toughest and most experienced of men. So it continued month after weary month. Spirits soared briefly as the sun returned. Any hopes the men nurtured of reaching open water and continuing on their intended journey were soon dashed – the frozen sea was always moving, the force of the pack so violent that it seemed only a matter of time before the ship was torn apart.

In mid-October open water came in sight for the first time in nine months, but within a day or so the pressure of the ice made itself felt again and inevitably the ship began to leak. On the 27th the dawn broke clear and bright. The temperature gauge read –8.5°F (–22.5°C) as the men began to stir. Later that day the ice dealt *Endurance* a crippling blow, forcing her stern up, and at the same time a floe ripped away her rudder and sternpost. She sank a little, like a wounded prize-fighter, braced for the next onslaught which buckled her decks upwards. As her keel tore away

Weddell seal

the water flooded in. Thick oak beams that had seemed indestructible cracked and splintered like matchsticks. Gone were any notions that the brave little ship might somehow pull through on this, her maiden voyage – she was done for, and the men could only watch their home and refuge break apart in front of their eyes. That afternoon Shackleton gave the order to abandon ship. The dogs and whatever supplies had already been readied were moved to the ice. The Boss was last to leave, hoisting the blue ensign of the Royal Navy to the accompaniment of three hearty cheers from the attendant party on the ice. They were 550 km (350 miles) from the nearest land.

Adélie penguins wander among storm-tossed ice rubble (washed up on a beach) at Robertson Bay, Cape Adare.

Out on the Ice

They camped on the ice in five tents, confiding to their diaries not the doubts they must all have been experiencing regarding their own chances of survival, but their grief for their ship. For Shackleton there could be no time for regrets, no turning back; his mind was focused on transforming seemingly impossible circumstances into the possible, announcing to the men that within the next few days they would set out to march northwest towards Snow Hill Island and Robertson Island, dragging three of the lifeboats and their supplies on sledges. All but their most prized possessions would have to be abandoned, the load limited to just 2 lb (less than 1 kg) per man. Shackleton showed the seriousness of his intentions by dumping a handful of gold sovereigns and his gold watch onto the ice, with silver brushes and dressing cases, and then salvaging only the flysheet, the 23rd Psalm and some verses from the Book of Job from the Bible that Queen Alexandra had given him.

A few days later an advance party of four set out to try to beat a path through the maze of ice rubble to make life easier for the 15 men hauling the first of the lifeboats, while the dog teams ferried smaller loads back and forth. These were uncertain times for everyone. Gentle Tom Crean was forced to shoot three of the four puppies that he had lovingly nurtured over the previous months, and McNish's pride and joy, 'Mrs Chippy' the cat – the ship's mascot – met the same fate, something for which the irascible carpenter never forgave Shackleton. The going soon proved impossible – the ice so hummocked and ridged that the men managed less than 3 km (2 miles) in three days of backbreaking effort before realizing that they could never reach Snow Hill Island under such circumstances.

The only alternative was to wait on the ice until leads opened up to allow them to continue by boat, something that might still mean months of waiting. Three tonnes of provisions were shifted from Dump Camp, where *Endurance* had been abandoned; they were then ferried by dog teams to the wheelhouse that had been removed from the ship and repositioned at their new home, named Ocean Camp. Key men such as Crean and Wild were spread among the crew to bolster spirits and calm frayed nerves in the tents. This was not what some of the men had signed up for – the reality of 'hazardous journey' and 'safe return doubtful' now had a new meaning for everyone. Shackleton realized that he would have to call on all his guile and leadership abilities, nurturing his men according to their individual and collective strengths and weaknesses. The scientists among them were seen as a bit bookish and vulnerable to teasing by the crewmen, so the Boss took them under his wing, along with Frank Hurley, the expedition photographer, and the navigator Hudson, who could be argumentative.

Shackleton's men camped on the ice

Shackleton's plan now depended on the remorseless drift of the pack to take them in a northwesterly direction towards Paulet Island, 600 km (400 miles) from their current position. Paulet is an ancient volcano where Captain Carl Anton Larsen – the founder of the whaling station at Grytviken – and his party had survived the winter of 1903 after their ship *Antarctic* had suffered a similar fate to *Endurance* (the men were eventually reunited with expedition leader Dr Otto Nordenskjold and the rest of the party, and rescued by *Uruguay*, an Argentine vessel that had

ABOVE

Sunset at 60°S. All but the most ice-hardened vessels have eventually to retreat northwards to escape the pack ice as summer draws to a close.

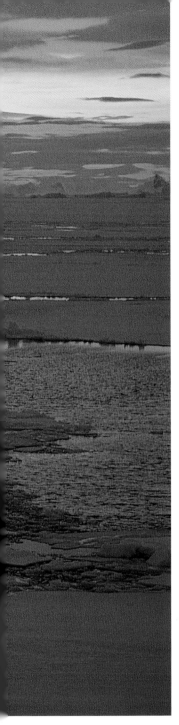

come in search of them). Larsen had built a hut on Paulet, but apart from the shelter it would offer there would be the bonus of much needed provisions – Shackleton knew this because he had helped provision the relief operation twelve years earlier. From Paulet a party of Shackleton's men would continue west to the Antarctic Peninsula, where they could expect to find help from whaling vessels.

This hiatus gave Hurley the chance to retrieve his precious glass negatives and film. The young Australian was a bit of an enigma – cocky but immensely able, physically and mentally as tough and resilient as Crean and Wild – but Shackleton wasn't sure that he could count on his undivided loyalty and made a point of letting the younger man know how much he valued his contribution, in order to keep him on side. Hurley returned to the ship and hacked his way into the refrigerator, diving into the icy water to salvage the art that he had wisely soldered inside a double tin lining. He knew that weight would be a real issue when the time came to take to the boats, but in this case Shackleton not only relaxed his rule but sat with Hurley on the ice while he systematically smashed over 400 of the negatives documenting every aspect of the expedition, keeping only the best of the best – resoldering 20 colour images and 100 whole- and half-glass plates, plus an album of developed prints.

Shackleton wasn't simply being benevolent: he realized that Hurley's images would prove a priceless record of their trip, something to stir the public imagination back home – and help pay off his debts. One of his shipmates described Hurley as 'a warrior with his camera and would go anywhere or do anything to get a picture', and certainly Hurley was no ordinary photographer: brave, inventive, with a wonderful eye for composition and the abstract. His black-and-white photographs and ciné films of *Endurance* being crushed by the ice are hauntingly beautiful. Without them Shackleton's legacy would have been far less powerful and abiding.

Desperation

There would be no respite at Paulet Island after all; the Weddell Sea made sure of that, moving the men northeast away from land rather than in the westerly direction they had hoped for. As summer returned they awoke each morning crammed together in the most uncomfortable way, bathed in water created by the warmth of their bodies and the melting icy floor beneath the wooden boards they rested on. Outside conditions were sodden too, and the tensions of living on top of one another had long since begun to test their comradeship and patience: inevitably quirks of character jarred at times.

'Chippy' McNish continued to work his magic, weatherproofing the three lifeboats as best he could for the journey ahead, raising the sides of two of them. To say that he was innovative would be an understatement – he commandeered lamp wick, oil paints belonging to Marston, the expedition's resident artist, seal blood – whatever he could lay his calloused hands on to caulk the seams, utilizing every scrap of material he had managed to scavenge from the carcass of their ship. Thomas Orde-Lees, the storekeeper and distributor of rations, meanwhile did nothing to ease the gloom. Lees was the antithesis of Shackleton, negative in outlook, vociferous about their seemingly hopeless dilemma and always the last to get his hands dirty. The party's ski expert as well as being in charge of the aero-propelled motor sledges (which had been abandoned earlier), he was a bit of a snob who believed he was a cut above menial work and grumbled when forced to pull his weight, on one occasion developing a painful bout of sciatica and retiring to his bed after being obliged to shovel snow. He soon made himself thoroughly unpopular and the butt of his companion's jokes, and when his snoring proved too much for his tent companions he was ejected and forced to seek alternative accommodation alone in his store in the wheelhouse. Well aware that people like Lees could be dangerously unsettling to a group of men striving to keep hope alive, Shackleton, though not naturally vindictive, allowed the men to deal with him in their own way.

On 21 November, as the men relaxed in their tents, they heard the Boss yell, 'She's going', and emerged in time to see *Endurance* disappear bow first beneath the ocean. Though they had long since accepted her fate, it must nevertheless have seemed like a bad omen. With warmer conditions the ice became even more mushy underfoot and a maze of leads began to open around the floe they were camped on, though the pack as a whole showed no signs of breaking up sufficiently to release them into the boats. The strain was now telling on even the strongest and Shackleton succumbed to a painful bout of sciatica that confined him to his tent for two weeks. This was mental torture for someone who liked to keep a firm hand on the situation, ready to quash dissent before it could fester and spread.

Come December 1915, Shackleton announced they would try for another march across the ice, a decision that caused much muttering among the men. Midsummer's Day fell on the 22nd, which was to be celebrated as Christmas. The following day they would set off at three in the morning when the ice was hardest. Wet and hungry, the men floundered around in the slushy ice. Inevitably grumbling turned to something more

serious and McNish refused, in the bluntest of language, to go on. Shackleton eventually defused the situation by announcing to the whole crew that they would be paid up to the day they reached safe port, and as such were still bound by orders despite the loss of their ship. Two days later, after a week in which they had travelled just 13 km (8 miles), Shackleton gave the order to stop marching and retreat to more secure ice where they established Patience Camp.

The months dragged on, food became scarce and more dogs were shot to provide additional rations for the men – they had already been forced to plunder the dogs' food. The Antarctic Circle came and went and the third lifeboat was dragged to Patience Camp with supplies previously abandoned; seals and penguins were worryingly scarce at times and blubber to fuel the stove was running low. Cocoa was finished, tea and flour in short supply, winter almost upon them once again. On 30 March the last of the dogs were shot and the younger ones eaten, bringing to an end an invaluable source of comfort for the men – the dogs had become characters in their own right, providing an emotional connection to a more normal way of life.

By now they were getting close to open water, with the pack breaking up around them and at the mercy of strong currents. The sea and sky were once again alive with animals and birds – land couldn't be far away. Shackleton had to

Adélie

Adélies breeding at Paulet Island, an extinct volcano
off the northeast tip of the Antarctic Peninsula.

Icebergs are calved by ice sheets, ice shelves and glaciers
along the coastline of the Antarctic continent. Driven
by ocean currents, tides and winds they drift at speeds
up to 5 kph (3 mph) for up to 25 km (12½ miles) a day.

decide when to make a break for it and abandon the ice; to go too soon could spell disaster. They rafted along on the floe, a triangle of ice barely 110 m (120 yards) long, and on 9 April – 15 months after becoming trapped in the ice – the Boss gave the order to launch the boats into the heavy swell. Their goal was now Elephant Island, and as the wind changed they made a dash for it, desperately trying to keep the boats to the open leads, ice churning around them, threatening to crush them at every turn. That night the men retreated to the ice to sleep and at one point a crack appeared under the sailors' tent, pitching two of the men into the freezing water. As one of them struggled out again unaided, Shackleton hoisted the other man – still in his sleeping bag – back onto the ice before the opening slammed shut again.

The misery of it all – wrapped in clothes designed to keep out cold but not water, the chaffing of wet clothes against battered skin, the saltiness adding to the discomfort. For month after month the men had subsisted on a diet of seal and penguin, supplemented by meat from the dogs; it had left them weak and bloated, longing for variety, whether it took the form of pudding, jam or fresh vegetables, and starved of the very carbohydrates that they now needed in order to row for their lives. It was so cold at times that they could hear the crackle of water freezing as their sodden clothes set solid, burning and lacerating their hands and feet. Everyone showed the first signs of hypothermia and Shackleton mounted a suicide watch; his men were fading fast with some of them incapacitated. Somehow he had to keep their hopes alive, digging into the sledging rations that had been set aside for their overland journey in more optimistic times and had until now been kept in reserve.

By this time Hudson had broken down; Blackborow's feet were in such a bad way that they rendered his legs useless (he would later have to have the gangrenous toes removed from his left foot), and to add to everything else they were desperate for fresh water. Many were suffering from dysentery, their bodies erupting in painful boils, lips swollen and raw, hands blistered from the oars. Wild – a man not given to exaggeration – noted that 'at least half of the party were insane, fortunately not violent, simply helpless and hopeless'. At one point Worsley was so exhausted, having not slept for more than 90 hours, that he dozed off in a crouched position while navigating, prompting one of his companions to kick him hard in the head to stir him. Think about that for a moment and you realize just how dire the situation had become. They bobbed around in the ocean for a week, sick to their stomachs, rowing and sailing in a desperate bid to survive, with the Boss standing resolutely in the prow like a warrior king, leading by example, determined not to be beaten.

Somehow they made it to Elephant Island and landed, having spent the last two day and nights without hot food or drink. It was a crazy moment. They had survived 170 days on an ice floe, and it was 497 days since any of them had set foot on land. They staggered around like drunkards, falling to their knees and kissing the ground – one even ran amok with an axe, frenziedly killing seals. There was little time for rejoicing, though: their position was still precarious; they would have to move again. By morning many of the men had had enough and were close to rebellion; some had to be forcibly dragged from their sleeping bags and set to work. The only thing on Shackleton's mind was how to get them safely home: reaching Elephant Island might have saved them from the ice, but nobody knew where they were and there was little chance of anyone stumbling upon them here. They faced certain death unless help could be summoned.

An Incredible Journey

The only realistic hope was if they could reach the whaling stations on South Georgia: there Shackleton knew he could find help. But South Georgia was 1,300 km (800 miles) away and surrounded by the roughest seas in the world, with 120 kph (80 mph) winds and 18-m (60-ft) waves. An impossibility? Not to someone like Shackleton. He set McNish to work shoring up one of the lifeboats, the *James Caird*, a boat just 1.5-m (5-ft) wide and under 7-m (22-ft) long, to make her as weatherproof as possible. He chose five men to accompany him – Crean, Worsley, Vincent, McNish and McCarthy – leaving Frank Wild to keep hope alive for the 22 men whose only shelter would be the upturned hulls of the two remaining lifeboats, perched on a spit of land barely 30 m (10 ft) wide and less than 3 m (9 ft) above the high-tide mark, lashed by waves and utterly exposed to the elements. Already weakened by their relentless diet of meat, they would still have to rely on penguins and seals for the bulk of their food. Pleasures were few – tobacco and a hearty singsong often being enjoyed from the depths of the sodden sleeping bags that the men occupied for 17 hours at a stretch when the winter darkness closed in. Before long even the tobacco had run out, defying all their inventiveness in eking out diminishing supplies.

Shackleton and his shipmates set sail on 24 April 1916 with two masts and four oars as their allies. Though they had a sextant and a chronometer they saw the partial sun only four times to take readings. Ice was their constant companion and they were perpetually wet and cold, with three men resting in sleeping bags cramped below deck, while the other three braved the most atrocious conditions as they bailed, steered and adjusted the sails. A massive wave nearly destroyed their boat, and as they neared the precipitous shores of South Georgia more waves threatened to smash them to pieces against the jagged rocks. But they were not to be denied, hauling ashore on 10 May 1916, 17 days after leaving Elephant Island. Through sheer bloody-mindedness and faith in their leader they had prevailed, with navigator Frank Worsley the hero of the day.

Salvation was now at hand but for one last obstacle. They had landed at King Haakon Bay on the uninhabited southern coast of the island, which is vulnerable to the prevailing winds and depressions that roar in from the Drake Passage and the Antarctic continent, the same brutal elements from which the men had just escaped. Knowing this, the Norwegians had wisely built their whaling stations among the sheltered bays on the far side of the island. Vincent and McNish were done for and probably could not have

OPPOSITE

Icicles on an iceberg, Paradise Bay, Antarctic Peninsula. Antarctica produces more than six times the number of icebergs than the Arctic, and the average size of bergs is much larger too. Each Antarctic iceberg averages 1 million tonnes of pure fresh water.

Shackleton's boat journey

survived another day at sea, so Shackleton decided to leave them with McCarthy; on 19 May he set off with Worsley and Crean for a hike of 35 km (22 miles) as the albatross flies across uncharted mountains towards the whaling station of Stromness – the alternative was an unthinkable 240-km (150-mile) journey by sea. They carried as little as possible, leaving even their sleeping bags behind, taking a stove, food, McNish's adze as an ice axe and a length of rope.

Fate must have been smiling on the three men, for by chance they chose the only two clear nights of the entire winter for their trek. Aided by screws that McNish had driven through the soles of their boots they safely completed a 36-hour slog over treacherous terrain. To put this achievement in perspective, in 1964 a well-equipped team from the Combined Services, starting fresh with plenty of food and equipment, had the utmost difficulty in repeating the journey and at one point nearly lost three men in an avalanche. What Shackleton and his two weary companions had accomplished was little short of a miracle.

It was almost 18 months since they had bade farewell to the whalers at Stromness, full of hope for a successful endeavour. Now they were back – unrecognizable, but alive. A strange new reality enveloped them – a war was still being fought; on the other side of the world millions of men had died. Worsley set out with a relief ship to bring the three men in from King Haakon Bay and the Norwegians insisted on recovering *James Caird* – this had been, after all, a journey to stir the heart of the most experienced sailor and everyone wanted the chance to celebrate an epic of navigation and daring. McNish, Vincent and McCarthy went straight back to England, but Wild and Worsley stayed on with Shackleton to help rescue the men stranded on Elephant Island. It took four attempts before they could reach

them; on one occasion they got to within 160 km (100 miles) before being forced back by the elements. Finally, on 30 August, four months after leaving the tiny island, Shackleton stepped ashore to be reunited with his men, while the Chilean steam tug *Yelcho* waited to take them home. All 22 had survived, thanks in large part to Wild's deft man-management. Like the Boss, Wild knew how to strike the right balance, insisting on routine and discipline to create a sense of order and purpose, but encouraging sketches and singsongs to ease the boredom and bolster morale.

The story doesn't end there. On arrival in Buenos Aires Shackleton was given news of his Ross Sea Party, whose job it had been to lay depots for the intended crossing of the continent. The party had had no way of knowing what had happened to Shackleton and had suffered their own version of hell. Their ship *Aurora* had broken free from her mooring and then had been kept from returning by the pack ice. Three men had died. Shackleton set out – successfully – to bring the survivors home.

Death of a Hero

In a speech delivered at a recruiting meeting for the war held in Sydney in March 1917, Shackleton was at his most persuasive: 'Death is a very little thing – the smallest thing in the world. I can tell you that, for I have been face to face with death during long months. I know that death scarce weighs in the scale against a man's appointed task.' As far as Shackleton was concerned if you signed up for whatever purpose in life – exploration or war – you stuck it out, did your best and then if necessary cranked it up a notch or two, drawing on reserves of courage and

Explorer with emperor chicks

stamina that you could never have dreamed possible. Neither regret nor fear of failure could be countenanced. The only way to survive Antarctica when it turns against you is to have someone like Shackleton to lead the way.

In 1921, with the war finally over, eight of Shackleton's men joined him on his last voyage of adventure, with South Georgia once again playing a pivotal part in the story. Shackleton couldn't settle at home – the war had changed everything and he felt he lacked a role. He needed a challenge, and the one he knew best was the ice. The aims of the expedition were vague, with talk of circumnavigating the continent.

The Boss was destined never to achieve that ambition, nor to return to England. He was struck down by a massive heart attack aboard the *Quest* as she lay at anchor off Grytviken on 5 January 1922. Macklin, the expedition doctor and one of Shackleton's closest friends in later years, performed the autopsy, noting that the heart was like that of an old man, a condition no doubt exacerbated by the stresses and strains of years of exploration. He was just 47.

Emily Shackleton declined the offer to have her husband's body brought back to England. She knew that he had always been happiest when off adventuring among the snow and ice and that his last resting place should not be the claustrophobic confinement of an English churchyard. He is buried in the Whalers' Cemetery in Grytviken, South Georgia, on a gentle rise overlooking Cumberland Bay, the sweet musty smell of fur seals permeating the air. Here, the headstones provide a window into the bleak existence shared by many who have lived in these parts. The earliest graves hold the remains of men from a ship called *Esther* who died of typhus in 1846. Others commemorate another outbreak of typhus at the whaling station in 1912,

while William Barlas, Magistrate of South Georgia, was killed by an avalanche on 2 September 1941. The most recent grave is that of Felix Artuso, an Argentine casualty of the Falklands War, who died on 26 April 1982. And high on the hill directly behind the cemetery is a cross erected to the memory of 17 men who drowned when their fishing vessel, *Sudur Havid*, sank off South Georgia in 1998.

When visiting the cemetery tradition dictates that you pay your respects to Shackleton in the time-honoured fashion: tots of rum and Guinness (he was, after all, an Irishman) are decanted, a eulogy is read and a toast offered. On the back of his headstone are engraved the words of Robert Browning: 'I hold…that a man should strive to the uttermost for his life's set prize.' Hardly surprising that the man who wrote these words should have been one of the Boss's favourite poets.

It is impossible to look at portraits of Shackleton – the strong, square-set jaw and resolute eyes – without pondering the qualities that made him such an inspirational leader; his courage and spirit of adventure seemed to cast a spell over his men. Today he is very much the dominant figure of the heroic age, his charismatic personality eclipsing that of Scott and Amundsen in the public's imagination. This is the age of Shackleton 'mania', as one old Antarctic hand termed it, admitting that in 1964, freshly arrived in Antarctica with the British Antarctic Survey, he went to Shackleton's grave searching for courage while suffering a particularly agonizing attack of toothache. Today there are books, scholarships, Imax movies and TV documentaries – even T-shirts – all eulogizing Shackleton's powers of leadership. The Boss would no doubt have approved: he was a showman who courted attention, knowing it was the passport to further adventures.

Certainly his story continues to inspire each new generation and his grave is like a magnet for the few who journey this far. In 2005 Karen Gaye Walker, granddaughter of Francis William Shackleton of Auckland, left her own tribute to her famous relative:

> I had a dream to honour your life by planting roses on your grave. Your persistence and determination, your value of life has inspired our family, your distant relatives in New Zealand, to emulate your courage.

We are all inspired by heroes and the aura cast by Shackleton lingers on, so much so that on one of our many visits to South Georgia a group of us hoped to taste just a little of what his weary party had faced when they set out on that 36-hour trek. We hiked from Fortuna Bay to the old whaling station at Stromness, recreating under very different circumstances part of the overland journey that Shackleton, Crean and Worsley had been forced to make. The island can be sublimely beautiful in its summer finery, but this is a deceptive façade that can turn on you in an instant.

The land rises steeply from the shores everywhere on South Georgia, the interior of the island a maze of jagged mountain peaks, glaciers, ice fields and snow-covered valleys; a landscape sculpted in shades of black and white with a dash of earth brown. In places the walking is pleasantly

ABOVE

Stromness whaling station, South Georgia – abandoned in 1965. In 1914 Shackleton and two companions made their memorable trek across South Georgia to reach Stromness and raise help to rescue the men marooned on Elephant Island.

easy, cushioned by a dense mat of tussocky grass and mosses, which in the low-lying areas gives way to sponge-like peat, soaked in the abundant meltwater. There is an eerie silence. You expect to hear moorland birds – grouse, partridge, pheasant – but the land is bereft of bird song, except perhaps for the harsh cry of a skua passing overhead. The rocks are sharp-edged and brittle, cleaved apart by freeze and thaw, in places split into patterns that resemble a stack of cards or floral decorations.

The ghosts of Shackleton and his men surrounded us – poorly dressed and dog-tired from the accumulated effects of the long months of deprivation and stress, how exhausted they must have felt. We had the luxury of walking over hard frosted snow that leaves the faintest imprint – not the wearisome powdery soft stuff that sucks the energy from your legs, dragging you down 30 cm (1 ft) at a time, making you struggle to pull your foot free, at times pitching forward on to your face. But they just had to keep going – the lives of others depended on it. By now they had grown accustomed to taking risks and as Worsley wrote later, 'When men are tired as we were their nerves are on edge, and it is necessary for each man to take pains not to irritate the others. On this march we treated each other with a good deal more consideration than we should have done in normal circumstances. Never is etiquette and "good form" observed more carefully than by experienced travellers when they find themselves in a tight place.' Snug in our gortex, mittens and warm hiking boots, revelling in the scenery, the pure clear air – something Shackleton, Crean and Worsley would have had little time to appreciate – we could only try to envisage the stark reality of their desperate march.

Shackleton would have chuckled perhaps to know that his reputation has lived on here at South Georgia, and that his gift of empowering those around him to believe in themselves and live bigger lives continues.

gentoos

CHAPTER 6

The Great Leviathans

Shackleton's mix of gritty determination and courage act as the perfect foil to the harsh reality of Antarctica. The Boss was as enigmatic as the continent, as hard as nails yet compassionate enough to give you his biscuit ration on a trek to the Pole because your need was greater than his. He could put you in your place just by looking at you, yet he loved to read poetry and to express his feelings in a lyrical way about that other Antarctica – a place of profound and surreal beauty embellished by the animals and birds that are so perfectly adapted to survive here. Yet even in Shackleton's time, human influence and disturbance were already leaving their imprint on the white continent, with the spirit of discovery and adventure offset against those who came here to exploit what nature had to offer – and to make money from it.

Blue whale. Named for its bluish-grey skin, the blue whale has a small hook-shaped dorsal fin far back on the body. They travel alone or in small groups of three or four.

Of all of the creatures to be found in Antarctica, perhaps the whales best represent the dilemma human beings face in balancing their own needs against those of wildlife and wilderness. Whales dominate the blue planet of the oceans, an environment covering nearly three-quarters of the Earth's surface. If ever there was a seascape to do justice to the great leviathans, then surely it must be the Southern Ocean.

Antarctic Whales

Whales are sentient beings, so large and outlandish in character and size that they capture our imagination and stir our emotions in ways that few other creatures can do. To see a whale is to be reminded of the drama of life on Earth, harking back to a time when giants ruled our planet.

The blue whale, Goliath of its tribe, is the largest animal ever to have lived, twice the weight of the biggest dinosaur, equivalent in size to a whole family of elephants, measuring 30 m (100 ft) in length and weighing up to 180 tonnes. Its tongue alone is 3 m (10 ft) thick and the weight of a bull elephant, and an adult blue whale can eat 3–4 tonnes of krill each day and live for 80 years (there is now evidence that whales may live far longer than this, perhaps even surpassing the oldest known land tortoises). It glides through the water as effortlessly as a bird on the wing, blowing spumes of moist vapour 6 m (20 ft) into the air as it surfaces from the depths of the ocean, exhaling with such force that the sound is audible to human ears 1 km (½ mile) away.

Before hunting commenced here, Antarctic whales represented the largest population of mammals by weight ever to have existed on Earth. The southern hemisphere is estimated to have supported four times the number of baleen

whalers flensing a carcass

whales as the northern, with around 1.1 million baleen and sperm whales in the Southern Ocean. But for over a century they were hunted with ruthless intensity worldwide, to service human ambitions. Not only did the oil from millions of whales light our world with lamps and candles – in London alone 5,000 street lights burnt by whale oil – it literally oiled the wheels of industry, lubricating the Industrial Revolution and acting as the catalyst for settlements that sprang up along the coasts of Europe and America. Major cities such as London, Liverpool, Dundee, Hamburg, San Francisco, New York and Boston all profited from the slaughter. Whale oil was like gold, and the race to exploit the abundant whale population left no room for consideration of the animals' future. Ironically nowadays visitors flock to the ocean to watch whales up close, showing the same fervour that they exhibit when heading off on safari on the African savanna – but for the whales this new enthusiasm may be too late. By the time the whaling industry went into decline in the 1960s, most of the Southern Ocean's whale species had been hunted to near the point of extinction – only 1,000–3,000 humpbacks were left and today there are no more than 12,000 blue whales worldwide. Some estimates put this figure as low as 5,000, whereas in earlier times Antarctica alone probably had nearly 300,000.

But it is not just the slaughter that is shocking. The demise of the great whales caused enormous disruption to the delicate balance of the whole marine ecosystem, making the krill, squid and fish on which they fed more abundant, and thus increasing the numbers of other higher predators such as birds, seals and minke whales (which were too small to be of interest to the whalers until stocks of other species began to run low – only 2,000 minkes were taken before the 1970s). The penguins and seals, particularly the fur and crabeater seals, have been the major beneficiaries of these changes and, with the surplus krill now devoured by these species, the great whales may never have the chance of recovering to the populations witnessed in Antarctica by the early explorers such as Cook and Ross.

Diversity of Whales

Whales, with their smaller relatives the dolphins and porpoises, are known as cetaceans, from the ancient Greek word for whale, *ketos*. There are 78 species recorded worldwide, and while they may look like giant fish, they are in fact streamlined marine mammals: warm-blooded creatures that breathe air and give birth to live young. Their front feet have evolved into flippers, while the remnants of their back feet lie hidden beneath the skin, the massive tail fluke acting like a giant monoflipper, propelling them through

Sei (pronounced 'say') whale. These are the third largest (after the blue and fin) among the baleen whales. They travel singly or gather in small groups. Females are larger than males and grow up to 21 m (70 ft). Renowned among whalers for their speed, their populations were devastated during the whaling era.

the water with effortless grace at speeds of up to 80 kph (50 mph). To reduce resistance they mould themselves to the contours of their watery environment, flexing muscle, cartilage and skin to smooth the flow of water over their velvety skins, minimizing drag and turbulence.

The distinction between whales and dolphins is a purely arbitrary one, with the term 'whale' being used to describe the larger cetaceans – generally those that measure over 6 m (20 ft) – and embracing about half of the known species. Biologically cetaceans can more legitimately be divided into two groups based on the way their mouths are adapted for catching prey: 85 per cent of them belong to the suborder Odontoceti or toothed whales, which use their teeth to capture prey before swallowing it whole; the remaining ten species belong to the suborder Mysticeti and have sheets of filaments of a nail-like substance commonly referred to as baleen or whalebone suspended from the roof of their giant mouths to sieve plankton and small fish from the water.

Standing on the bridge of a ship as it cuts a path through Antarctica's ice-bound channels and open bays, passengers are always eager to glimpse one of these great creatures and the first sign that whales are in the vicinity is usually when one blows – exhaling air through its nostrils as it comes to the surface. Sometimes you can hear the noise from far away, at other times the whale may

ABOVE

Late evening off the Phantom Coast, Amundsen Sea. The pack is made up of ice floes which are constantly moving, at times creating openings known as leads. It is far less dangerous for most vessels to follow such leads than to attempt to force a way through the ice.

be so close that you can smell it – a cloying vapoury muskiness that leaves an oily patch on the surface of the water that seabirds such as the Antarctic prion are quick to spot, dipping low to feed on the nutritious droplets of oil. Despite the huge difference in size – the six species of baleen whales found in the Southern Ocean in summer range from the blue whale down to the minke, a mere 8 m (26 ft) long and weighing only 7 tonnes – to the untrained eye many whales look alike: huge dark blobs with the majority of their body concealed beneath the surface like icebergs – and size is generally not an easy thing to judge. Their appearance at the surface is often so fleeting that good binoculars are essential if you are to have a chance of telling them apart: you can quickly scan their outline and most importantly their fin – or lack of it – as they slice though the water. The fact that the southern right whale doesn't have a dorsal fin, blows air in two directions and looks like a big crusty submarine (as ornithologist Martin Gray described it to us) makes it one of the easier to identify. And if you ever come across a blue whale its slightly blotchy, denim-coloured hide almost matches the sea.

Other clues to look for are whales that spy-hop, poking their heads out of the water while they look around or display – this is something that killer whales, humpbacks and minke whales do quite frequently. A whale's wedge-shaped tail fluke is another good field characteristic – sei, minke and fin whales never show theirs ostentatiously, while southern right, sperm, blue and humpbacks do. The floppy lob-shaped dorsal fin of the sei whale is a giveaway and, even without the distinctive black and white markings of the killer whale, there can be no mistaking it, with males sporting a 2 m (6 ft 6 in) high dorsal fin – mighty impressive when you are in a zodiac at eye level to the water and you find that tall dark

fin suddenly scything towards you. To have an 18 m (60 ft) long humpback whale emerge from the depths at arm's distance from a rubber inflatable, to hear the whoosh of its breath as it dives again, is both a heart-stopping and an exhilarating moment for even the most experienced of zodiac drivers. But perhaps most memorable of all is when a party of a dozen minkes swarms around the zodiacs, cavorting among the ice floes, their long, flat snouts emerging next to the boats at times, that large eye upturned questioningly.

Many whales commute between the Antarctic, where they can find food during the summer months, and the more tropical waters further north, where they breed and give birth. They can go for long periods without feeding and during their winter sojourn they fast for several months – up to eight in some species.

To undertake such lengthy migrations, long-distance wanderers like the humpback 'feel' their way along the ocean depths by echolocation, navigating the contours of the seabed; some make their way through the submerged mountain ranges of the mid-Atlantic ridge which stretches for 16,000 km (10,000 miles) from Iceland to Patagonia, providing a guided tour of their migration routes to their offspring. Deep within their brain they possess a 'compass' that enables them to sense the rotational forces of the planet, tracking the path of the sun and the position of the moon and its tidal pull, guiding them unerringly back to their breeding grounds. Here the male humpbacks compete for females with the power of their songs and the rhythmic movements of their bodies, cutting through the water, spinning and riding the waves.

Human language struggles for ways to describe the magnificence of these displays: spy-hopping, lob-tailing (lifting their flukes into the air and thwacking them down) and slapping the water with enormous paddle-shaped flippers. But how can the word 'breaching', for instance, possibly convey the power and athleticism of a whale bursting from the ocean, defying gravity in a spectacular leap into the sky, twisting and pirouetting like an Olympic diver, a waterfall of spray cascading from its massive body as it topples back into the sea, displacing tonnes of water in the process and leaving its human audience speechless with joy.

Beneath the surface a courting couple seem to caress each other without touching – twisting and turning in a sinuous slow-motion dance as they glide past, fanning the water towards one another. When the time is right to mate male and female brush against each other with their pectoral fins, rising up and out of the water, pressed together like one being. Anything from 11 to 16 months later depending on the species, a single calf (twins are very rare) is born into the soothing ocean environment. The mother gently nudges her offspring to the surface, rolling on to her side to allow it to suckle, using special muscles to pump litres of rich, fatty milk directly into its mouth.

Among the things that have always fascinated people about whales and dolphins – and key to how they communicate – are the sounds they make, though many whale species are silent (to human ears at least). In fact, the ocean is alive with sound, albeit very different to the sounds we are familiar with on land: the rasping of fish feeding on coral, the muffled snapping of shrimps, fish drumming their air-bladders, the metallic clicks uttered by dolphins – and, most hauntingly beautiful of all, the extraordinary song of the male humpback whale. In the olden days sailors hearing these strange calls echoing and amplified by the wooden hulls of their ships believed them to be haunted by spirits of the deep, and in a sense they were.

Humpbacks and many other large whales dive to great depths, using low-frequency sounds to map their position in the ocean and keep in contact with others of their kind over hundreds of kilometres – using sound as deftly and surely as other animals use sight. And dolphins are known to scan their surroundings using their own organic sonar by focusing a fatty lens in their melon-shaped head – housing twin cerebral cavities – allowing them to transmit two finely tuned, multi-directional sound beams as high-frequency bouncing clicks of up to a thousand per second that act like radar, penetrating the darkness and picking out the tiniest details. This enables them to build up a sound picture through precise echolocation, mapping their position relative to the surface and the ocean floor, helping to pinpoint obstacles and alert them to the presence of prey. The other category of sounds are those used by individuals to communicate with each other, ranging from the soft rhythmic tapping of sperm whales to the swirling eerie howls of the humpbacks. It is these sounds that have captured the imagination of humans, as musical in their way as birdsong.

The toothed whales and baleen whales feed in very different ways, with the latter scooping up their food, either by swimming through dense concentrations of small prey – particularly swarms of krill – with their mouths open or by taking in vast quantities of water and then using their massive tongues to expel it, leaving their food trapped on the baleen filaments. Toothed whales, by contrast, are adapted for taking fish and squid. Sperm whales are the champion divers, sometimes hunting giant squid with tentacles as long as 10 m (33 ft) in the cloying darkness of the ocean floor. To do this they dive to depths of 1,000–2,000 m (3,300–6,600 ft), remaining submerged for more than an hour if

ABOVE
Killer whales or orcas are the largest of the dolphins, with distinct markings, black above and white below. They travel in small groups or pods with the dominant male recognizable by his large triangular dorsal fin. Capable of great speeds, killers often travel in a close-knit group in a line abreast.

OVERLEAF
Skuas at sunset, Bellingshausen Sea. South polar skuas have been recorded near the South Pole, making them the most southerly birds on Earth.

necessary, accommodating the dramatic changes in pressure by collapsing their ribcage concertina-like along articulated joints to help resist the force of a quarter of a million tonnes of dense water at the bottom of the ocean. Not only do whales have huge lungs to suck in massive quantities of air before diving, their blood and muscles absorb oxygen in vast quantities and they can shut down the movement of blood to non-essential organs, allowing it to flow mainly between the heart and the brain.

Killer whales or orcas are sometimes referred to as the wolves of the sea and are found in every ocean, with around 160,000 in the Southern Ocean, each individually marked in black and white, the perfect colours for the white continent. Some 7 m (23 ft) long and weighing 8 tonnes, they are the largest of the dolphins: quick, enormously strong and inquisitive, living in family groups or pods. Aggression is virtually unheard of within killer communities, yet they are the only cetaceans known to kill other whales, chasing them down in packs – co-ordinating

their attack and harassing their victims to the point of exhaustion, ramming them and then ripping into them with their sharp teeth. They often feast on the tongue of a large whale or its calf and then abandon the carcass to the scavengers; the paddle-shaped tails of some humpbacks are tattooed white-on-black with the teethmarks of killer whales, which have no natural predators. Sometimes a pod will charge in a looping run towards an ice floe, setting up waves to wash seals off the slick surface into the water. And Norwegian killer whales are known to employ a 'carousel' feeding technique, corralling shoals of herring into a tight ball by releasing bubbles or flashing their white bellies, and then slapping at them with their tail flukes to stun or kill 10–15 fish at a time.

Despite the fears these impressive creatures stirred among early explorers – Shackleton's men were always anxious whenever they emerged among the pack ice – there are no documented accounts of them killing humans, though one did once grab a surfer before letting him go again.

There is flexibility in their feeding regime, and though the culture of preying primarily either on fish or on mammals holds true from Norway to the Antarctic, in the vicinity of the Crozet Islands, in the Southern Ocean off the southeast coast of Africa, the killers switch according to the season, taking southern elephant seal pups for as long as they remain at their breeding grounds and when they leave switching their attention to fish. These different populations have evolved different traditions, speak a different 'language' and do not interbreed with other communities.

The Great Slaughter

Fascinating and complex as they are, whales have traditionally been viewed as little more than a commodity. The history of whaling goes back thousands of years: there is archaeological evidence from South Korea suggesting that whales were killed with harpoons as early as 6000 BC and records of people hunting whales off the coast of Persia in 2000 BC, while the origin of commercial whaling can be traced to Basque fishermen operating in the Bay of Biscay around the eleventh century. From there it spread north along the European coast to Spitzbergen and reached Greenland by the beginning of the seventeenth century, with British, Dutch, Danes and Germans all involved.

By the early eighteenth century a substantial whale fishery had evolved in Britain's North American colonies, with vessels competing with European whalers in the traditional whaling grounds of Greenland, pursuing their quarry southwards to the 'southern whale fishery'. Not to be outdone, British whalers were soon competing in the South Atlantic, and they claimed to be first around Cape Horn in the

1780s to begin whaling operations in the Pacific, followed soon afterwards by the Americans. During the next 30 years whaling spread to all parts of the Pacific and Indian Oceans, including the waters around New Zealand and Australia. By the middle of the nineteenth century nearly a thousand whaling ships were plying their trade across the world's oceans, employing 70,000 men, all driven by the same objective – to hunt down the sperm and right whales, pursuing them in small rowing boats with hand-held harpoons, muskets and side arms. The crews of the whale ships were usually paid a 'lay' or share of the value of the catch, with the master typically receiving 10 per cent and crewmen one eightieth. The 9-m (30-ft) long whaleboats were carried by the mother ship until needed, then lowered into the water. They were powered by oar or sail with a crew of six and steered by an oar located over the stern, with a harpoon secured by 300 m (1,000 ft) of rope. It was dangerous work – a single flick of a whale's tail could smash a small boat.

Of the toothed whales, only the sperm whale was extensively hunted, due to its great size and the copious semi-liquid waxy oil known as spermaceti found in its enormous head – whalers thought that this was the whale's 'sperm', hence the name. The purpose of spermaceti is still debated: it has been suggested that it helps in echolocation; that the effect on the wax of temperature changes aids buoyancy; that it insulates the whale's hearing and brain from the cold of the ocean deeps. What is certain is that this is one of the purest forms of oil, clear and white, and does not film over or go rancid. While not edible, it proved ideal for making candles and cosmetics; for lubricating machinery that had to operate at high temperatures and pressures; and for automatic transmissions and watches. The fact that the sperm whale didn't sink when killed

A minke whale plunges beneath the surface. Minkes are the smallest and most abundant of the rorquals; they are quick and often found close inshore within the pack ice, far from open water. With the decline in populations of the larger whales, the minkes have in recent times been targeted by Japanese whalers for 'scientific' purposes, and their meat sold in shops. Minkes typically occur singly or in small groups, although they sometimes gather in their hundreds where plankton is abundant.

added to its value. The whalers targeted females with young and the bachelor pods of immature males that gather in warm tropical waters during the southern summer. Adult male sperm whales spend the summer in colder polar waters and initially these huge and powerful creatures proved too dangerous to hunt.

Apart from the fast-moving, deep-dwelling sperm whales, the whalers concentrated most of their efforts on the large, peaceful and relatively slow-moving, coast-loving right whales, which were easiest to kill and butcher. This combined with the fact that they too floated when killed made them the 'right' whales to target – as did the large quantities of oil that could be extracted from their thick layer of blubber, along with high-quality 'whalebone', which was much sought after by the fashion industry for the manufacture of corsets and the struts that held umbrellas and voluminous hooped skirts open. In the first 70 years of the nineteenth century American whalers pursued and killed nearly 200,000 right whales throughout the world's oceans; the species was soon hunted to near extinction in the north Pacific. Next it was the turn of the humpbacks, which also favour coastal waters, but fight when caught and often sink when killed. Before long they too were brought to the brink of extinction in Europe and other northerly regions.

Neko Harbour, Antarctic Peninsula. Though they left few records, the sealers and whalers were responsible for exploring and naming some key landmarks in this region.

With whales on the decline in their traditional hunting grounds, whalers took increasing interest in the reports from explorers of the large numbers of whales to be found in the Southern Ocean. James Clark Ross visited the area between 1839 and 1843 and encountered numerous southern right whales – at one point south of the Falklands he had 30 whales within view at the same time. The whales allowed ships to pass within touching distance, and in the case of the humpbacks sometimes actually approached vessels. Here, surely, was a lucrative industry just waiting to be exploited, in seas barely 900 km (600 miles) from a British possession. But tempering these early accounts was the bleak picture the travellers painted of ice-filled seas and hardship.

An Englishman named Charles Enderby was the first to try his luck at whaling in the Southern Ocean, founding a whaling outpost in 1850 at the northern tip of the remote Auckland Islands to the south of New Zealand. Enderby arrived with 300 hopeful colonists and established what became known as the Enderby Settlement, offering work, money and food to the local community of Maori and their Moriori slaves who had moved from the Chatham Islands to settle on the Auckland Islands in 1843 and had since eked out a meagre existence in this cold, harsh environment by subsisting on seals and albatrosses. Enderby's venture, which embraced shore-based whaling, ship repair and refitting as well as the provision of fresh meat and vegetables, was to prove an expensive failure: in the first year the whalers, desperately trying to match the pace of the fleeing leviathans while attempting to kill them with harpoons launched by hand from wooden catcher boats, managed to capture only a single pregnant female. By the end of 1852 Hardwicke (as the Enderby Settlement became known) was deserted; the acid nature of the peaty soil made it almost impossible to cultivate and the Maori and Moriori moved on to Port Adventure on Stewart Island at the southern end of New Zealand.

The interest in Antarctica that had prompted Britain, America, France and Russia to send national expeditions south between 1819 and 1845 was on the wane: there was little, it seemed, to be gained in terms of either colonial expansion or commercial enterprise in the frozen south. The discovery of petroleum in 1859 helped make whale oil a less valuable commodity over the next few decades; between 1850 and 1872 the number of ships engaged in whaling dwindled from 400 to 72. There was still a heavy demand for baleen driven by the fashion industry, but the only whale that could supply it in commercially viable quantities was the right whale, whose northern population had been virtually wiped out. Once more people's attentions turned to the south.

During the summer of 1892–93, four vessels (known as the Dundee fleet) sailed to the Weddell Sea. Though scientific discovery was part of the expedition's remit, the real purpose was to explore the region's commercial potential. It was now 50 years since Ross's journals had alerted the world to the possibility of whaling here, and the majority of right whales he had observed had long since been killed in their winter retreats among the fjords and bays of Patagonia. The whalers were forced to turn their attention to the humpbacks, or try to hunt the fast-moving blue, fin and sei whales – difficult and dangerous work. But with whalebone selling for £3,000 a ton, men were willing to take the risk (though with scant return in this instance), and there were always the seal rookeries to plunder if all else failed.

By this time a key development had taken place that would give the drive to plunder the Southern Ocean's whale population added momentum, hastening the time when even the quickest and most powerful of the whales would attract the attention of the whalers. A Norwegian called Svend Foyn had transformed the harpoon into a far more lethal device: a heavy iron lance armed with an explosive grenade and fired from a cannon mounted on the bow of fast, steam-powered catcher vessels. Like the killer whales the catcher vessels hunted in packs, with the harpoon aimed at the middle of the whale beneath the dorsal fin, exploding deep inside its body and destroying the heart and lungs, sometimes with sufficient force to kill it outright. The tip of the harpoon had hinged barbs to anchor its prey while it was winched up from the depths, with a system of springs known as the accumulator helping to absorb the resistance created by the desperate thrashing of the dying animal and the buffeting of the sea. Once at the surface compressed air was pumped into the carcass to keep it afloat.

By the turn of the century this lethal combination of firepower and steam-driven (later diesel-driven) catcher vessels saw the remaining whale stocks dwindle rapidly in waters around Europe and North America. No whale, regardless of size, was safe, with little or no thought given to preserving numbers by limiting catches. Soon even the mighty blue and fin whales had nowhere left to hide – not even in the Southern Ocean.

It took another Norwegian to successfully open the whaling industry in Antarctica – Captain Carl Anton Larsen, the man who had wintered on Paulet Island in 1903. The remote southern lands held no fear for him. At a banquet held in his honour in Buenos Aires Larsen

regaled his rescuers with stories of the thousands of whales he had seen, wondering why they weren't already being exploited. The following year he was back with a loan of £40,000 and a licence from Britain to begin whaling at South Georgia under the auspices of an Argentine company, basing his operation at Grytviken, within the shelter of Cumberland Bay. Larsen chose a Norwegian crew equipped for business with a single catcher boat and a shore station to render the blubber into oil. The advent of these factories heralded a new era. Shore stations or moored factory ships could 'process' the whales brought alongside by the catcher boats.

Finally the Southern Ocean, the world's richest whaling ground, was conquered: during their first year of operation Larsen and his men accounted for nearly 200 whales, mostly humpbacks. In those days there were so many whales that the whalers often didn't even have to leave the bay to hunt them. Soon the beaches were littered with rotting carcasses, the stench overpowering, the water stained red by their blood. But that was a small price to pay when set against the money to be made. Grytviken must have throbbed with life – and death – the sounds of heavy machinery, scenes of men hard at work flensing (stripping the blubber from the giant carcasses). Either due to the rigours of their existence or by dint of the money they saved many whalers retired in their forties, having earned two or three times what they could have hoped for among the poor rural communities in Norway.

At Larsen's prompting, in the summer of 1905–06 the Norwegian whaling entrepreneur Consul C. Christensen sailed a factory ship named *Admiralen* to New Island in the Falklands, then on to Admiralty Bay in the South Shetlands. Within a few years Chilean, Argentine and British whalers were all operating in the

Minke whale emerging at the surface of the pack ice with a characteristic smooth arching of the back.

area and shore stations were soon established around the South Shetlands, the South Orkneys and elsewhere on South Georgia, providing work for numerous floating factory ships and catcher boats. In the 1912–13 season alone nearly 11,000 whales were taken. In later years whaling interests prompted Britain and Norway to make territorial claims to protect their interests, and profits were such that the British Government soon put a tax on every barrel of oil extracted from whales taken in their territory.

In due course the Norwegians developed a more sophisticated kind of factory ship, with a slipway opening at the stern and the capability of processing several whales aboard at once, streamlining the whole operation. The first of

these, *Lancing*, arrived in the Antarctic in 1926. The lifeless carcass was hauled to the loading ramp, where it was met by a set of massive steel jaws that locked into its flesh; held fast in this manner it was winched up onto the flensing deck, where men in spiked boots armed with long-handled, scythe-like knives would scale the flanks of the whale mountain, deftly cutting off strips of blubber 3 m (10 ft) long. These were then dragged to the mouths of gaping manholes that swallowed the meat, depositing it in rotating drums armed with spinning blades that rendered the bloody stew to mincemeat, then steam-heated it until, after four hours, the blubber and oil separated (later still the oil was filtered and centrifuged).

Soon ocean-going factory ships were common – some the size of aircraft carriers – equipped with giant freezers, ensuring that not one part of the whale carcass was wasted: the skeleton was ground down for animal feeds and fertilizers, the oil collected for glycerine to manufacture into explosive nitro-glycerine or glycerol for lipstick; some of the inner organs distilled into pharmaceuticals. Parts of the whale were used as sausage skins and drum skins; as wax crayons and pigment for artists; as the basis of soaps and detergents; as gelatine for coating film. The jaw cartilage was preserved as a delicacy, the tail flukes eaten raw, the meat carved into steaks or rendered into soup. In addition to corsets and umbrellas, baleen filaments proved strong enough and flexible enough to use as watch springs, in toys and upholstery, as springs in the first typewriter, for brushes and brooms, in linoleum, tennis-racket strings, medical trusses and surgical stitches.

Between 1927 and 1931 more than 14,000 whales were killed and processed in the Ross Sea area alone. Increasingly whaling fleets were catching predominantly smaller whales and now realized that stocks of even these were dwindling; there was a glut of whale oil on the international market, the world was in the grip of an economic depression, petroleum was increasingly available and electrification was widespread in Europe and America. But with the development of hydrogenation of liquid oil to produce fats for soaps and margarine whale products still found a market and the killing continued with whaling fleets from Britain, Norway, the United States, Japan and Germany scouring every corner of the Antarctic. Then the Second World War gave us the jet turbine, which would have yet another profound impact on whaling – specialized oil to cope with the high

operating pressures and temperatures of jet engines could not easily be distilled from petroleum, but sperm whale oil proved ideal. It is estimated that between the two world wars up to 45,000 whales a year were slaughtered, and as late as 1960–61 over 41,000 whales were processed by three land stations and 21 factory ships into whose giant maw most of Antarctica's remaining blue and fin whales disappeared.

The development of the ocean-going factory ship meant that whales could be killed in the open ocean or near to ice floes, winched aboard for flensing in as little as an hour, enabling the whaling industry to operate beyond any nation's territorial restrictions. This soon sounded the death knell for the onshore whaling industry – the shore stations probably accounted for no more than 10 per cent of the total number of whales killed in Antarctica. By 1965 Grytviken had been abandoned: between its founding and its closure 175,000 whales were killed and butchered here. A year later Leith Harbour shut its doors, drawing to an end an industry that had prospered on South Georgia for 60 years.

Today, the old whaling stations are mournful places – ghost towns. Recently Grytviken has been the focus of a massive clean-up campaign costing £6 million, removing toxic asbestos and unsafe structures from among the ruins of the old buildings to make them safe for visitors. The massive rusted fuel tanks provide a decrepit reminder of those days, along with the pretty wooden church where visitors can still ring the bells to celebrate their visit – stirring dreams of their own, perhaps. The decaying wreck of *Petrel* and two other old whalers once powered by steam and fuelled from giant coal bunkers lie marooned along the jetty, abstract patterns of rust and paint decorating their hulls. The silence is broken only by the guttural belching of

Whale bones, Antarctic Peninsula, a poignant reminder of the millions of whales that were slaughtered in the Southern Ocean in the first half of the 20th century.

cent of the humpback population – 250,000 animals – butchered for their meat and oil before they received official protection in 1966. By the late 1960s Japan and Russia were the only whaling nations and even today Japan continues to take hundreds of whales – mainly minkes – in the name of scientific research. By 1973 the number of baleen whales had dropped to 500,000, representing a staggering loss of biomass – a decline from 45 million to 9 million tonnes due to the bigger whales having been hunted most severely.

elephant seals and the gentle lapping of the waves. Penguins and seals have reclaimed the beaches, and visitors tread carefully so as not to disturb a slumbering elephant seal, while the fur seals generally announce themselves with a snuffling cry of alarm long before you reach them. The only signs of whales are giant bones littering the shores, bleached by the elements, an echo of the past.

The slaughter of the whales during the twentieth century was of such magnitude that its effects are still being felt today, a biological tragedy of epic proportions. Many whale species were reduced to just a fraction of their natural populations – by the late 1980s estimates based on direct sightings of the southern right whale pointed to fewer than a thousand in Antarctic waters – and despite protection in more recent times such slow-reproducing species have struggled to recover. Two million whales were killed in the Southern Ocean alone, with 95 per

Attempts to stem the number of whales being hunted and to regulate the industry date back to 1946, the year when the International Whaling Commission (IWC) was established; in 1975 measures were proposed to try to limit catches to sustainable levels, though in the subsequent 30 years the IWC permitted 1.5 million great whales to be killed. With whale populations worldwide in serious decline, the decision was taken in 1982 to ban all whaling – except for 'aboriginal subsistence'– beginning with the 1985–86 season. A huge Southern Ocean Whaling Sanctuary was established in 1994, but this has not stopped whaling entirely and there are currently concerted attempts by pro-whaling nations such as Japan, Norway and Iceland to have the ban overturned and commercial whaling resumed – indicating that there are those who will always view Antarctica and its resources as exploitable. You need look no further than the history of whaling to realize that this last great wilderness and its wildlife are far from secure.

CHAPTER 7

The Antarctic Peninsula

The Falkland Islands and South Georgia are visibly alive with seabirds and other animals – summer is their moment and to see them during that season is to see them at their most vibrant and beautiful. For many people, though, stopping here would leave their journey to Antarctica incomplete. Heading further south towards the Antarctic Peninsula – the northernmost tip of Antarctica – there is one objective only: to see ice, to satisfy the longing for a glimpse of the white continent, the place the explorers struggled to reach and which for so long had been beyond their grasp.

Depending on ice conditions, it takes one or two days to reach the Antarctic Peninsula from South Georgia across the Scotia Sea; two if you head directly across from Ushuaia over the notorious Drake Passage, a journey of almost 1,000 km (600 miles). While sailing south, people gaze in awe and fascination as icebergs appear on the horizon for the first time. Some are transfixed by the beauty of it all, iPods plugged into their ears, squeezing every last drop of emotion from the moment, their music adding a soaring refrain to match the mood. There's nothing strange about that: Scott and his

ABOVE

Adélie penguin porpoising – a technique that allows it to travel fast on the surface. Penguins are superbly adapted to the water – compact and streamlined, heads retracted to reduce resistance, wings modified as powerful flippers, and legs positioned well back on the body with feet acting as rudders.

men carried a gramophone and a pianola to Antarctica, and when Shackleton's men were forced to leave precious possessions behind on the ice to lighten their load, one of them, Hussey, was allowed to keep his banjo to provide 'vital mental tonic'.

At first all that lies ahead is an unbroken expanse of ocean. Far off in the distance a whale blows and is gone again. In places the water's surface is broken by the silhouettes of porpoising penguins and seals, hinting at how far from land these creatures can travel. Then eventually the South Orkneys and South Shetlands appear out of the mist to the north and northeast of the tip of the Peninsula. These two clusters of islands, together with the neighbouring South Sandwich Islands and South Georgia, form the spine of a submerged mountain range linking the Transantarctic Mountains with the Andes of South America – an archipelago known as the Scotia Arc that reaches 540 km (335 miles) into the Southern Ocean.

This is the chance for more landings and more penguins: 5 million pairs of chinstraps breed on the South Shetlands, and Bailey Head on the cinder flanks of Deception Island's ancient caldera is home to the single largest colony in the region, the massed ranks of birds acting like noisy commuters hurrying about their business on a crowded street as they hike back and forth between rookery and sea. At the northeast end of the South Shetlands is Elephant Island, where Shackleton's men sought shelter while he headed for South Georgia and salvation on that legendary small-boat journey. Occasionally you can land here, but more often than not the weather is too rough and the fog too thick to permit it. Even so, the proximity is sufficient to conjure images of what lay in store for those men in the coming months.

The Importance of the Antarctic Peninsula

The Peninsula itself evolved around 65 million years ago (mya) and, with its spiny tail stretching north towards more temperate climes, it is now bounded to the east by the vast expanse of the frozen Weddell Sea and to the west by the warmer Bellingshausen Sea, buffeted by fierce winds. Volcanic activity gradually subsided along the northern end of the Peninsula 3 mya, though in parts of Antarctica ancient volcanoes still murmur and rumble. If you visit in the summer, the Peninsula has a benign beauty that is picture perfect, the most glorious amalgamation of snow-capped mountains set against clear blue skies:

form sculpted by sunlight and shadow. Due to the purity of the atmosphere at this end of the world the ultraviolet light of the sun's rays is so intense that it toasts the skin. The scenery has a familiarity to it, a touch of the Swiss Alps or parts of Alaska, yet on a grander scale, the missing element being the green wash of trees and foliage. There will be no burst of autumn colour when the days begin to shorten.

Here the comparisons end – Alaska for all its grandeur is within reach of a warm cabin with oil-fed heater to take the edge off the night chill, an aircraft close at hand to swift you safely home. The Peninsula is far more remote. Even so, in terms of isolation it is just the tip of the Antarctic iceberg, quite different in character from the bulk of the continent. It is too cold for vascular plants to flourish and only two species are found here; even a footprint pressed deep into moss beds more than 2,000 years old may last for ten years in such a hostile environment, with lichens growing at just 0.5 mm ($\frac{1}{50}$ in) a year.

Adelaide Island, Antarctic
Peninsula. The Antarctic
Peninsula is composed of
Mesozoic, Tertiary and
younger glacial rocks.
The mountains here are
connected to the Andes
by a submarine ridge,
which includes active
volcanoes in the South
Sandwich Islands.

By November the pack has usually retreated sufficiently around the rugged coast of the Peninsula and its complex network of surrounding islands to reveal narrow, rock-strewn beaches between land and ocean. The wealth of animal life to be seen at this time of the year is almost overwhelming, comparable in places to some of the sights that make South Georgia such a highlight. Though perfectly adapted to life in the water, penguins and seals must still come ashore each year to lay their eggs or deliver their young. This is their moment in the sun, the snow and ice melting sufficiently for seals to haul ashore and penguins to return to their rookeries, breeding cycles compressed to allow for the fact that wintry days will return soon enough. There is a sense of comedy about the scene, the penguins waddling around like old men with arthritic knees while seals 'callumph' caterpillar-like as if trying to move while confined to a snug sleeping bag as they head back to sea.

There are numerous landing sites where visitors can step ashore and observe the spectacle. Many such places bear the imprint of the early sealers and whalers: Neko Harbour, for instance, was named after a whaling factory ship that operated along the Peninsula in 1911–12 and again in 1923–24. The harbour was first seen and charted in 1897–99 by Baron Adrien de Gerlache, leader of the first fully scientific Antarctic expedition and the first to winter – the expedition responsible for charting much of the Antarctic Peninsula.

Neko Harbour is a good place to see gentoo penguins, the snow slopes carved into a honeycomb of highways defined by the march of a thousand clawed feet, deepening and widening as the season progresses, providing well-trodden pathways between the exposed patches of rock where the penguins nest and the sea that nourishes them. Later in the season the rookeries become so inundated with guano that pristine pathways and clean white penguin feathers turn a pinkish-brown with krill stains.

Though neither king nor emperor penguins breed along the exposed beaches of the Peninsula or the South Orkneys and South Shetlands, the three Pygoscelis or 'brush-tailed' penguins – the

Penguins are most easily identified by their head markings. Chinstraps (opposite) have a narrow black line running from the chin and beneath the eye. Gentoos (below left) are the largest of the brush-tailed penguins and have a white bandanna across the forehead. Adélies (below right) have black heads and a white eye-ring.

gentoos, chinstraps and Adélies – add their own unique brand of mayhem and colour, noise and smells to make this an overpowering sensory experience. Wherever you land penguins seem to dominate proceedings, swarming over the hillsides and rock faces like feathered ants, transforming the snow-clad terrain into a mass of heaving, breathing collective life as they reclaim rookeries occupied seasonally for hundreds of years.

The three species are sufficiently different from one another to be easily recognizable, yet not large enough to be mistaken for a king or an emperor and lacking the stylish head plumes worn by rockhoppers and macaronis. Gentoos have a distinctive white headband, while the chinstraps have a black strap running under their white chin and the Adélies have a black face and sparking blue eye-ring, all of which probably help to enhance courtship and aggressive displays – and to prevent interbreeding. They have different temperaments, too: the gentoos, for example, are rather mellow and tolerant of one another, probably because they stay longer at their colonies, so spend more time together; this makes them the easiest for researchers to handle. All three species overlap on the Peninsula and on

BELOW

Chinstraps on an ice floe. Chinstraps winter at sea beyond the edge of the pack ice. They are usually the last of the three brush-tailed penguins to return to their breeding colonies in late October/ early November.

OPPOSITE

Chinstrap penguin about to regurgitate food to two chicks. Chicks are covered in a greyish down at birth. Adults forage around nearby ice floes for krill.

the South Orkneys and South Shetlands, avoiding unnecessary competition by breeding at slightly different times, foraging in different areas – and at different depths of the ocean – and wintering in different locations. Their lifestyles have proved so successful that between them the three brush-tailed penguins have until recently accounted for nearly 90 per cent of all Antarctic birdlife in terms of biomass.

Adélies are true Antarctic penguins, ranging further south than any other species. They feed on krill at the ice edge, spending seven to ten days at a time away from their nest site, and this is why you don't generally find them along the more northerly regions of the Peninsula – it is too far for them to travel between their nest sites and the pack ice further south. The gentoos are at the other end of the spectrum and have the widest and most northerly range of the three species, with a circumpolar distribution as far north as 54°S. They are primarily coastal, preferring to avoid the pack ice and feeding inshore near to their breeding colonies for as long as these remain ice free – all year if possible. This explains why the bulk of gentoos are found further north, on the Falklands and South Georgia, and why the southern gentoo population nesting on the Peninsula breeds later. Chinstraps meanwhile occupy the middle ground, returning to the open sea of the Drake Passage after breeding and spending the winter there, feeding offshore and mid-ocean, with the Peninsula acting as the centre of their distribution.

One way these close relatives avoid competition is by selecting different locations within suitable breeding colonies and staggering their arrival. At King George Island in the South Shetlands, for instance, the Adélies come ashore in early October as strong winds and currents help break up the sea ice, preferring windswept

knolls and ridges that become snow free early in the season. Ice-free nest sites are at a premium, with nests crammed as little as 75 cm (30 in) apart. The gentoos meanwhile tend to build larger nests than the other two species and seek lower-lying, flatter areas where they can space themselves 1 m (3 ft) or more apart. The chinstraps arrive a few weeks after the Adélies, when the slopes are clear of snow and ice. These are the mountaineers among the *Pygoscelis*, hiking up rocky knolls and cliffs, digging in with their powerful clawed toes and leaning into the steep slopes, using their ice-axe-like beaks to pull and lever themselves upwards to reach their nests.

Despite everything, disputes between the species do sometimes occur. Occasionally an Adélie will try to pirate a chinstrap's nest site and lay eggs before the rightful owner arrives and, though the two penguins are similar in size,

Newly fledged Adélie penguins on an ice floe, waiting to enter the water. Young inexperienced birds such as these are especially vulnerable to (attack by) predators such as leopard seals.

chinstraps are champion brawlers and are quick to assert their rights, pecking and slapping with their flippers until the intruder gives way. American ornithologist Robert Cushman Murphy summed up the different temperaments of the three species perfectly: 'Gentoos turn tail, Adélies stand their ground, but chinstraps charge!'

Male Adélies arrive first at their rookeries, unerringly homing in on the nest site they used the previous year and taking responsibility for most of the nest-building and maintenance. If there is snow covering the nest the male will dig it out, lying on his belly to melt away the snow while waiting patiently for his partner to arrive. Time is of the essence and if she hasn't appeared within two weeks he will find a new mate. Courtship and copulation quickly follow. Once the female has laid her two eggs and is ready to head back to the

sea she often searches for stones to fortify the nest, and it seems she is prepared to do whatever it takes to get them.

The newspapers had a field day a few years ago when a study on Adélie penguins found that at this point females sometimes offer sex to a non-partner with the intention of stealing a stone from his nest. The females seem to have discovered that they can hoodwink inexperienced single males who are occupying nest sites on the periphery of sub-colonies late in the courtship period. The female approaches with head bowed – normally an invitation to sex among established couples. Then when the male moves aside, instead of the female settling on the nest and adopting the mating position, she pilfers a stone and heads back to her own nest. This pattern may be repeated a number of times, and occasionally the female does allow the male to mate with her, but as this tends to happen after egg-laying it doesn't compromise the breeding success of established pairs.

All three species lay two eggs that are incubated for 35 days and, unlike the rockhoppers and other crested penguins, they all attempt to raise both chicks. As with most penguins, everything has to be accomplished quickly, refined and abbreviated to within roughly a two-month period in the case of the chinstraps and Adélies. By this time the chicks are fully moulted and ready to go to sea, gathering along the beach until one plucks up sufficient courage to dive in – then the rest of the party hurries to follow. At first they swim on the surface until they seem to get the hang of this strange watery environment and then they are gone. Losses from various causes can be as high as 50 per cent during the chicks' first winter, but if they survive they will return to their birthplace and start breeding when they are three to four years old.

The fact that gentoo chicks take three to four months to fledge, rather than two, is one reason why they are not found as far south as the chinstraps and Adélies, where the season is shorter, and probably why they are far less numerous than the other two species. But with the effects of global warming bringing warmer temperatures in recent years and less severe ice around parts of the Peninsula, the gentoos have prospered, increasing by an order of 600 per cent since 1976. The worrying decline in the Adélie population that has been tracked by scientists working at the American research base at Palmer Station has proved to be a blessing for the gentoos and chinstraps, who are increasing in numbers and replacing their cousins at breeding sites in a broad sweep across the western Peninsula. For the first time in 800 years gentoos are breeding in the vicinity of

Palmer. Where krill stocks are in decline (and the reasons for this are discussed more fully in Chapter 10) the gentoos and chinstraps take more fish and squid – you can see this from their guano, which is more whitish green than krill-stained pink under these circumstances – showing an adaptability in their diet that the Adélies do not seem to have. This, combined with a later breeding regime affording greater protection from spring snow meltwater, and the more open water that gentoos and chinstraps prefer, appears to be the reason for the extension of their range.

When the Adélie population first began to decline no one was quite sure why: no one realized at that point just how critical the pack ice was to the survival of these penguins, nor that they were destined to become an extremely sensitive measure of the health of the Antarctic ecosystem and the effects of global warming on the region. The pack ice acts as their feeding platform in winter – they dive into the water via leads in the ice when within reach of rich feeding sites. Without the ice they simply cannot survive.

gentoos and Adélies

There are other factors at work, too. The melting of the sea ice allows water vapour to escape into the atmosphere from the open ocean, increasing the amount of snowfall along the Peninsula. Come springtime the snow melts and the Adélies, being the first to arrive and breed, are most at risk from the consequences – the flooding of nests and drowning of eggs and chicks. With fewer chicks surviving, the population is plummeting: one study site near Palmer Station has documented a 70 per cent decline over the past 30 years, a loss of 10,000 breeding pairs since 1975. The Adélies, it seems, are 'hard-wired' by instinct to return to the same breeding sites that have served their species for millennia, apparently unable to adapt to the changing conditions as their relatives can. They are not alone. As we have seen, there have been declines of up to 80 per cent in some rockhopper colonies in the Falklands as their food supply – the Patagonian squid Loligo – has migrated further south to colder regions due to global warming or been compromised by overfishing.

ABOVE

Gentoo feeding a large chick. Chicks gather in crèches at four to five weeks, allowing both parents to forage at sea. Unlike other penguins, young gentoos continue to be fed after fledging and may still be resident at the moulting area as late as March.

Predation

With so many birds gathered together, the rookeries are always likely to attract the attention of predators, and it is the lack of mammalian predators that has allowed penguins to dispense with flight and to flourish throughout the southern hemisphere. Their young, though, are still vulnerable to avian predators such as skuas, giant petrels and gulls, which will take eggs and chicks whenever the opportunity arises. Skuas often stake out territories within penguin colonies and take up to 20 per cent of eggs and a similar number of chicks, though their predation varies from year to year according to location and season. The tendency of chicks to huddle together in crèches from when they are three to four weeks old helps to deter predation and to keep them warm – it also allows both parents to go to sea to forage, and can occur only once the chicks are able to recognize their nest site and their parents. At this time the skuas look for easier prey. In more northerly climes less hostile to human settlement, introduced species have also had a devastating effect on bird colonies, with cats, rodents, mustelids and reptiles taking eggs and chicks.

The periphery of the colony is the most dangerous place for a breeding bird to nest – if you are at the edge your eggs and chicks are easier to target, and this is often where the least inexperienced birds are forced to try to breed. Nesting in the centre of a colony means enduring repeated pecks and wing slaps from your neighbours each time you leave and return to your nest, but this is a small price to pay if it increases your chances of raising your offspring. Clumping together in large colonies probably helps to synchronize breeding – everyone is in the right place at the right time, with the added benefit of safety in numbers. Chinstraps, kings and macaronis all nest in massive colonies, with the macaroni probably the most abundant of all – there are some 5 million pairs breeding on South Georgia and a total world population of up to 10 million pairs, including a million pairs of the closely related royal subspecies.

Though penguins need not fear a life-threatening encounter with a mammalian predator on land (though very occasionally fur seals do kill penguins on land – and at sea), they face their most formidable adversary when they enter the water, for this is the domain of the leopard seal, an opportunistic hunter clad in a silvery-grey pelt flecked with dark spots on throat and flanks. It is not uncommon to find a leopard seal resting on one of the ice floes as you cruise the waterways, giving you the chance to admire the ultimate Antarctic predator, which though sighted as far north as 21°S is usually a denizen of the sea ice. Leopard seals were fortunate to be spared the attention of the sealers, who prized the luxuriant coat and the easy availability of the colony-dwelling fur seals, and their only natural predators are the killer whales.

Leopard seals have a wicked, almost snake-like smile when they yawn, exposing teeth that befit the only seal that regularly hunts warm-blooded prey. Their long, pointed canines and incisors are

RIGHT
Leopard seal with gentoo penguin. The leopard seal's spotted throat and shoulders give it its name. These are solitary predators, targeting exit and entry places at penguin rookeries. Having caught their prey, they shake it violently, in the process turning it inside out and making it easier to feed on.

clearly designed to grab and tear, and the jagged cheek teeth have interlocking cusps to cut through flesh or gulp mouthfuls of krill before expelling the sea water through the valleys of their teeth. The leopard seals' predatory ways make them quite unlike any other seal you might meet in Antarctica. There is something about the way they look at you with those big, alert, dark eyes – they have the presence of a creature that lives by killing.

With so many penguin breeding sites dotted along the Peninsula, these are favourite haunts for leopard seals during the summer. The leopards possess the longest flippers of any seal, helping to propel them through the water at lightning speed, and they regularly patrol the shallows at the places where newly fledged penguins gather at the water's edge. Life is tough for these inexperienced birds. There is an understandable nervousness for first-time swimmers, with a degree of jostling and uncertainty, and once you have seen a leopard seal in action you know why any penguin might appear nervous about entering the water. The reward for the leopard seal is a penguin stomach stuffed full of krill; they flay their victim, thrashing it on the surface of the water in the manner of a crocodile breaking apart a gazelle, to the point where the penguin is torn to pieces, turned inside out even, making it easier to devour. The scraps are then left to the petrels and gulls, with sea stars and ribbon worms taking their turn when the feathered remains reach the ocean bottom.

To see a leopard seal swimming in a leisurely curve around a zodiac is mesmerizing: over 3 m (11 ft) and 400 kg (900 lb) of pent-up energy, all fluid, languorous movements, twisting and pirouetting under the boat as if in contemplation of what it might hold. It is hardly surprising that so many crabeater seals bear a patchwork of old lacerations the width of a leopard seal's jaws on their blonde coats – aside from the wounds that

the males inflict on each other during fights over breeding females. Leopard seals attack crabeater, Weddell and fur seal pups, while around South Georgia they prey on elephant seal pups too, with the lucky ones living long enough to bear the scars from their encounter. The seals have only a brief window of opportunity during the breeding season to catch such easy pickings as young penguins and seal pups, and analysis of leopard seal faeces from Couverville Island showed a diet of 80 per cent krill, along with the occasional remains of blue-eyed shag, fur seal and penguin. At Palmer Station krill accounted for around 40 per cent of their diet. Fascinatingly, samples taken from a leopard seal's whiskers can reveal three years of feeding patterns.

Like the leopard in Africa the leopard seal hunts alone, roaming so widely that scientists know little about their biology. Females give birth to a single pup between November and January, and you occasionally see a mother and pup hauled out on an ice floe during these summer months, though pups are independent at a month old and must then fend for themselves. Leopard seals spend the winter further north, frequenting the sub-Antarctic islands, where some of them breed, and reaching as far as the coasts of South Africa, South America, Australia and New Zealand, with numbers estimated at anything from 200,000 to 400,000 individuals worldwide.

Shackleton described the leopard seal as a 'fierce, handsome brute', and his storeman Thomas Orde-Lees had reason to agree when one suddenly lunged at him from between ice floes while he was skiing, then tracked him from below, prompting Frank Wild to shoot it. There is certainly no question that these impressive creatures are potentially hostile to any perceived intrusions on their domain by competitors and they have punctured zodiac inflatables before

Adélie penguins emerging from the Ross Sea, north of Cape Washington. The ability to leap high out of the water like salmon enables them to reach the safety of ice floes, putting them out of reach of predatory leopard seals.

now, though generally they seem more curious than predatory where human beings are concerned. However their formidable reputation was enhanced in 2003, when scientist Kirsty Brown was grabbed by a leopard seal while snorkelling off the Peninsula, then pulled under and drowned, the only recorded fatality. A number of underwater photographers have found themselves feeling less than comfortable while filming leopard seals, using their bulky camera as a barrier between them and the seal to try to ensure that things don't turn nasty. All predators deserve our respect and when we intrude on their environment it has to be on their terms – or not at all.

Antarctica is an environment like no other and has some harsh lessons for humans. Our presence this far south is so recent that it underlines just how unsuited we are to a life of such bitter cold, and even today, with all the inventiveness of modern technology, we have much to learn about how to survive here, conditions that the emperor penguin has embraced over millions of years of evolution. And it was an attempt by three of Scott's men to learn more about these extraordinary birds in the depths of winter that nearly cost them their lives.

Disintegrating icebergs at Paradise Bay, Antarctic Peninsula. Icebergs gradually break apart forming smaller chunks of ice known as 'bergy bits' and 'growlers' – which are still hazardous enough to endanger most vessels.

CHAPTER 8

A Winter's
Journey

In December 1922 a book was published that is considered by many to be the best travel book ever written. *The Worst Journey in the World* is the work of Apsley Cherry-Garrard – 'Cherry' to his friends – a member of Scott's ill-fated 1910–13 *Terra Nova* expedition and one of three men to make what became known as the 'Winter Journey', a trek to the emperor penguin colony at Cape Crozier, a little bay between the Ross Ice Shelf and Ross Island. *The Worst Journey in the World* is much more than a riveting tale of exploration under the most extreme conditions. It captures perfectly all the elements that made the Antarctica of those days such an extraordinary and compelling land,

blending scientific enquiry, the quest for 'priority' in being first to the Pole, endurance and a way of life in which friendships were tested on a daily basis and acts of courage and heroism were commonplace. It has become a metaphor for what intrigues people about the white continent, an intimate exposé of both its harshness and its appeal, and of the men who sought to unravel its secrets. When you finish reading it you don't have to be an emperor penguin to know what they must have gone through.

The trio who undertook that journey could not have been more different. Cherry-Garrard, the son of landed gentry with no great need to follow

RIGHT
'Man-hauling' across the ice. The 'heroic age' of Antarctic exploration lasted from 1895 to 1922, with the death of Shackleton traditionally marking its end. During this time the continent, which had previously been virtually unknown, was extensively explored and charted and the South Pole reached.

a profession, had studied Classics at Christ Church, Oxford before switching to Modern History. Oxford stimulated his interest in exploration and opened his eyes to the world of men like Scott and Amundsen. In 1907, during his final year, Cherry's father died, leaving his only son as heir to several estates and ensuring him a handsome income. Thoughts of studying law soon yielded to the greater urge to travel and explore, a means of escape – even if only temporarily – from the family pressures that would burden him in later life. A chance meeting the following year with Edward and Oriana Wilson at a cousin's Scottish shooting lodge was to prove a turning point for the 22-year-old Cherry.

Dr Edward Wilson had been a pivotal member of Scott's first expedition south in 1901–04 during which he was Scott's close friend and right-hand man, a paternal figure to whom people could turn for advice without fear of judgement or condemnation – 'Uncle Bill' to one and all. A keen ornithologist and naturalist, as well as an artist of considerable skill, he was the expedition's chief scientist. Though somewhat retiring by

nature, he possessed great zest for life, was physically fit, athletic and, above all else, steady. Impressed by Cherry's intelligence and enthusiasm, Wilson was sympathetic to the younger man's strong desire to join the *Terra Nova* party, not least because of a deep loyalty to Cherry's cousin, Reginald Smith, with whom he shared a great affinity and who had published the book of Scott's first expedition. Wilson knew that there was no vacancy for Cherry among the expert scientific staff but that there was the possibility of enrolling him as an 'adaptable helper' with an interest in natural history. Cherry let it be known that he would not expect a salary (expedition finances were not in the most robust of health), and in due course paid £1000 for the honour of joining.

The third member of the 'Winter Journey' party was Lieutenant 'Birdie' Bowers, a Royal Navy officer who had learnt his trade in the Merchant Marine, earning his nickname for his enormous beaky nose. He was immensely strong and as fit as any man on the expedition, possessed of phenomenal mental and physical

LEFT

Emperor penguins on sea
ice, Cape Washington,
Ross Sea. Some 40
emperor nesting sites are
known to be scattered
around the periphery of
the continental mainland.
By November the
penguins begin to
abandon their rookeries
and return to sea to
rebuild their energy
reserves after the rigours
of raising their chicks.

stamina. A devout Christian, he drew strength in adversity from a rock-solid belief in his maker and in his mother, whom he worshipped.

Antarctica was to give purpose to Cherry's life; here in the clarity of the crystal desert he suddenly knew who he was, or perhaps rather what he wanted to be. He enjoyed the comradeship and the jovial banter, and felt secure away from the responsibilities of everyday life, freed among this small party of men from the shyness and anxiety that had always lurked in the shadows of his complex personality. For the first time he had a clearly defined role; people depended on him and it brought out the best in him. He had never felt so alive – and never would again. Yet he so nearly didn't make the cut. The doctors were concerned about his fitness: he was so short-sighted that, as he himself describes it, 'I could only see the people across the road as vague blobs walking.' Fortunately Wilson had a word with Scott, and Cherry was allowed to join the expedition on condition that he was prepared to take the additional risk imposed by his impediment. His official position was assistant zoologist to Wilson with the chief responsibility of skinning the bird specimens they collected. This would allow Wilson to devote more time to painting than he had managed on Scott's first Antarctic expedition.

The Winter Journey was prompted by Wilson's desire to investigate the extraordinary life of the emperor penguin, a bird that breeds under the most hostile conditions known. At the time just how hostile the conditions are, and how remarkable these birds are, was only beginning to become clear. Wilson already knew more than most men about the emperors – he had been to Cape Crozier before, but that had been in the summer. If he was serious about observing their breeding habits, there was no alternative but to travel to the rookery in the depths of winter. The challenge was not to be underestimated – there is nowhere on Earth more elemental and unforgiving to humans than Antarctica in winter.

Other explorers besides Wilson had been to Cape Crozier before the Winter Journey. Charles Royds had travelled there by sledge in October 1902 while serving on Scott's *Discovery* expedition, to prepare the way for the relief ship, and it was at this time that Reginald Skelton had become the first man to discover a breeding colony of emperor penguins, coming back with three chicks and some egg fragments. Royds had then volunteered to return (Wilson was occupied with the final preparations for the journey south with Scott and Shackleton) and it was he who secured the first whole egg, found lying frozen in the snow, and noted that the young penguins had already left the colony as early as 8 November. At the beginning of September the following year Wilson, Royds and four seamen found about a thousand emperors clustered on the fast ice – an area of sea ice attached to land and surrounded by the more transitory pack ice – at the foot of towering and precipitous ice cliffs. Wilson returned again in October, gathering some chicks at a later stage of growth and a lot of additional information about their behaviour.

Wilson was not one to exaggerate, but the wry understatement apparent in a letter written to his father hints at the reality of his experiences: 'Bird-nesting at −62°F [−52°C] is a somewhat novel experience. Those journeys to Cape Crozier were pretty average uncomfortable, even for the Antarctic. It has been worth doing; but I am not sure I could stand it all over again.' Little did he imagine that he would return nearly ten years later, in infinitely more testing conditions.

BELOW

Emperor penguins with chicks on fast ice. Emperors breed on fast ice during winter so that their chicks can benefit from the nearby abundance of food available in the spring and summer months.

Though Scott's expedition has ultimately been remembered as a race for the Pole, Wilson was first and foremost dedicated to his work as a naturalist and a painter. He expressed the wish to his father that his monograph on the emperor penguin should be a classic – which indeed it turned out to be, forming part of the scientific reports of the expedition published by the British Natural History Museum. In a letter to his wife written on 7 June 1911 he said, 'We want the scientific work to make bagging the Pole merely an item in the results.' He was determined if possible to help solve one of ornithology's leading questions: 'How did birds evolve from reptiles?' The emperor penguin was seen as

crucial to this enquiry – the missing link perhaps between birds and reptiles.

The emperor had first been formally described in 1844 on the basis of pickled remains brought back by James Clark Ross. By the end of the nineteenth century some scientists had become intrigued by the belief that an embryo passes through the stages of its evolutionary history as it develops. With the emperor penguin thought to be the most primitive bird in existence, examining its embryo would surely help to shed light on the evolution of birds in general. At the time many people believed that penguins were distinct from other modern birds while sharing the flying dinosaur as a common

ancestor (in fact we now know that penguins diverged from late Cretaceous birds which existed before the dinosaurs became extinct). Wilson hoped to find vestiges of teeth in emperor penguins, something that would link them directly to the Jurassic dinosaurs. Examining the embryo might also help answer the question of whether feathers had evolved from reptilian scales or were of independent origin. The cost of this line of enquiry was a potentially suicidal journey to collect penguin eggs at an early stage of their development.

The First Stages

Wilson had hoped that the expedition might be able to establish its winter quarters at Cape Crozier itself, but the seas proved too rough and it was impossible to find a suitably sheltered landing spot. Instead, Scott based himself at a rocky point at the southern end of Ross Island, then known as the Skuary, but later renamed Cape Evans, 107 km (67 miles) from the penguin colony. Wilson and his two companions were going to have to walk the rest of the way, negotiating a path across the formidable Ross Ice Shelf or 'Barrier', as it was known in those days.

The Winter Party set out on 27 June, man-hauling two 3-m (9-ft) sledges packed with 360 kg (790 lb) of equipment and six weeks' worth of provisions. Cherry voiced the fears that anyone would have felt when he wrote, 'Five days later and three men, one of whom at any rate is feeling a little frightened, stand panting and sweating out in McMurdo Sound.' The darkness was total except for the glow cast by the moon and the aurora, together with the tantalizingly brief and faint twilight of midday. For Cherry

there was the added problem of his short-sightedness. His spectacles soon proved worthless, fogged and iced up in seconds by his breathing, leaving him virtually blind. As if that wasn't enough, on only the second day out he made the mistake of removing his mitts to haul his sledge over the fractured ice along the Barrier's edge, resulting in all ten fingers becoming frostbitten. Within a few hours he had blisters 5–8 cm (2–3 in) long on every finger and 'for many days those blisters hurt frightfully'.

It didn't take long for the three men to discover that sledging in these conditions would be no gentle glide across the ice. The ice was crumpled and buckled into ridges, hummocky ice with steep-cut drifts (sastrugi) which soon capsized one of the sledges. For much of the time they could barely make out what lay ahead. Their only sanctuary from the elements was a double canvas tent which, when the wind wasn't blowing a blizzard, should have been relatively

LEFT

Bowers, Wilson and Cherry on the eve of their departure on the Winter Journey to Cape Crozier in 1911 (the first journey of its kind in Antarctica – nobody had proceeded overland in winter before).

easy to pitch – it certainly had been in the spring, summer and autumn sledging journeys. But now every time they wanted to cook a meal they had to pitch the tent as a windbreak just to light the primus stove. There was nothing cosy about going to bed, either – they could hardly wait to get out of 'their shivering bags' the following morning. The only respite was breakfast, as it meant that with a bit of luck it would be 17 hours before they had to get back into their sleeping bags.

At times the going was painfully slow – barely 2–5 km (1–2 miles) in a day. Clear starlit nights were a blessing and at times their spirits were buoyed by the magnificence of the aurora spreading swirling curtains of colours across the sky. They stood – or lay flat on their backs in the snow – to marvel at its displays of orange and lemon-yellow suffused with green and blue which at times covered two-thirds of the sky. But there was only so much relief to be garnered from moments such as these. Both Cherry and Wilson suffered frostbite to their feet. It went without saying that they remained stoic in their travails and Wilson, referring to Cherry's blistered fingers, remarks, 'But he takes them all as a matter of course and says nothing at all about them….' Each man was expected to tough things out in the knowledge that he could rely on his companions to sustain him in the brutal conditions. Wilson and Bowers were always careful not to complain and their writing gives away little of how difficult things were. The truth of the matter is voiced by Cherry, and it is his honesty and willingness to reveal his most intimate feelings that make his story so appealing:

> The horror of the nineteen days it took us to travel from Cape Evans to Cape Crozier would have to be re-

experienced to be appreciated; and any one would be a fool who went again: it is not possible to describe it. The weeks which followed them were comparative bliss, not because later our conditions were better – they were far worse – but because we were callous. I for one had come to that point of suffering at which I did not really care if only I could die without much pain. They talk of the heroism of the dying – they little know – it would be so easy to die, a dose of morphia, a friendly crevasse, and blissful sleep. The trouble is to go on…

The constant darkness put a different complexion on everything. Even the simplest of tasks was a trial and it took the men hours to get going in the morning – if one can call it morning, because any sense of time became somewhat meaningless in the darkness. Hauling the sledges was toughest on the more compact patches of snow and ice, made even worse because the surface was roughened by deposits of ice crystals. Instead of the sledge runners melting the crystals, they could only advance by grinding them over and over; conversely, in soft snow the difficulty was accentuated by the men's feet sinking at every step. When it became impossible to haul both sledges at once, they relayed them by 'daylight' from eleven in the morning till three in the afternoon, then by candlelight from 4.30 to 7.45, limiting their progress to just over 5 km (3 miles) a day in temperatures ranging from –48°C (–55°F) in the morning to –54°C (–66°F) at night. Mostly they navigated with the help of Jupiter. When the wind picked up they wore 'nose nips', bits of wind-proofed fur to protect their noses that proved the greatest of comforts. Despite the terrible conditions Bowers methodically recorded temperatures, took sledge-meter readings to measure how far they had travelled, noted the condition of the ice on the Ross Ice

Shelf and the nature of the auroras. His cheerful 'never say die' attitude must have been of great comfort to Wilson, who was acutely aware of his responsibility in proposing this venture, and to Cherry, who embodied all the frailties of human nature – and the courage. Make no mistake, for all his foibles Cherry had loads of heart and had already proved himself to be a powerful sledger, using the strength and stamina that had seen him chosen to row for his college's first four at Oxford – no small achievement.

Each man was equipped with a reindeer sleeping bag with an eiderdown lining as a reserve. Cherry's bag proved too large to keep him warm, so he turned it hair-side out and stuffed his down bag inside as a lining. But the exertions of walking or simply moving around and breathing caused moisture to accumulate on their bodies, soaking their clothes and sleeping bags, which froze when exposed to the cold, then melted again when they got warm. Little wonder that the bags came to represent such misery for much of the time.

Conversations could take a week to complete. 'We were very silent,' says Cherry, 'it was not very easy to talk: but sledging is always a silent business.' Quiet they may have been but it did not stop them constantly worrying about their feet – trudging on ice meant moving slowly, chilling feet encased in frozen finnesko – reindeer-skin boots stitched with gut. The soles of the boots were made from the thick skin of the reindeer's forehead, with the grip of the hair giving the best purchase on the ice. They were only too well aware that if any one of them became crippled with frostbite the whole party would be in danger, and Wilson, being a doctor, kept a close eye on each of them. Toes, heels and soles were carefully examined whenever they camped and they used their oil-fuelled lamp to thaw and dry

their socks, mitts and finnesko before putting them on again in the morning. At night they donned a change of dry footwear. Wilson urged caution, reminding the others again and again to do things slowly so as to avoid injury and conserve energy.

By early July the going was very tough indeed. They had slowed to about 2 km (a mile or so) a day, scant reward for seven or eight hours of man-hauling. A bank of fog often obscured the way ahead as they struggled to relay the heavy sledges – back-breaking work, and far harder to keep feet and hands safe in temperatures that now regularly plummeted to –57°C (–70°F). At times there were no landmarks to guide their path, just a disorientating and confusing nothingness as they did their best to avoid patches of fractured land ice and pressure ridges riddled with cracks and crevasses. They struggled to keep out of the line of blizzard, choosing the lesser evil of eddying winds, deep snowfall and fog, with the creaking and groaning of the ice all around them.

The Winter Journey had been a chance for Scott to experiment with the composition of his men's diet – food was heavy and took up space, so the less the better when the time came for a trek to the Pole. Breakfast was tea, biscuit and a highly nutritious form of dried meat known as pemmican – originally a food of the North American Indians consisting of dried lean caribou or buffalo meat mixed with fat and berries; lunch was biscuit and tea (with Cherry and Wilson adding extra butter to see if it would give them more energy), and supper was pemmican, biscuit and a mug of hot water – woefully few calories for such strenuous work. Cherry soon found himself craving more food and increased his biscuit ration, while Bowers, who had chosen to raise his protein intake,

found he could not stomach pemmican three times a day, so cut back. Both Cherry and Wilson then altered their diet, with Cherry being allocated more butter and Wilson more biscuit. They agreed that 12 oz (330 g) pemmican, 16 oz (450 g) biscuit and 4 oz (120 g) butter a day was an 'extremely good ration', something that today makes one shudder with hunger. But regardless, meals helped breathe life back into their weary bodies, balancing the mind-numbing work of hauling the sledges and fighting the wind and ice.

Cape Crozier

On the evening of 15 July they eventually reached their destination, aided by what little moonlight and daylight there was. They pitched camp and immediately set to work building a rough stone hut 250 m (800 ft) above the place where the emperors breed on the fast ice. Bowers as always was eager to get the job done, driven by his seemingly endless reserves of strength and

BELOW
The sexes of emperor penguins are similar. They are seldom seen in sub-Antarctic waters and are

totally independent of land. After the breeding season they moult and disperse to the surrounding waters.

determination, disappointed that he could not finish the whole enterprise in a day, rather than the three that it took them. Their new home was a combination of solid rock walls covered with moraine gravel and an outer coating of ice slabs, roofed with canvas with an upturned sledge as a cross-beam. It had a sloping aspect, with a canvas entrance flap at the lee end and the more robust end acting as a buffer against the weather; at 2.5 m (8 ft) wide, it was just sufficient for three men to lie in their sleeping bags side by side. Every crevice was packed with snow to keep the elements at bay – or so they hoped. Despite all their efforts at weatherproofing, when a gale started to blow, snow drift and gravel dust poured in.

By now their precious supply of oil was running short, too – they had used four of their six cans and were getting low on the fifth. They promised themselves that they would keep the last can for the homeward journey, in the belief that they would be able to fuel a blubber stove with penguin fat while in camp to save oil fuel for the primus stove during the return trek. It was essential they reach the emperor rookery as soon as possible, but that would test their resolve all over again. They set out on the 19th, wearing crampons on their boots and pulling an empty sledge, struggling across snow slopes and pressure ridges – a chaotic pile of ice blocks and drifts – and then clambering along the edge of the ice cliffs and rock cliffs which rose 30 m (100 ft) or more to form the background to the rookery. It was a race against time if they were to achieve their objective and still return to the hut before what little light was available in the middle of the day vanished. They roped themselves together in case the ground collapsed beneath them – which it often did – and used the sledge as a platform to cross soft and rotten-looking snow bridges. For Cherry it was even more of a nightmare, being

virtually blind when unable to use his spectacles (it was −38°C/−37°F and too cold to prevent them fogging up), and he found himself endlessly blundering in and out of rifts and crevasses as his companions tried to find safe passage ahead. In the end they ran out of time.

The following day they set out again and by chance stumbled on the path that Wilson and his companions had used ten years earlier to take them down to the foot of the ice cliffs, to a point where they could get onto the sea ice. By now they could hear the emperors calling and knew they were close. But first they had to lower themselves over a 3–4 m (10–12 ft) drop, requiring Cherry, the least nimble of the three, to remain on the high ground to help the others clamber down on ropes. Imagine then the disappointment they must have felt to see a compact group of only a hundred emperors standing under the cliffs. Nonetheless, Bowers and Wilson quickly caught, killed and skinned three of them to fuel their blubber stove. Some of the birds were incubating eggs on their feet and tried to shuffle away. In doing so, many lost their eggs and the men were able to collect five of them.

Ten years earlier there had been between one and two thousand penguins at Cape Crozier during September and October, and now Wilson thought that many birds must simply not have arrived yet, and that the eggs they had collected had probably been laid only within the last week or two. Some of the penguins were so anxious to incubate something – anything – that they scooped up rounded pieces of egg-sized ice, and in the gloom both Bowers and Wilson picked up these dirty rounded 'ice eggs', thinking them to be the real thing. They watched in fascination as one bird that had lost its egg in the confusion returned and picked up an ice egg, tucking it inside its cosy brood pouch. The men carefully placed the five eggs in fur mitts and tied them round their necks for safety. Later poor Cherry smashed both the eggs he had been entrusted to carry while blundering about on the icy ground. Ironically his misfortune was to prove a blessing, as the fats from the broken eggs made his mitts much easier to thaw out on the return journey. At least the men could bolster their spirits in the knowledge that they had blubber to cook their meals for a number of days without broaching their last can of oil.

By the time they got back to the hut the weather had worsened and as if they weren't already suffering enough hardship a glob of red-hot oil spat in Wilson's eye as he tended the stove – an injury that left him unable to stifle his groans of agony throughout the night. He later told his companions that he thought his eye had gone. The blubber stove got mixed reviews from the men, providing them with a welcome source of heat but at the cost of choking them with smoke and covering everything in a layer of oily soot.

It was now 21 July and they had been away for 25 days. By the following day the weather was truly awful and, as Cherry describes it, 'Then there came a sob of wind, and all was still again. Ten minutes and it was blowing as though the world was having a fit of hysterics. The earth was torn in pieces: the indescribable fury and roar of it all cannot be imagined.' Wilson kept trying to reassure the others that things must improve. But when Bowers emerged from the hut he saw to his horror that their tent had been blown away. They had been careful to pitch their tent in the lee of the hut so that they could dry out some of their gear in it. They had then dug the tent into the snow and ice, weighing it down with a tank filled with supplies and equipment that was too heavy for a single man to move easily. But with winds blowing at force 9–10 nothing could stand in their way.

Fortunately all their clothing and equipment were still there, bar two flat parts from the bottom of the cooker, but, already exhausted by their exertions and lack of sleep, the three men were faced with the prospect of attempting the homeward journey without the shelter of a tent and with only a meagre supply of oil – a truly horrifying predicament. They had always hoped to find and kill a large seal to provide an abundant source of oil and to use the skin to supplement the canvas roof of their hut. But this might mean waiting in vain, consuming valuable supplies and lessening their chances of returning alive. If they failed to find their tent they would have to improvise some form of protection from the canvas awning they had used to roof the hut.

They dozed fitfully as the wind continued to roar around them. 'Storm force is force 11, and force 12 is the biggest wind which can be logged,' wrote Cherry. 'Bowers logged it force 11, but he was always so afraid of overestimating that he was inclined to underrate. I think it was blowing a full hurricane.' To add to their burdens, the blubber stove was giving trouble. Before they had finished heating the water for their meal, the feed pipe came unsoldered, rendering the whole stove useless. They carefully decanted the last of the blubber oil into tins and lamps in case their candles ran out and so that they would still be able to thaw and dry their socks. Thankfully they still had the primus stove and so were able to finish cooking breakfast.

There was no escaping the gale and at noon on the next day, 23 July, the canvas roof of the hut was ripped from its mooring and torn to shreds. It was Wilson's birthday and they spent it huddled in their sleeping bags, no doubt wondering how it would all end. Snow quickly piled up inside the hut and the sledge that had acted as a support for

BELOW

Pack ice, Ross Sea. Unlike glacial ice, sea ice such as this is saline and forms by crystal growth rather than by compressed snow. In winter it insulates the ocean; in summer it reflects 80 per cent of solar radiation, delaying the warming effects of the sun.

the roof fell across their bags, with several of the heavy stones landing on Cherry and Bowers. They lay there listening to the pistol-like report of the shredded canvas flapping in the wind, aware that the sole surviving piece of canvas was the one forming the floor of the hut. Wilson envisaged them having to dig a hole in the snow and ice at the end of each day as a shelter, but in his heart he knew they could never survive the return journey in these conditions without a tent. In the meantime they dared not have another meal because of the need to ration the oil supply. Wilson and Bowers sang songs and hymns, and paddled their feet to try to keep going, with Cherry doing his utmost to join in.

Every so often they gave each other a friendly thump to fortify their resolve.

By the morning of 24 July the storm had started to abate. It was two days and two nights since they had eaten their last meal. They struggled out of their sleeping bags and made their first attempt to search for the tent, but were soon forced to give up. Huddled together with the floor cloth pulled up over their heads so that they could get the primus stove going, they brewed tea and made a hot meal of pemmican which, despite the addition of hairs from their sleeping bags, penguin feathers, dirt and debris, tasted delicious. As the first glow of light pierced the darkness they set out again and this time as Wilson and Cherry stumbled around they heard a shout from Bowers. He had somehow located the tent about 1 km (½ mile) away at the bottom of a steep slope. Miraculously it was virtually intact. Their relief must have been overwhelming.

Not wanting to waste time trying to improvise a new blubber stove in a roofless hut they began to prepare for the journey back to Cape Evans. Wilson realized that they had attempted the near impossible in the darkness of midwinter, but was nevertheless disappointed that they had failed in their main objective of spending time observing the behaviour of the emperors. He felt they had 'achieved nothing but disaster'. Their sleeping bags were now so ice encrusted that he feared they might not offer sufficient protection against really low temperatures when they recrossed the dreaded Barrier.

They determined to leave the following day, stockpiling everything they could for a future journey to Cape Crozier. They then loaded rocks and one of the sledges on top of the depot and tied a note concealed in a matchbox to the handle of the pick-axe, giving the date on which they were leaving and noting that they were all well. Nearly 45 years later members of the Commonwealth Transantarctic Expedition rediscovered the shelter, and Wilson and his companions would have been gratified to know that Cape Crozier has become an important site of oceanographic and ornithological research, with particular interest in the ecology of emperor and Adélie penguins.

A Miraculous Return

By now the men were suffering from chronic fatigue – food deprivation too. Bowers was still much the strongest of the three, but the lack of sleep relentlessly wore Cherry down, while Wilson 'looked very bad'. Many was the time when one or other of them dozed off during mealtimes as they perched on their sleeping bags and huddled over the cooker. As they headed for

BELOW
Emperor penguins courting. Pair bonding involves head bowing and trumpeting calls.

Male emperors incubate a single egg for a period of around 65 days, and brood the chick for up to 10 days. (Females return to the colony around the time of hatching.)

home they had once again to endure the prospect of near darkness and no landmarks to guide them, just the vague and indistinct silhouettes of slopes. At one point Bowers disappeared down a crevasse and was saved only by his sledge harness, which was designed to withstand just such a mishap; he remained suspended over the 'bottomless pit' until his companions could rope him up little by little, their fingers suffering terribly in temperatures approaching –45°C (–50°F). It was so cold and uncomfortable in their sleeping bags that wherever possible they preferred to keep going, though Wilson insisted that they should rest up for seven hours in their bags each day, even if sleep was impossible. The bags were in such a sorry state that they dared not roll them up for fear of having them break in pieces, so they loaded them full length on the sledge 'like three coffins'. As it was, the bags were already broken in several places through the struggle to get into them when they were frozen solid. The men would stuff some of their gear into the mouths of the bags to make it easier when the time came to push their feet inside. Cherry had pulled the eiderdown lining from his sleeping bag while struggling to get his feet out and then found it impossible to reinsert it. Eventually he accepted Bowers' generous offer to take his lining, which he had not needed inside his own fur bag.

They rose at 5.30 a.m., took lunch at 2.30 p.m., camped at 6 and turned into their bags at 9 or 10 p.m. Their hands gave them the most trouble and by morning their mitts were so wet that they froze the moment they turned out. Even tying the tent door proved difficult. Their feet also suffered whenever the going was soft, forcing them to trudge slowly along. A bank of fog formed where the cold Barrier air met the warmer sea ice, making it even harder to see.

But crossing the Barrier also meant that the end was in sight, and the three exhausted men arrived back at Cape Evans on 1 August, 35 days after setting out. Cherry had a blurred memory of men in pyjamas and dressing gowns trying to remove his frozen clothes. In the end they had to cut them off and by the morning they were a sodden mass weighing 11 kg (24 lb).

Scott wrote in his diary:

> Wilson is disappointed at seeing so little of the penguins, but to me, and to everyone who has remained here the result of this effort is the appeal it makes to our imagination, as one of the most gallant stories in Polar History. That men should wander forth in the depth of the Polar night to face the most dismal cold and the fiercest gales in darkness is

LEFT

Emperor penguin swimming underwater. Emperors are deep divers, preying on fish and squid at depths of anything from 50 m (165 ft) down to 265 m (870 ft). The bulk of their diet is fish, though they also make shallow dives for krill under the ice floes.

something new; that they should have persisted in this effort in spite of every adversity for five full weeks is heroic. It makes a tale for our generation which I hope may not be lost in the telling.

Emperor Penguins

Nothing can more clearly illustrate how unfitted humans are to survive in Antarctica than attempting a journey such as this, particularly before the invention of all the sophisticated equipment that we now take for granted. Even the emperor penguins – kitted out with a combination of the finest feather suit, with longer and denser feathers than any other penguins, and a thick layer of blubber as a cushion against the elements – are driven to the point of exhaustion and starvation as they struggle to raise their chicks. Indeed, the only thing that can rival the endurance displayed during the Worst Journey in the World is the story of the emperors themselves. Their

Emperor penguins tobogganing. Although they are built to swim more than walk comfortably for long distances, by using their feet and flippers to propel themselves along and steer, penguins can move surprisingly rapidly over ice and snow.

very existence is a tribute to nature's inventiveness, its ability to come up with a plan to cope with even the most extreme environments.

Like all penguins, emperors spend most of their lives at sea, inhabiting the sea ice at latitudes between 66°S and 78°S, and breeding in some 40 colonies scattered around the continental coasts, with a total population of 195,000 breeding pairs. Almost half of these are in the Ross Sea region, where human disturbance may have been responsible for a 50 per cent decrease in numbers. The ice is a barren environment, offering not a

scrap of material for nest building, so a flat solid surface is essential to emperors, and colonies choose areas of stable fast ice. These areas are often spectacular – a backdrop of towering, grounded icebergs helping to prevent the break-up of the ice while the emperors are in residence. Cape Crozier is considered a typical site, situated as it is in the lee of ice cliffs, craggy hills and bergs. The emperors reach the sea via leads in the ice, often breeding close to perennial polynyas – stretches of open water surrounded by ice, caused by the katabatic winds that roar down to the coast

from the Polar Plateau or the storms that force ice away from the shore. They also use cracks made by the tide, and even seal breathing holes.

Those are the bare facts of where the emperors live, but the reality of their winter existence is indescribably bleak, as Wilson and his companions found out, with temperatures as low as –62°C (–80°F) and winds howling at speeds of more than 160 kph (100 mph). As winter closes in, finding a mate is the first priority for the emperors and display calls are vital for bonding and pair formation. To help with this, emperors and kings have evolved a 'two-voice' system, with calls utilizing two frequency bands simultaneously, courtesy of two small membranes located near the lungs that allow them to vary pitch and tone. The hauntingly beautiful contact call, which Wilson called trumpeting and which confirmed to him and his companions that they had arrived at Cape Crozier, is made with the bill pointed skywards.

The fact that the male emperors are forced to huddle together like the best of friends to stay warm in winter is probably the reason they are noticeably less feisty than other penguins (except during pair formation and chick feeding) and they rarely resort to physical aggression, no doubt because they do not stake out territories or defend a nest. They are equally social at sea, diving and surfacing together, co-ordinating their search for food and in the process helping to lessen each individual's chances of falling victim to predators such as leopard seals and killer whales.

Most of Antarctic's wildlife heads north before winter sets in, to escape the unforgiving conditions. But emperors are large birds and it takes them longer to raise their slow-growing chicks than smaller species, so to ensure that the young fledge during the summer when food is at its most abundant and easily available they are

forced to begin their breeding cycle at the beginning of winter. Having their chicks fledge before they are fully grown reduces the time of dependency to five months.

To prepare for their ordeal emperors spend January until March searching for food in open water or fishing beneath the sea ice to build themselves up to peak condition. An emperor penguin shuffling about on the ice in its bulky winter coat is a clumsy-looking, corpulent creature – it may have dignity, but not grace. But watching emperors gliding through the water, necks drawn back against their sleek bodies, feet stretched out behind them, is altogether another matter. These are master divers that can submerge deeper than any other bird, pursuing their prey to depths of up to 450 m (1,500 ft) and at speeds of up to 10 kph (6 mph), powered by long, trim wings or flippers beating at 25–50 strokes a minute and covering nearly 5 m (16 ft) with a single beat. Mostly they forage in open water over the continental shelf or in ice-free leads and tidal cracks, and scientists use satellite tracking devices attached to the penguins' backs to record their journeys. Most dives last 2–10 minutes and emperors will dive to the very bottom of the sea, pursuing their prey in total darkness. A single foraging journey of up to 1,000 km (625 miles) is not uncommon, with chick-rearing birds known to travel even further – up to 1,500 km (1,000 miles) before returning to their breeding colony.

In late March or early April, as the new sea ice begins to form, days become shorter and the arrival of winter darkness prompts the emperors to begin their long march from the ocean to their traditional breeding colonies, a journey of up to 150 km (100 miles) across the ice. This is an epic event – a thin dark line of birds threading their way between towering icebergs and ice cliffs like

OPPOSITE

Emperor penguins waiting to take to the water. Leopard seals are a potential danger for all penguins, so they are naturally cautious about entering the sea.

participants in an ancient pilgrimage. Their arrival is highly synchronized, with males appearing a few days before the females. Both sexes must now fast until they return to the sea: in the case of females this will be some 40 days after their arrival, while males are confined to the ice until the end of incubation – approximately 115 days without feeding. Such commitment relies on strong pair bonds and emperors sometimes mate with the same partner for three or four years, though the majority select a new partner each year. This may be partly due to the short time the pair spend together and the lack of territory – a territory provides a fixed abode and meeting place, helping to reinforce the pair bond – and perhaps because of the unusual sex ratio of 40 per cent males to 60 per cent females. The surfeit of females no doubt accounts for the preponderance of trios consisting of two females and one male which form temporarily, though females will invariably end up breeding with the previous year's mate if he is available and, as in other penguins, males mate with only a single female each season.

During April and May prospective breeders perform a carefully co-ordinated sequence of displays and calls. There is a beauty and solemnity to these displays – a gentleness and deftness of touch – that is universal in its appeal. The calls are complex, with male distinguishable from female even by the human ear, and in the main consist of repeated rhythmic songs separated by periods of silence when the birds assume an almost trance-like state. This 'pre-laying silence', as it is known, helps the pair to conserve energy and lessens the chance of confusion – by continuing to call they might attract more potential mates. It is therefore likely to deter trio formation and the disruption of established pairs. Although they have no territory

ABOVE

Emperor penguins splashing into water from an ice floe.

as such, each pair maintains a sense of inviolable space around themselves; any stranger that comes within pecking distance is considered to have breached an invisible barrier and is duly chastised.

Egg-laying is synchronized in each colony, with all the females laying a single greenish-white egg weighing about 400 g (1 lb) within a week or two of one another. The appearance of the egg prompts frequent calling and mutual displays of head-circling and bowing, behaviour that is seen again when the egg hatches, helping to ensure that chicks imprint on their parents sufficiently for adults and young to recognize

each other at feeding time. Having already lost 25 per cent of her body weight, the female now leaves her partner and disappears into the darkness, returning to the sea to feed and recover her energy. The male will not see his mate again for nearly two months.

Through May and June and on into July the assembled males face a gruelling test of endurance, forming scrums of a thousand birds – 5,000 even – as they attempt to combat the effects of inconceivable privation. Temperatures drop to between –25° and –50°C (–13° and –60°F) as katabatic winds merge with hurricane-force

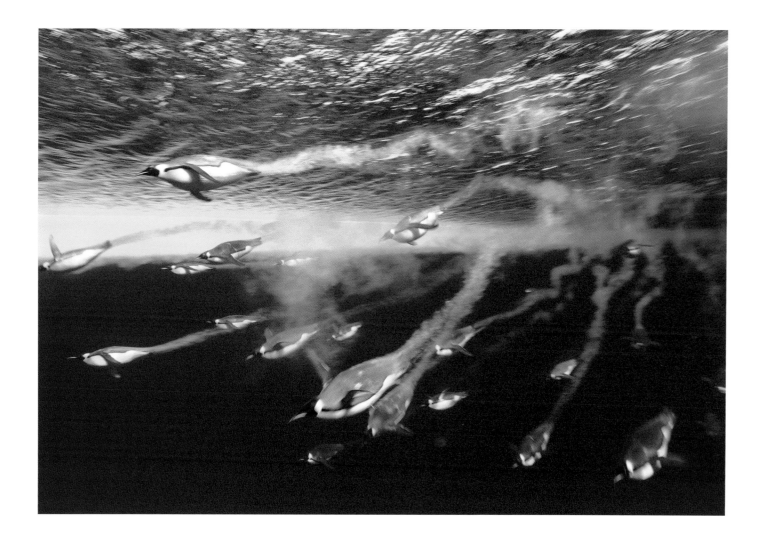

storm winds of only slightly lesser intensity. All the while the precious egg is tucked protectively within the father's brood pouch – a warm fold of featherless skin richly supplied with blood vessels that encloses the egg like a warm glove with the 'thermostat' set to 35°C (96°F). Balancing an egg on their feet means that the males are greatly restricted in their movements – they do little more than shuffle along like old-age pensioners. To conserve energy even further, the male's body temperature drops several degrees during the first two weeks of his ordeal, enabling him to prolong his fast. Sometimes the penguins are blown over like skittles by the sheer force of the storms howling around them, but still they endeavour to keep the egg safe, at times lying flat on their tummies for respite. It was during this difficult period in the emperors' breeding cycle that Wilson and his companions were struggling to reach Cape Crozier, and at times like this dozens of eggs may become separated from their owners and lie frozen on the ice.

One of the most memorable and awe-inspiring sights in nature is that of hundreds of male emperors pressed together in the depth of winter, isolated in the darkness. This is an ancient

ritual, refined by evolution to maintain life under the most testing conditions. The huddle, or 'tortue' as it is known, is like a single living organism, barely moving, but over time the birds exposed to the worst of the wind and cold on the outside make their way to the warm centre, and those that have felt the warmth at the core of the huddle emigrate slowly to the margins to take their turn with the elements, blanketed by snow. At times the emperors are forced to double their metabolic rate to cope with the intense cold and winds that can descend on them at any moment out of the darkness, and by huddling together they can maintain the temperature at the heart of the tortue by 10°C (18°F) and reduce the wind chill to just 5–10 per cent of what a single exposed individual would have to suffer.

Miraculously, three-quarters of the eggs hatch, in mid-July to early August. The chick weighs around 320 g (12 oz) and immediately begins to utter a high-pitched whistle that becomes individually recognizable to its parents within a few days. If everything has gone according to plan the female returns to the colony at around this time. By now conditions are very different from when she left. New ice forming during winter has doubled or even trebled the distance she must walk or toboggan to reach her mate, a trek undertaken during continual darkness and among gale-force winds. Yet somehow she manages to navigate her way home. Meanwhile the male has been burning his energy reserves to keep himself and the egg warm, in the process losing 35–40 per cent of his body weight. But despite his prolonged fast, if the chick hatches before its mother returns he is able to feed it, regurgitating a nutritious secretion from his oesophagus. Just how nutritious is borne out by the fact that a chick is able to double its weight on this food alone. But by now the father is close to

the limit of his endurance. If the female does not appear soon he may be forced to abandon the egg or newly hatched chick and make a life-saving dash to the sea to find food.

Fortunately, in most instances his mate appears at the appointed time and, having identified one another, the pair exchanges duties. The male hurries back to the sea, one last energy-sapping trek across the ice before he can begin to replenish his reserves, leaving the female to feed the chick on the partly digested krill, fish and squid she has gathered at sea. She continues to brood the chick for the next 24 days; the male then returns, his strength restored, and tends the chick for the following week, after which the parents alternate feeding trips. By the time the chick is a month old it is ready to leave the warmth and safety of the brood pouch, and from around six to seven weeks starts to form crèches with other chicks. The pack ice is by now breaking up, allowing the adults to make shorter and more frequent feeding trips to satisfy the appetite of their growing youngster, with each chick receiving up to a dozen feeds per parent. Orphaned chicks are doomed, as no adult will tend a chick that is not its own.

In early November the chicks begin to moult into their juvenile plumage so as to complete the process before the sea ice disintegrates beneath them. Only when they have acquired the waterproofing and insulation afforded by their permanent plumage will they be able to survive at sea. The adults stop feeding the chicks while they are still covered in down and it is at this point that the young leave the colony: the average fledging period is about 150 days, with larger chicks moulting earlier and faster. To the casual eye they look too small to survive – only around half their adult weight. Most newly fledged birds are the same weight as adults, but with the

Emperors gathered on sea ice near Cape Washington, Ross Sea. The Ross Sea is the most southern breeding ground of both emperor and Adélie penguin.

emperors there is simply too little time for that. It is vital that the young are ready to take to the ocean during the summer, when the annual bloom in plankton helps ensure that there is plenty for them to eat.

The annual variation in the distribution and amount of sea ice is often the difference between success and failure for breeding emperors, determining how far adults have to travel to find open water on foraging trips, but despite the enormous challenges around 60 per cent of the young survive. If the sea ice breaks up before the chicks are ready to fledge 90 per cent may be lost, and with global warming increasingly making itself felt this situation is destined to become more common.

Between November and February the adults undergo a post-nuptial moult lasting 30–40 days before returning to sea, trekking 10–60 km (6–40 miles) to reach water. Young emperors reappear at their natal colony when they are four years old; females begin to breed at five and males at five to six years old. Just how well adapted these birds are to their extraordinarily harsh environment is borne out by the fact that adults suffer very low mortality – 5 per cent annually – and live for around 20 years.

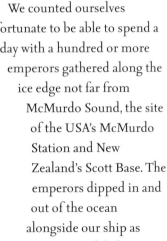

We counted ourselves fortunate to be able to spend a day with a hundred or more emperors gathered along the ice edge not far from McMurdo Sound, the site of the USA's McMurdo Station and New Zealand's Scott Base. The emperors dipped in and out of the ocean alongside our ship as passengers took helicopter

gentoo

flights to the dry valleys – ancient polar deserts covering 3,000 sq. km (1,160 square miles), slumbering in the shadow of the Transantarctic Mountains. These starkly beautiful valleys cut through the mountain range to terminate along the coast of the Ross Sea to the east of McMurdo Sound. There are three of them – Victoria, Wright and Taylor – each carved by ancient glaciers that were stifled as the land was uplifted, marooned in their dryness from the rest of the ice-covered continent. Katabatic winds evaporate any snow transported here by moist easterly winds before it can form into water, making these valleys dryer even than the Sahara Desert. The ever-opportunistic skuas are the only birds patrolling these desolate reaches, picking over the carcasses of the seals and penguins that have the misfortune to wander inland in the wrong direction and starve to death, their mummified corpses sculpted by the ceaseless winds.

The Mars-like landscape has remained virtually unchanged for millions of years with rocks carved and polished by windblown sand and snow – a land where it never rains. But while the dry valleys appear inhospitable to life they are not entirely so: there are ephemeral streams and lakes formed from glaciers nurturing lichens, mosses and microscopic organisms eking out a living among the bare rock, meltwater pools and streams, hinting at perhaps the kind of primordial world where life on Earth began. Fossils found here such as *Lystrosaurus* – an animal that could not swim – match with similar finds in Africa and India, further evidence for the existence of Gondwana, the supercontinent that fragmented to leave Antarctica so many millions of years ago. This is truly an ancient land, where nature has had to use all its extraordinary ingenuity to enable animals and plants to

survivc. Of all of them, the emperor penguin provides us with the most powerful emblem of fortitude, to match the exploits of those three intrepid explorers who sought out the penguins in the quest for knowledge.

• • • • • • •

We were now within reach of the last stage of our journey, a mere helicopter ride away from Cape Evans, where in 1911 Scott prepared for his ultimate assault on the South Pole. Scott was not alone in his dreams and aspirations. The Norwegian explorer Roald Amundsen had decided to make a race of it.

CHAPTER 9

Race for
the Pole

Roald Amundsen was the outstanding explorer of his era, a born adventurer destined to achieve spectacular success in both the Arctic and the Antarctic. As a teenager he read voraciously on polar exploration, challenging himself with the stories of his heroes to the extent that he took to sleeping with his bedroom window wide open even in the depths of winter, and exploring the hills and mountains around his home in Oslo, honing his skills on snow and ice. He soon found that dreams and building up one's physical fitness were only the beginning. A disastrous winter journey with his brother across a range of mountains west of Oslo nearly cost him his life. Frozen, starved, snowbound and frightened, he learned the dangers of poor preparation and that success required meticulous planning before you set foot out of doors. Chastened but undeterred, he opted to spend time in the Norwegian army to toughen himself up before deciding that if he was serious about being an explorer he needed to learn how to command a ship. He had noted that in the annals of Arctic exploration leaders were rarely ships' captains, so that once at sea the expedition was under divided command, a situation that might easily lead to disharmony.

In 1894, at the age of 22, Amundsen joined a whaling vessel to gain the experience necessary to become a licensed mariner. Three years later, he offered his services to Adrien de Gerlache's Antarctic expedition and was appointed second mate of *Belgica*, setting out from Antwerp in August 1897. But things did not proceed as planned and in no time the *Belgica* found herself trapped in the pack ice, making the expedition the first to winter below the Antarctic Circle – circumstances that some believed de Gerlache had intended from the outset. The enterprise was ill-prepared for such an event and the men soon found themselves short of winter clothes and

rations. The deprivation and stress proved too much for at least two of the crew, who became insane; another was lost overboard and one officer succumbed to heart failure. At one point all but three of the crew fell victim to the old enemy, scurvy, and with the expedition in disarray it was left to Amundsen and the American explorer Dr Frederick Cook to rally the men.

This was the moment Amundsen had been preparing for all his life. Calmly and methodically he and Cook set to work, organizing parties to hunt for seals and penguins while others fashioned clothes from blankets to help keep them warm. After months of hardship they managed to dig, hack and blast a path through the pack to an open lead – only to find themselves blocked once again by the ice. But finally, on 14 March 1899, 13 months after she had become beset, *Belgica* emerged from the pack ice.

The following year Amundsen obtained his skipper's licence and could begin planning his own expedition. As a youngster he had been fascinated by the story of the British explorer Sir John Franklin, whose unsuccessful search for the Northwest Passage was a tale of courage and hardship – and ultimately death – in pursuit of his objective. Discovery of the Northwest Passage – a navigable water route across the top of North America, linking the Atlantic and Pacific Oceans – had been a dream of nations and explorers since the discovery of the New World.

Achieving the goal for which Franklin had given his life was the challenge that Amundsen had long set his heart on. He was wise enough to know that his expedition needed a scientific purpose if it was to get financial backing. Polar magnetism was his choice of scientific endeavour and to this end he practised navigation in the North Sea and studied terrestrial magnetism before setting off. He bought his own ship, Gjøa, a 47-tonne herring boat, and

OPPOSITE

Tabular iceberg, Drygalski Ice Tongue. Named after the German scientist and explorer Erich von Drygalski (1865–1949) who was the leader of the German Antarctic Expedition of 1901–03 in the 'Gauss'. Icebergs can be trapped in the sea ice, slowing their rate of decay.

with a crew of six men left Norway in 1903, he then completed two years of work on polar magnetism among the ice that would keep scientists busy evaluating the findings for the next 20 years.

Eventually Gjøa succeeded in navigating a way through the frigid Arctic waters to become the first vessel to complete the Northwest Passage, but was then forced to endure a third winter lying up at winter quarters near King's Point. By now Amundsen was convinced that the indigenous people of the polar regions were the key to survival there: he learned how to drive a team of dogs and made a collection of traditional clothing – polar-bear pants, sealskin boots, Arctic hare socks and fur-lined anoraks. Then in October 1905, rather than wait for the winter to end, he left his companions and journeyed 1,300 km (780 miles) by dog-sledge to Eagle City, a tiny outpost on the border between Alaska and Canada, to announce his triumph to the world.

The experience gained from long-distance dog-sledging and time spent with the Eskimo would prove crucial to Amundsen's later expeditions. Aged 36 and buoyed by his success, he was ready to attempt the greatest of Arctic adventures – to be the first man to reach the North Pole. The plan was to drift over the Pole in a ship frozen into the ice covering the Arctic Ocean, a feat that Amundsen's mentor, the great Norwegian explorer Fridtjof Nansen, had attempted in the mid-1890s. In fact Nansen generously agreed to lend his ship *Fram* for the endeavour. But late in 1909, when Amundsen's preparations were well under way, the Americans Frederick Cook and Robert Peary cabled to say each had claimed to have reached the North Pole.

Amundsen's response to this news was typical – triumph or defeat, discovery or disaster, he was always ready to respond with a new plan. With the North Pole no longer a consideration, the only

Adélie chick

challenge left to a man of Amundsen's ambition was the South. Initially he kept his change of plans secret from his financial backers, his crew – and from Scott, who he knew was already on his way to Antarctica in his ship *Terra Nova*. Instead, he let it be known that he would still attempt to reach the North Pole for 'scientific purposes'. He set sail from Norway on 9 August 1910 with a hundred Greenland sledge dogs (a breed descended from canines that had accompanied immigrants from Siberia some 5,000 years ago) and sufficient material for a hut to house ten bunks and a kitchen – evidence for anyone who cared to think about it that he was in fact not headed north. Having crossed the equator the crew were informed of the change of plan and by the time Scott reached Melbourne in October he found a telegram awaiting him: 'Beg leave to inform you proceeding Antarctica, Amundsen.'

The two men were very different. Scott was a career naval officer who had fallen under the ambitious gaze of Sir Clement Markham, a key member of the Royal Geographical Society with a burning desire to see a British-led expedition be the first to conquer the South Pole. Markham believed that this was a challenge for a young man of stamina and resilience, and so he appointed Scott leader of the National Antarctic Expedition of 1901–04, aboard *Discovery*. This was the making of Scott – after two winters in Antarctica, having personally made a balloon flight over the frozen continent and sledged to 82°17'S with Wilson and Shackleton, he returned to England a national hero and was promoted to the rank of captain. Though it was always his ambition to be first to the Pole, he also deserves credit for his scientific endeavours.

He and his men recorded data on weather and climate, collected geological and biological specimens and mapped and surveyed as much as possible of the terrain they discovered.

Scott's success fired his ambition and he immediately began to plan a second expedition, this time funded by public contributions, with the aim of bettering Shackleton's furthest south. The more than 8,000 men who applied for positions were eventually whittled down to a shore party of just 32 and a similar number as ship's party. But in Amundsen Scott faced an adversary who would prove to be an even more formidable opponent than Shackleton.

The Race Is On

Early in 1911 *Fram* reached the edge of the Ross Sea at a place known as the Bay of Whales. Here, 3 km (2 miles) inland on the ice, Amundsen established his base. He had chosen with foresight – every step travelled across this desolate landscape required the utmost effort and the Bay of Whales was 100 km (60 miles) closer to the Pole than Scott's headquarters at the other side of the ice shelf. Both parties now busied themselves checking and familiarizing themselves with equipment and supplies, then set about laying depots for the journey to the Pole the following

Adélie penguins trekking across the pack ice. The males are first to arrive at the breeding colonies, sometimes walking 100 km (60 miles) across the ice to get there.

spring. As winter closed in they bided their time, waiting for the sun to return in August. But even then it was too cold to set out; Amundsen made a false start and was forced to wait a further two months before conditions improved, while Scott's party was still unable to set out because, despite advice to the contrary, he had insisted on using ponies as well as dogs to drag heavy equipment and supplies on sledges.

With the benefit of hindsight the race was over before it began. Amundsen didn't just look the part of a polar explorer. Photographs of him among the snow and ice show him balanced comfortably on skis and dressed in animal furs, exuding confidence and completely at home in his surroundings. He had a face hewn from stone, hinting at a fierce self-belief and steely will, and was driven by a keen sense of purpose. To this he added painstaking preparation and planning, applying the lessons he had learned from the Eskimos and equipping his men with reindeer-fur boots and loose-fitting, light and waterproof fur garments, while Scott and his men wore heavy woollen clothing which became damp and uncomfortable in the cold. Skiing was second nature to the Norwegians, and the use of dogs was something that Amundsen had believed in from the start. Scott by contrast knew that many of the dogs were destined to die from starvation, exhaustion, exposure or accidents, and more than anything he loathed the practice of killing dogs for food once they had served their purpose. He viewed them as intelligent individuals, as friends and companions, whose 'murder' he did not wish to contemplate. Besides, ponies had a good track record – Shackleton had used them for his 'furthest south' and Scott could not have known that they were ill-equipped to endure the more extreme cold that he and his party were about to suffer.

There was another reason that Scott decided against taking dogs on the final stages of the attempt on the Pole, and it says as much about the era in which he lived as it does about the man. Honour and duty were priorities for Scott and his companions, and in Scott's case at least the idea of man-hauling – pulling loaded sledges harnessed to their bodies – held great symbolic value, regardless of how exhausting it might be for everyone concerned. 'In my mind no journey ever made with dogs can approach the height of that fine conception which is realized when a party of men go forth to face hardships, dangers, and difficulties with their own unaided efforts, and by days and weeks of hard physical labour succeed in solving some problem of the great unknown. Surely in this case the conquest is more nobly and splendidly won,' he wrote.

Amundsen had no such scruples. He set out with his four companions on 19 October 1911, equipped with four lightweight sledges pulled by 13 dogs apiece. Initially they had a relatively easy time of it, until they reached the Axel-Heiberg Glacier with its crevasses and ridges of frozen ice, where the going proved much tougher. The glacier was their chosen pathway through the mountainous Queen Maud Range and the great central plateau beyond. Once on the plateau their choice of equipment and method of travel paid handsome dividends and they made good progress. The plan for survival was ruthless in its simplicity – as the men travelled they shot the weaker dogs; in all two-thirds were killed to conserve food and to provide meat for the working dogs and the men.

On 7 December the party reached Shackleton's furthest south of 1909 – 88°23'S. By now they were down to 17 dogs and three sledges, lightening their load still further by establishing their last supply depot. At 3 p.m. on 14 December 1911 they reached

ABOVE

Antarctica – a photographer's paradise. As the sun descends slowly towards the horizon in summer, the changing light creates a cloak of colours from orange to pink, purple and mauve that bathes the landscape in the softest pastel shades.

the South Pole, where they erected a small tent topped with a Norwegian flag. Inside they left two notes, one addressed to Scott telling of their success, the other for the King of Norway in case they failed to return. They stayed at the Pole for three days, making absolutely sure that they had reached their goal, taking readings and making observations, with three of the men setting out in different directions for 20 km (12 miles) to verify that they had 'encircled' the Pole.

By contrast, for Scott and his men there was only hardship. Within a few days of their departure from Cape Evans on 24 October the advance party was forced to abandon the motorized sledges that Scott had hoped would speed them on their way south, which meant they had to man-haul the heavy loads earlier than expected. The issue of the sledges illustrates the contradictions in Scott's thoughts on exploration; he was always keen to test and embrace new technology – balloons and motorized sledges – yet allowed himself to be distracted from his goal by issues of the heart and 'doing the right thing'.

Scott and the support parties whose job it was to lay supplies for the return journey left on 1 November – two weeks after Amundsen. Bad weather and difficult ice conditions hounded them from the start, with repeated snowstorms making pulling the heavy sledges a painfully slow business. The choice of ponies rather than dogs proved a disaster. Of the 19 taken on board in New Zealand, two never even made it ashore and, despite careful nurturing by Lieutenant Oates, fierce blizzards quickly took their toll as the bitter wind-blown snow penetrated the ponies' shaggy coats as they floundered belly-deep in the drifts. One by one they died or were shot and eaten. Within five weeks all were dead.

There was no respite, with blizzards pinning the entire party down in their tents, eating away at their precious supplies of food and fuel. On 9 December they struggled to the foot of the Beardmore Glacier, a maze of fractured ice leading up the Transantarctic Mountains, the route pioneered by Shackleton in 1908–09. They lingered long enough to set up a depot of food on the lower slopes and then bade farewell to one of the support parties and the dogs. One of the things driving Scott on was the fear of failure; the weight of expectation of a great nation was a heavy burden for any man, let alone one who suffered from bouts of depression, accompanied by the deep-seated belief that he was somehow not worthy, that he was idle by nature and that life was a constant struggle. Tormented by such thoughts, there were times when he doubted his own leadership abilities. Perhaps it was this that made him so fiercely competitive when it came to man-hauling, and somewhat intolerant of others' failings.

man-hauling sledges

Disappointment and Despair

Scott will always remain an enigmatic character. As Cherry-Garrard wrote, 'And not withstanding the immense fits of depression which attacked him, Scott was the strongest combination of a strong mind in a strong body that I have ever known. And this because he was so weak.' ... 'But few who knew him realised how shy and reserved the man was, and it was partly for this reason that he so often laid himself open to misunderstanding.'

On 4 January 1912, just 250 km (150 miles) short of the Pole, Scott sent the last of the support parties back to Cape Evans. For the final stage of the journey he chose his old friend Edward Wilson, cavalry officer 'Titus' Oates, Petty Officer Edgar Evans, a bull of a man whom Scott had long held in high esteem for his strength and toughness, and Lieutenant 'Birdie' Bowers. Bowers was a late addition to the party – he had impressed Scott with his dogged determination and for having been such a source of strength and inspiration to Wilson and Cherry-Garrard on the Winter Journey. People have questioned the wisdom of Scott's decision. The tent was designed for four, including an extra man added to their discomfort as well as costing them additional time and fuel when cooking their food. What they gained was pulling

LEFT
Tabular iceberg held fast among the ice, Drygalski Ice Tongue. Once calved, many icebergs remain grounded on the ocean floor and stay close to the continent, lasting for many years.

power (in a race for the Pole) even though just a few days earlier Bowers, the man who never complained, had been told to stash his skis at the glacier and was now forced to proceed on foot. Some 17 km (11 miles) from the Pole it was Bowers who spotted a black flag tied to a sledge bearer. It was over; the Norwegians had beaten them to it.

The following day, 17 January 1912, they reached the Pole. 'This is an awful place and terrible enough for us to have laboured to it without reward of priority,' Scott wrote in his diary. Who knows what effect the disappointment must have had? Even the most stoic of the men would have found it near impossible to turn for home with anything other than a sense of foreboding.

Oates, who had served in the Boer War and still had shrapnel embedded in one of his legs, was by now suffering terribly with his feet. Evans had frostbite to fingers and nose, and Wilson was grappling with the agonies of snow blindness, according to entries in Scott's diary dated 25 January – the same day that Amundsen and his men arrived safely back at the Bay of Whales, having covered almost 3,000 km (1,860 miles) in 99 days. The Norwegians too were suffering various degrees of frostbite, windburn, snow blindness and exhaustion. There had been no provision for collecting scientific specimens, no survey of their route. But they had returned victorious and brought eleven of their dogs back alive.

Soon the brief Antarctic summer would retreat again, bringing even lower temperatures than on the outward journey. As Scott's polar party made their way back down the Beardmore Glacier they once more had to find a path through the icy crevasses and fissures, a task akin to hauling a sledge over the devastation of a collapsed building. But this didn't stop them from adding almost 14 kg (30 lb) of geological specimens to their already overladen sledge – loyalty to their scientific

endeavours precluded that, and these fossils proved central Antarctica once had tropical conditions.

Evans by now was a shadow of his indomitable self – a bone-deep gash to his hand that he had tried to conceal from his companions was in a terrible state; frostbitten and half-crazed from exhaustion and the effect of repeated falls he eventually mercifully slipped into a coma and died in the tent. Thereafter there were days when the four survivors managed to travel 15–16 km (9–10 miles), but on others it was 8–10 km (5–6 miles) at best over a surface that Scott described as being like 'desert sand'. All of them were showing signs of scurvy and each time they reached a depot they were dismayed to find the oil cans only partially full – the precious fuel had evaporated or leaked out due to faulty seals. Oates's feet were now so painful that he could barely get his boots on in the morning. The pattern of suffering and misery that they had witnessed with Evans began to repeat itself, adding to their burden. Oates could no longer pull the sledge and fell further and further behind. He begged to be left, but the others refused. Finally, on 16 or 17 March, he announced to his companions, 'I am just going outside and may be some time.' With that he stumbled out of the tent and into the blizzard, never to be seen again.

All three remaining men were suffering from frostbitten feet, with Scott noting in his diary, 'Amputation is the least I can hope for now.' By 20 March they estimated they were only 18 km (11 miles) from One Ton Depot – a massive stash of supplies that due to bad weather conditions had been established 30 km (20 miles) further from the Pole than Scott had hoped. Pinned down by a blizzard they were unable to make a dash for it and eventually ran out of fuel and food.

Scott made the last entry in his diary on 29 March 1912. Eight months later, in November

OPPOSITE
Antarctica – a world of ice. It is formations like this that adds a sense of unreality to a journey to Antarctica.

Tabular iceberg, Ross Sea. Every year around 2 million tonnes of ice calve from the Antarctic Ice Sheet as icebergs, while glaciers also add their share of icebergs to the Southern Ocean.

1912, a party of his men from Cape Evans including Cherry-Garrard, who had always hoped that he might be included in the polar party (and might have been, despite being so young, if Scott hadn't determined to take Oates) found the tent, with the frozen bodies of their companions inside. They removed the tent poles, leaving the men as they had found them, covering the spot with a cairn of snow blocks. A wooden cross was erected on Observation Hill overlooking Cape Evans, and at Cherry's suggestion it was inscribed with a line from Tennyson's 'Ulysses', befitting the extraordinary courage the men had shown: 'To strive, to seek, to find, and not to yield'.

Cherry was to torment himself in later years with the thought that he might have been able to save his friends from their icy grave. On 26 February 1912, with wintry days closing in on them, he and the Russian dog driver Dimitri had set out with two teams of dogs to trek the 225 km (140 miles) south to One Ton Depot. The aim was to ferry additional food to the depot and to escort the polar party in more speedily if they met. The two men waited at One Ton Depot for six days, unable or unwilling to continue south due to the weather and for fear of missing the others. There were no additional dog rations at the depot and, as Cherry had been told not to sacrifice any of the dogs to facilitate further travel south (Scott wanted them for sledging journeys the following season), he and Dimitri turned for home on 10 March, confident that Scott's revised estimate of an April return to Cape Evans would prove correct and there was no need to worry – Scott had originally reckoned on being back at One Ton depot on 20 March and home at Hut Point on 27 March but, taking into account how much the weather had slowed them, he had amended this schedule before sending the last of the support parties home.

Months later, when the awful truth was laid bare before him inside the tent, Cherry was devastated. For him there would be no fading of memories with the passing years, no easing of his feelings of guilt in not continuing the search for his companions, two of whom – Wilson and Bowers, to whom he had become close during the Winter Journey – he worshipped. At one cruel stroke the sense of comradeship that had given Cherry the confidence to believe in himself and live the life of his choice was snatched from his grasp.

The Explorers' Legacy

While it has become popular to denigrate Scott, his poetic way with words helped to create a story like no other. The manner of Scott's death and the power of his words have made Amundsen the forgotten man of Antarctic exploration, overshadowing his achievements to the extent that outside his native country his name is little known.

There are those who say that a conspiracy of silence followed Scott's death, helping to make him a hero when in truth he owed his fate to incompetence. But for a nation that was already losing an empire and would soon be fighting for its life in the war to end all wars, with thousands of young, terrified soldiers entering the living hell of the trenches, Scott's exploits must have made stirring reading. Whatever the truth might be, stories such as Scott's, Shackleton's and Amundsen's – and those of the brave men who suffered alongside them – still carry a message for us today. They reveal what is possible when all seems lost, and show that even when there is no hope people can find a way of being that inspires others long after their deaths. No stories of survival against all the odds – or of death – can compare with tales crystallized in the icy furnace of the great white continent.

CHAPTER 10

The Pack Ice

There will always be some prepared to measure their courage and endurance in remote corners of the world – doing it the hard way – but for the most part exploration has now given way to science as the main objective in Antarctica and is key to our understanding of this complex and fragile environment. The International Geophysical Year (IGY) of 1957–58 was a turning point in promoting a new way of viewing our world, a chance to examine in detail the remotest parts of our planet – the atmosphere, outer space, the ocean depths, Antarctica – prompting scientific co-operation on an international scale and embracing areas rarely visited and poorly understood. In the course of IGY 54 research stations, observatories and laboratories were established in the Antarctic.

This visionary endeavour paved the way for the drafting of the Antarctic Treaty the following year and set a new trend in forging a more global view of issues that ultimately affect us all. It was to blossom into a truly international initiative, with scientists around the world co-ordinating their observations on geology, glaciology, seismology, oceanography and the atmosphere. Millions of kilometres of the Earth's surface were surveyed from the air. Sir Vivian Fuchs and Sir Edmund Hillary led a Commonwealth Transantarctic Expedition across the continent, accomplishing a feat that had been the dream of Sir Ernest Shackleton and his men some 40 years earlier. Hillary and his New Zealand companions were the first people to reach the South Pole by surface traverse since Scott, though under very different circumstances – they ploughed across the ice on snow tractors.

Science in Antarctica

The human population of Antarctica consists mostly of scientists and other base personnel. In winter the scientists are in the minority, with the bulk of residents being mechanics, electricians and technical specialists such as the electronic and ventilation engineers required to keep the stations and their scientific equipment running. Operating in Antarctica is a costly business – in 1999 America spent $200 million in the region (a mere $16 million of that allocated to science), though to put that figure into perspective it represents just one-fifth of the cost of a B1 Bomber.

Many of the passengers on cruise ships show a keen interest in the work of their countrymen in these far-off outposts, and a visit to at least one scientific base is part of most itineraries. This can be frustrating for wildlife photographers when time ashore is so brief and they would like to spend more of it with the penguins and seal colonies. But there is much of interest to be found in the bases and besides, several of them are situated among colonies of penguins totally unconcerned about all the people moving through their abode – so long as you stay a sensible distance from them and allow them to choose if they want to come closer, which they often do.

One of the most startling discoveries made by scientists in Antarctica has been the large seasonal reduction of ozone from the atmosphere that can be traced back to the early 1970s. When the British scientists Joe Farman, Brian Gardner and Jeff Shanklin first became aware of the problem in 1982 they were so surprised that they thought that either their instruments or their calculations were wrong – or that there was a hole in the ozone layer. When the findings were reported in a paper published in 1985 in *Nature* they sent shock waves through the scientific community. Scientists had been looking for such a trend for a decade, but had expected to find depletion levels of 2–3 per cent – not the nearly 60 per cent loss reported from the

British base at Halley on an ice shelf in the Weddell Sea. NASA too had been monitoring ozone levels worldwide via satellite, but had failed to pick up on this phenomenon until they went back through their records and were able to confirm the British data, as well as providing the evidence that it was true for most of the Antarctic continent, not just the Halley area.

Ozone occurs throughout the atmosphere, but is mainly situated in what is known as the stratosphere, some 10–20 km (6–12 miles) above the Earth's surface. It is produced by sunlight splitting molecules of oxygen (O_2) into atomic oxygen (O), which then combines with oxygen molecules to form ozone (O_3). This mainly occurs in equatorial regions and the ozone is then circulated to polar areas, where it accumulates. Ozone is vitally important to life on Earth, absorbing much of the harmful ultraviolet (UV) radiation produced by the sun which would otherwise damage the cells of living things – small amounts of UV cause sunburn, but larger quantities can induce cancer and cataracts. Just as worrying, plankton populations vital to ocean ecosystems are particularly susceptible to the adverse effects of UV light, an excess of which may compromise plant growth in general (scientists at Palmer Station have found a 10–20 per cent decline in phytoplankton growth due to increased UV associated with the ozone hole). One of the reasons it took 2.5 billion years for life as we know it to appear on Earth is that this is how long it took for a protective covering of ozone to form between us and the sun.

The main reason for ozone depletion during the past 30 years is man-made chemicals – the chlorofluorocarbons (CFCs) and other halogen compounds used in fridges, air conditioners, aerosols, fire extinguishers and solvents. CFCs are carried by wind systems throughout the atmosphere, where in the presence of icy clouds and intense sunlight they release the chlorine and bromine atoms that destroy ozone.

The total amount of ozone in the stratosphere has declined at a steady 3 per cent per decade for the past 20 years, with a much larger decrease over the polar regions. The reason for the especially rapid depletion in Antarctica is the whirlpool of high winds known as the polar vortex that spirals around the South Pole, helping to trap and chill the air during the darkness of winter and leading to the formation of cloud particles of ice or nitric acid, both of which provide surfaces suited to the chemical reactions that promote the destruction of ozone. At its peak in the spring and early summer, the extent of the hole is such that it exposes the southern regions of South America, Australia and New Zealand to higher than normal levels of harmful UV light. Concerns for both our own health and that of the planet led in 1987 to 43 of the major CFC-producing countries signing the Montreal Protocol, leading to the phasing out of CFCs and other halogen compounds by 1996 – and requiring that all the world's nations cease using CFCs by 2006. While it is unlikely that this aim has been entirely achieved, it has already resulted in signs of improvement, though it will probably take around 70 years until recovery is complete. To complicate matters, global warming, caused by a build-up in carbon dioxide from the burning of fossil fuels in industrialized nations, is likely to cool the stratosphere further, leading to even more ozone depletion.

In the past people have questioned the high cost of conducting science in such remote regions as Antarctica, perhaps wondering whether the science is just a pretext for ensuring a presence on the continent, with a view to gaining future benefits from its valuable resources. Discoveries such as the hole in the ozone layer show just how vital and cutting-edge this research can be.

The study of the Southern Ocean is proving equally important, revealing the complexity of the lives of the creatures that dwell here and helping to warn about the damaging consequences of our actions – even when they originate many thousands of kilometres away. The effects of global warming are probably as dramatically evident in the polar regions as anywhere else on Earth, highlighting how crucial it is that science is allowed to prosper here. And a fascinating long-term study on Adélie penguins at the United States' only base north of the Antarctic Circle is reason enough to make Palmer Station a popular stopping place for passenger ships cruising along the Peninsula.

Krill – one of the world's most abundant animals and the primary food of whales, penguins, seals and many birds. It is estimated that there are 500 million tonnes of Antarctic krill in the Southern Ocean, and without it the ocean's ecosystem would collapse.

Palmer Station and Torgersen Island

Palmer Station is located on the southern end of Anvers Island off the Antarctic Peninsula, and may be reached via the Gerlache Strait and a spectacularly narrow waterway known as the Neumayer Channel. To the southwest is yet another pictorial favourite, the beautiful Lemaire Channel.

During summer Palmer is home to 40 people, a quarter of them women and half of them scientists working on around 15 projects; the number of residents shrinks to 12 in winter. The station was opened in 1968 and has accumulated over 30 years of data on meteorology and the marine ecosystem that is now proving invaluable as an indicator of trends influenced by global warming. Just how fragile this environment is was underlined in 1989 when the Argentine ship *Bahía Paraíso* took a wrong turn on leaving Arthur Harbour and foundered on rocks, spewing tonnes of oil into the sea. The hull of the vessel is still visible in the crystal-clear waters adjacent to

the harbour, a stark reminder of an environmental disaster. To give just one example, when the ship went down it destroyed large quantities of limpets, causing a noticeable decline in the local population of the kelp gull, Antarctica's only gull.

There are five 'canyons' hidden deep beneath the ocean around the Peninsula where upwelling of saline nutrient-rich water means that birds and other animals can benefit from predictable sources of the phytoplankton that feeds the whole ecosystem. This is one reason why the area around Anvers Island is such a magnet for wildlife – within 4 km (2 ½ miles) of Palmer there are 45,000 breeding pairs of penguins, according to 1999 figures, and all six species of Antarctic seals – fur, southern elephant, Weddell, Ross, crabeater and leopard – as well as large numbers of whales during summer: on a good day you can see minke, sei, fin and humpbacks.

A tour around the base offers up the friendly face of science, with keen and knowledgeable people anxious to share the results of their work. This is an opportunity to see some of Antarctica's

BELOW

Weddell seal at rest in the pack ice. Among the largest of the true seals, Weddell males can dive to depths of over 700 m (2,300 ft). Underwater they are very vocal as a way of attracting mates and deterring rivals.

OVERLEAF

Adélie penguins among a maze of ice, Cape Adare.

hidden wildlife up close, creatures that live beneath the sea surface such as white worms 15-cm (6-in) long which secrete enzymes to dissolve food scavenged on the floor of the ocean. There are also starfish, sea spiders, krill and the sponges and tunicates that replace coral in these cold waters, all displayed in salt-water tanks. In one of the tanks amphipods swarm ant-like over the body of a krill, and in the ocean these would in turn provide food for birds such as the tiny Wilson's storm petrel.

Monitoring the effect of global warming in these regions is a high priority at Palmer. Records show that during the 1990s temperatures at nearby Torgersen Island increased by 4.5–5.5°C (8–10°F), with fluctuating pack-ice concentrations, break-up of ice sheets and higher than normal incidences of massive icebergs – all as a result of increasing temperatures. Meanwhile the Marr Glacier, situated behind Palmer, has been retreating by 10 m (33 ft) a year, with new islands emerging underneath it. These findings have implications for many species living in these regions, particularly, it seems, the Adélie penguins.

Dr Bill Fraser co-ordinates one of the longest running studies on Adélie penguins at Torgersen. He and his colleagues have been able to monitor

the effects of tourism on Antarctic wildlife – something else that people have become concerned about recently. Certain areas of the penguin colonies are off-limits to act as a control for their results, with flags making it clear where visitors can and cannot go. The good news is that the increasing numbers of tourists do not seem to be affecting the breeding success of the penguins at all, and this appears to be the case throughout Antarctica. The bad news is that, as we saw in Chapter 7, the Adélies are suffering the repercussions of the warmer conditions, particularly the effect that this is having on krill populations, their main source of food.

Torgersen is a maze of jagged slate-grey rocks, decorated in places with bright orange lichens and delicate stems of green descampsia grass, their growth fuelled by the nutrients in the thick coating of guano droppings. The increased amount of UV light is having a harmful effect on grass growth, though the warming trend is compensating for that to some degree. Piles of limpet shells mark the shore where kelp gulls have feasted – untouched by predators, these blue limpets can live for 60 years – and early in the season the island is blanketed with snow and ice. By the time the penguins are ready to return to sea the snow has long since melted and the brooding volcanic rocks make bleak viewing, with weak or late-fledging chicks the only penguins to be seen, standing motionless among the moulted feathers scattered like confetti over the ground. Researchers refer to late in the season as 'dead penguins in the dark' time, for by then the majority of successful breeders have raised their chicks and headed back to sea as the hours of daylight diminish. The offspring of late breeders are almost certainly doomed.

For some of the base personnel the end of summer signals the completion of their tour of duty and, while there are those who love this way of life, everyone knows what it means when someone gives you 'a 20ft stare in a 10ft room' or confesses to being 'toasted' by the end of a season. Bob Burton, a former British Antarctic scientist, lecturer and Antarctic devotee, told how in the old days when it all got a bit too much 'you could always go and have a chat with Ginger, a very sympathetic cat', though Ginger was eventually declared persona non grata and shipped out to the Falklands. Sled dogs, that other source of comfort and companionship in the heroic era, have long since gone from all Antarctic bases, partly for fear that they might introduce canine distemper into the seal population. One British base commander of long experience of men and ice had pared his recruiting technique down to the bare essentials: 'Married? – No. Engaged? – No. Any attachments? – No. Good you'll be no trouble.' While the remedy for the recipient of the inevitable 'Dear John' letter was to present him with a broom handle concreted into a boot (as in 'getting the boot'), with the aim of encouraging him to race around putting holes through doors to ease the hurt, after which everyone retired to the bar to get the poor chap plastered.

One shouldn't for a minute, though, doubt the seriousness of what is achieved down here. The Adélie penguins have become Bill Fraser's life's work and the pack ice holds the key to their prosperity. They have evolved hand in hand with this frigid environment; it has made them what they are – krill specialists. Emperors, too, need the sea ice: if it breaks up too early they may lose their chicks, which cannot survive at sea until they have developed their waterproof coat. Alternatively, if the ice is too thick, the emperors must travel further to reach the sea to find food. Bill Fraser reports that one emperor study colony in his area is on the verge of extinction, declining rapidly from around 300 breeding pairs to just nine.

OPPOSITE
Adélie penguin, Cape Adare. Penguins are averse to warm sea water, restricted in range to the cold waters of the southern hemisphere – which is why there are no penguins in the Arctic. Auks occupy the equivalent position to the north (they are excellent divers, though they are not flightless).

If phytoplankton and krill are the foundations of the Antarctic ecosystem, then the pack ice is its bedrock, the lifeblood of the system, for it is here that larval krill seek sanctuary. Each autumn as the temperature plummets in late March or early April, the sea surface freezes, beginning its advance in sheltered bays around the southernmost reaches of the Weddell, Bellingshausen and Ross Seas. The pack expands in all directions like a giant white amoeba, a seemingly lifeless entity reaching out to the north at the rate of 57 sq. km (35 square miles) a minute until by August it covers an area of nearly 20 million sq. km (8 million square miles), doubling the effective area of Antarctica. Snowfall thickens the ice layer, making passage by ship even more hazardous and difficult by increasing friction at the surface.

It seems ironic that warmer conditions are making Antarctica more accessible to humans, while compromising the future of some of its wildlife. Over the past half-century the western Antarctic Peninsula has recorded the largest temperature increases anywhere on the planet – around 6°C (11°F) – far exceeding the scientists' computer models and making the climate more maritime than polar in character: warm and moist rather than primarily cold and dry. For as long as records have been kept, the waters surrounding this region have been known for their intense krill concentrations, with nearly half the Southern Ocean's stocks concentrated in a relatively narrow wedge between the tip of South Africa and the Antarctic Peninsula, which is one reason why this and the surrounding sub-Antarctic islands are such havens for wildlife. With the shift to warmer conditions the pack ice is forming later and breaking up earlier, with serious consequences for the krill.

The extent of the sea ice has always varied from year to year and season to season. In the past, in four out of every five years scientists at Palmer would witness particularly thick winter ice, with the pack reaching out into the Drake Passage. Now this happens only once or twice every five years. Similarly, the normal pattern of ice formation along the southern coast of the Peninsula now commences two or three weeks later in the autumn than it has done for the last 30 years or more. Corresponding to these changes, krill records concentrating in the Southern Ocean show a catastrophic drop in numbers – 80 per cent in the past 30 years over the entire Atlantic sector – prompted, it seems, by warmer temperatures whose effect has been particularly evident during the winter, a crucial period for survival of krill larvae, and threatening to tear the whole system apart.

Female krill are capable of producing 20,000 eggs each year and breed during the summer, from December to March. Their eggs are heavier

Adélie penguins porpoising. During the breeding season it is essential that they have easy access to rich sources of food.

than water and sink, with the larvae hatching at depths of 400–1,500 m (1,300–5,000 ft) before swimming towards the underside of the ice – most fish and invertebrate larvae hatch at the surface. The ice edge is critical, acting as a nursery for krill larvae and a shelter from foraging penguins, seals and whales. Here where the ice is thinnest the sunlight can penetrate most easily and this, combined with upwelling of nutrient-rich deep water along the continental shelf, allows ice algae to flourish.

During winter a yellowish cloud of algae remains locked in a labyrinth of unfrozen brine channels within the ice floes, sustained by sea water and nutrients. Krill slows its metabolism during winter, with adults and larvae foraging on the algae and bacteria beneath the pack ice all winter long; without it the larvae almost certainly couldn't survive. During summer, with a surge in phytoplankton numbers stimulated by the sun's rays, krill blooms in indescribable numbers, producing the greatest mass of living matter of any species on the planet, aggregating in blood-red superswarms of 30,000 per square metre (3,000 per square foot), with Southern Ocean stocks estimated at 1.5 billion tonnes – possibly more. If winter ice forms too late, as has been the case in recent years, then phytoplankton populations are diminished, and with less food for larvae there is a drop in krill numbers by the time summer returns: unlike adult krill, the larvae do not have sufficient fat reserves to sustain themselves if food is scarce. This decline has been mirrored by an increase in transparent jelly-like creatures known as salps, normally associated with warmer waters, and most krill-dependent predators do not eat salp.

Global warming is just one of the factors capable of compromising krill populations. Fears that the harvesting of krill for human use could lead to a damaging decline have so far proved unfounded: krill is certainly nutritious, containing 18 per cent protein, but tends to spoil quickly due to its high fluoride content, a problem that has now been solved. Even if it has not yet proved particularly appealing to human tastes, it is a valued source of organic fertilizer and animal food. South Georgia currently has a krill fishery, but if the area was overexploited it might not have the means to recover – the local population is not self-seeding and depends on recruitment of adult krill from other regions, in all likelihood areas along the western Antarctic Peninsula, which are already experiencing declines of their own. The harvesting of krill combined with the continued retreat of the pack ice have the potential to cause devastating changes to the ecology of the Southern Ocean.

Into the Pack Ice

To get a better understanding of what life must be like for the creatures who depend on the pack ice, you need to immerse yourself in it for a while en route to the Ross Sea and the broad body of the continent further south, as we did in November 2006, travelling for a month by sea on a semi-circumnavigation of the continent from Ushuaia in Argentina to Lyttelton in New Zealand. At this time of year the pack ice has retreated sufficiently to allow access to the continent's milder fringes, though visitors are always eager to experience the pack and are disappointed if the ice is insufficient to cast its frozen spell. Cruise vessels have varying degrees of ice-strengthening – many of them lead double lives, filling a primary role as research vessels during winter – but at present there is only one ship carrying passengers to these regions capable of tackling the pack head on without fear of retribution – the Russian icebreaker *Kapitan Khlebnikov*. This impressive ship, with its 45-mm (1¾-in) thick reinforced steel skirting and double hull, provides a mobile platform for passengers to experience a very different world to that of the Peninsula, offering the chance to travel in the footsteps of the explorers for whom the Ross Sea represented the launch pad for assaults on the South Pole.

We depart not knowing quite what to expect – this is our fourteenth trip to Antarctica, but we have not been this far south before. The pack reaches out in front of *Khlebnikov* until all around is white. This is first-year ice, formed during the last winter season, 1.5 m (5 ft) thick on average and fractured into a million irregular pieces by the wind and the currents, an icy jigsaw too vast to comprehend. The occasional metallic thump resonates upwards as a more obstinate piece of ice registers our intrusion into this frigid world, the ship's rounded bottom and low centre of gravity conspiring to push the ice down to the point where it meets the metal 'knife' concealed beneath the surface of the water, nicking it sufficiently forcefully for the weight of the hull to split it and push it aside. Under these

Ice sculpture. Nature has always provided the inspiration for artists and photographers, and the early explorers marvelled at the beauty of this frigid and alien world.

conditions *Khlebnikov* can maintain progress with just three of her engines powering her along – later she will need all six to negotiate a passage through to the Ross Sea.

The temperature has dropped another degree or two, enough to chill the fingertips and dissuade all but the most tenacious from staying long on the bow. The wind is picking up and has an icy bite to it. The going is slow, exacerbated by a 50-cm (20-in) deep blanket of snow that increases friction, along with the thick pressure ridges that have appeared where ice floes have collided. Crunching through the ice costs time and fuel – the best way of course is to skirt around it, like Cook, but that is not our mission right now. We want to be surrounded in the ice for a while if we are to understand this surreal world called Antarctica, where the ice is both life and death.

For photographers, Antarctica this far south at this time of year means long hours of daylight. Soon there is no need to ask when the sun sets and rises, and little time for sleep as long as the sun is low in the sky and the colours are warm and saturated. Even when it isn't, the icescape proves irresistible, a thing of wonder in all its moods, whether white and grey or blue. At times the ship is barely moving, all is quiet, the ghostly shapes of icebergs floating past. *Khlebnikov* is now the most remote vessel on the high seas – it would take four days for another ship to reach us at our present position. Pushing through the ice gives this journey a sense of purpose, reminding you that you are merging with that other Antarctica, the Antarctica that Scott, Shackleton and Amundsen came in search of a hundred years ago. You have to keep telling yourself that this is Antarctica – all of this – an

ABOVE

Crabeater seal. Males sometimes engage in serious fights over females during the breeding season.

OPPOSITE

Khlebnikov approaches the Ross Ice Shelf. The retreat of the ice shelf is one of many warnings of the effects of global warming.

amalgam of land, sea and ice. Antarctica is all around us, in the air, on the ice and beneath it, in the sea and on the bare exposed rock; a masterpiece of design and implementation. There is detail here, too – ice sculptures formed by the constant movement of the pack ice, whites and blues, greens and greys – a palette of colours that most of us have never experienced before: pastel tones so subtle that no photograph or painting can convey their beauty. The ship seems to glide across the ice – a giant steel-hulled sledge bearing down, splitting and

fracturing the blanket of ice to create a mosaic of white etched on black.

In places icebergs have become enclosed and trapped by the blanket of ice sailing along until, freed by the wind and the currents, they continue on their journey north, gradually melting into the sea, a process that may take up to ten years. A light dusting of snow covers the ice rubble, softening the vision. The ship judders like a pneumatic drill, picking away at the ice front, reversing and then ramming into it, determined to force a way through. A lead

emerges out of the whiteness and a minke whale, trapped between the ship and the ice edge, bursts from the deep, rupturing the silky black surface of the ocean with a mighty whoosh as it races alongside. The whale is all streamlined grace, the white of its fins reflecting up towards us, green on black. Then it is gone, sucking in air through its blowhole, curving up before submerging, three spumes of water exploding into the air.

In places the ice floes are covered with crabeater seals, a species so numerous that it may well be the most abundant mammal on Earth besides ourselves, with perhaps 10–30 million of them – though make no mistake they feed on krill, not crabs (the misnomer may originate from a mistranslation from the Scandinavian). Their thick beige fur is torn and lacerated, patterned with old scars inflicted by leopard seals. Every so often a party of Adélie penguins emerges, seemingly from nowhere, inky black shadows against the whiteness, flopping onto their bellies and tobogganing away as the ship bears down on the pack. Occasionally a Ross seal is spotted – darker and more pear-shaped than the crabeaters, with broad round head and thick neck, weighing around 180 kg (400 lb) and possessing the largest eyes of any seal, designed no doubt to pick out the large squid that make up a sizeable portion of its diet. These are the least well known of the seals, inhabitants of the densest areas of the pack ice and circumpolar in distribution. They are sometimes referred to as singing seals, and they are certainly very vocal, which allows them to communicate their whereabouts to others of their solitary kind.

The weather, as one might expect, is fickle, one minute a chill brightness to the sky, the next it is snowing and a degree warmer. We are now at 72°12'S, the temperature is 5°C (41°F) and we have travelled 240 nautical miles through the pack ice en route to the Ross Sea. The visibility is down to 16 km (10 miles), snow is falling again with low clouds blotting out the sun. The ship is at the mercy of the ice, the leads determining our course and how fast we can travel, and though we carry 3,000 tonnes of diesel it is expensive to tackle the thicker floes and we need to conserve fuel whenever we can. People are getting anxious: we seem to be losing time and they are concerned as to what we will or will not see.

The Ross Ice Shelf

The faintest shadow emerges along the horizon, a distant grey smudge. The Ross Ice Shelf is in sight at last, the first substantial sign of the continent since leaving the Peninsula. We have travelled through the Bellingshausen and Amundsen Seas to get here, and are now confronted by the outer fringe of the Antarctic ice sheet, which conceals all but a tiny fraction of the bedrock on which it rests.

The Ross Ice Shelf – the 'Great Barrier' of Scott's day – is the largest ice shelf in the world, extending 500 km (300 miles) out over the sea, a massive floating tongue of ice the size of Texas and larger than France, located at the point where a huge indentation occurs in the Antarctic mainland, covering the southern portion of the Ross Sea. The shelf is nourished by glaciers and ice streams, and where it enters the sea it is up to 1,000 m (3,300 ft) thick. James Clark Ross was the first to see it in January 1841, naming it the Victoria Barrier and sailing along its 960-km (600-mile) coast in the hope of finding a way through. Perceptive man that he was, Ross recognized that this huge expanse of ice was floating – there was no tide line.

Everyone on board Khlebnikov falls silent as the expedition leader announces over the intercom that in the last ten years the ice shelf has retreated by 32 km (20 miles).

The barrier was a welcome sight for the explorers of the heroic age, a flat icy platform leading to the interior – and the Pole. Today its level surface provides a runway for aircraft, ferrying staff and supplies to and from the scientific stations, and a highway for vehicles capable of travelling over the snow. When the sun emerges it gives form to the shelf, a tabular sculpture rising 50 m (165 ft) in places above the surface of the ocean, its cliffs decorated with ice caves and fractured by crevasses. A helicopter appears overhead, disgorging people onto the top of the ice shelf where champagne awaits them to salute those who came before. From on high you really get to appreciate the immense thickness of the shelf, the jagged edge running away into the distance as far as the eye can see. The temperature drops another degree or two up here, the wind cutting through warm winter clothing like the sharpest knife, urging people back to the ship. A crevasse is located towards the lip of the ice shelf, and visitors are allowed to lie flat on their belly, safely attached to a rope and anchor, for a view into the cold blue maw. It is a thing of wonder, but for the explorers a crevasse, as wide as a ship in places, could be a death trap concealed beneath a blanket of soft snow, waiting to ambush men and dogs, pitching a sledge head first into the darkness. Navigating a way across or around such obstacles was just one of the many hurdles standing between the polar explorers and their objectives.

A few days earlier a single emperor had appeared out of nowhere and wandered across the sea ice towards the ship. We could only guess where it came from – probably a newly fledged youngster fresh from one of the fast-ice rookeries and looking for company; perhaps it had heard the noise of Khlebnikov's engines or the fracturing of the ice as it swam beneath the surface of the ocean and leapt up onto the ice for a closer look. While the king penguin almost rivals the emperor for size and is equally beautiful, the emperor has a quiet presence that is riveting, even when seen alone like this. It is completely unafraid and curious, moving towards the ship, which is conveniently wedged into the pack to allow people to step down onto the ice. Now they hurry down the gangway, cameras at the ready to record their meeting with this extraordinary visitor. The sight of strange creatures moving upright on two legs no doubt lends a degree of fascination to the moment for the emperor, too. Every so often it pauses as if in some profound reverie, or preens, running its long black bill through its dense white plumage. It glows a delicate yellow, drops of moisture gathered on its chest from tobogganing on its belly reflecting the light. Just occasionally it raises its bill to the sky and calls, a mournful nasal cry drifting on the breeze, fading. Nobody wants to leave, to break the spell that this solitary figure has conjured up out here among the pack ice, a speck of life marooned in all this whiteness – a fantastical bird, a creature of the imagination, the original polar explorer.

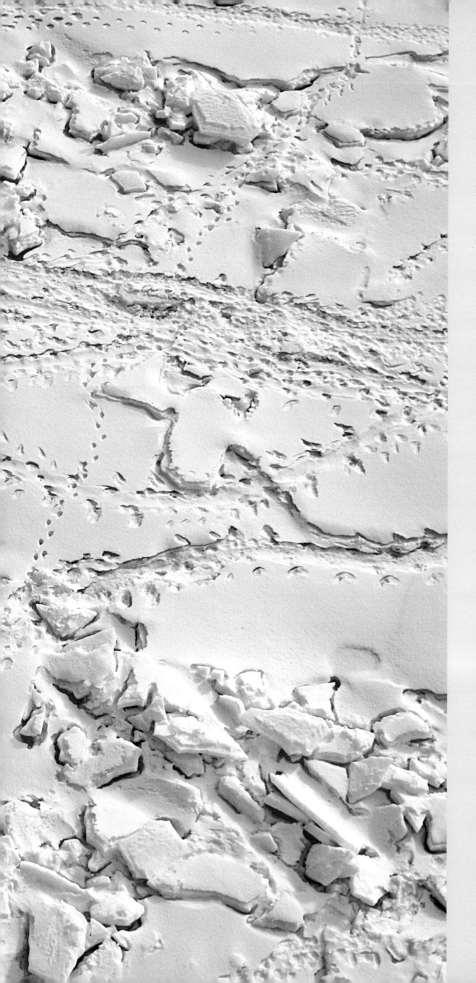

The Future

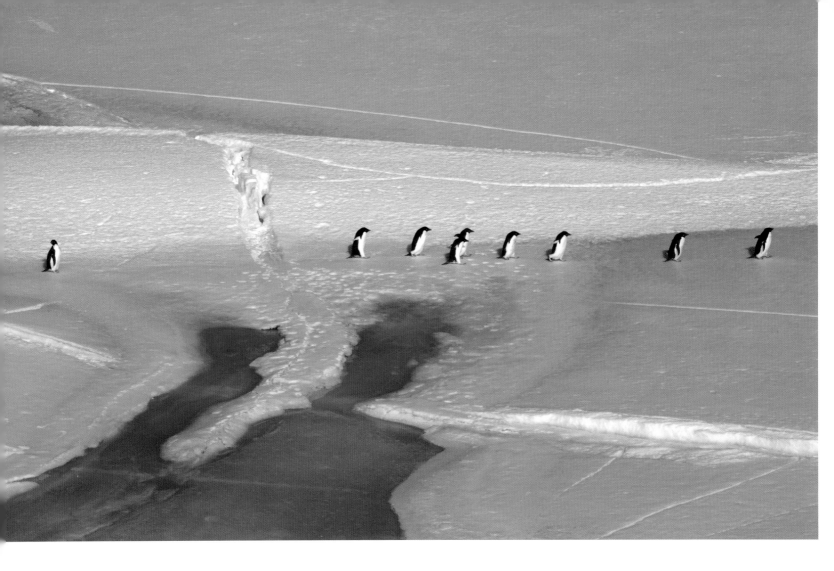

Antarctica is the last relatively unspoiled wilderness left on our planet, nature at its harshest, terrifying yet seductive in its power and beauty, as remote and mysterious as the oceans and outer space. But technology is rapidly catching up with these last frontiers, revealing their vulnerability to exploitation. This is particularly true now that we humans have exhausted so many of the more easily obtainable non-renewable resources closer to home. Fortunately a transformation in people's perceptions dating back to the 1980s and beyond has brought widespread recognition of the importance of our environment. Growing concerns about global warming, rising sea levels and the ozone hole have helped to forge an alliance between people from all walks of life: self-interest can now be added to the other less tangible reasons for protecting Antarctica.

Antarctica is no longer beyond our reality; the tales of the explorers and the revelations of scientists have given it form and substance, it has been mapped from the air and is no longer inaccessible by sea and land. Many now feel that wilderness areas such as Antarctica should be preserved regardless of any current or future use they might offer to us. Key locations in Antarctica are already designated as World Heritage Sites and ideally all of Antarctica should be accorded this status, thereby helping to cement the seed of global interdependence and international co-operation represented by the Antarctic Treaty that must continue to be nurtured if we are to succeed in protecting our environment.

The Antarctic Treaty is a remarkable document, setting out its ideals with great clarity, stating that Antarctica should be preserved for peaceful purposes, for science rather than exploitation. All claims to territory are held in abeyance – after all humans were never native to Antarctica, so it seems only right that it should remain stateless territory – and no new claims or additions to existing claims are to be undertaken as long as the Treaty remains in force. No military manoeuvres are permitted, no testing of conventional or nuclear weapons or dumping of nuclear waste, and the role of military personnel is limited to providing assistance to scientific projects only. Exploitation where it occurs – such as in the catching of krill – should take into consideration the effect that this might have on the ecosystem, with the offtake maintained at or below sustainable levels. Observers from member countries are entitled to free access to and scrutiny of all bases, ships, aircrafts and equipment, while people living and working in Antarctica are deemed to be the responsibility of their own governments (the status of visitors and people from nations that are not signatories to the Treaty remains unclear).

The USSR and USA emerged as key players in the early days of the Treaty, with Britain not far behind and Argentina, Australia, Belgium, Chile, France, Japan, New Zealand, Norway and South Africa all playing a part. Since then 15 other nation states have been recognized as consultative parties, having shown their willingness to conduct substantial research in Antarctica: Brazil, Bulgaria, China, Ecuador, Finland, Germany, India, Italy, the Netherlands, Poland, Peru, the Republic of Korea, Sweden, Spain and Uruguay. A further 17 have acceded to the Treaty as non-consultative parties: Austria, Canada, Colombia, Cuba, Czech Republic, Democratic Peoples Republic of Korea, Denmark, Greece, Romania, Slovak Republic, Switzerland, Turkey, Ukraine and Venezuela.

The Whaling Dispute

In the early 1970s cries of 'Save the Whale' became the voice of the fledgling environmental movement, forcing the issue into the public domain and reminding people that when the International Whaling Commission (IWC) was established in 1946 it was little more than a gentlemen's club for whaling nations, designed to regulate what had until then been a free-for-all – no rules, no quotas. But membership of the IWC is voluntary and any member can opt to register a formal objection to proposed regulations and thereby not be bound by them.

Utilization of living resources is a complex issue, touching on moral, cultural and political arguments, and nothing generates quite as much emotion among the general population – and the scientific community – as the 'harvesting' of charismatic creatures such as fur seals in Canada and Namibia, elephants in Africa – and whales across the globe. Pro-whaling nations such as Japan and Norway, with a long history and culture of whaling, were eager to keep their whaling operations solvent, continuing to exploit the loophole of 'scientific whaling' to kill whales. Japan insists that this is necessary for stock assessment and that the remit of the IWC is to manage whale stocks scientifically – not to prohibit their sustainable harvest. Despite the fact that whale products are no longer essential, and that some species of whales are already at risk from pollution and fishing activities, Japan is intent on lobbying the Convention on International Trade in Endangered Species (CITES) to reduce protection for more common species of whales on the grounds that it is obsolete, denouncing countries that take an ethical position against whaling as acting 'contrary to the IWC's object and purpose'. At the most recent meeting of the IWC, held in 2006, the pro-whaling nations failed to muster the 75 per cent majority required to lift the moratorium and allow the resumption of commercial whaling, but tellingly they found support from within the IWC's scientific committee, which now maintains that 'many species and stocks of whales are abundant and sustainable whaling is possible'. This has helped to reassure the sceptics and to break the supremacy of the anti-whaling lobby that has dominated the IWC for many years.

Such pragmatic views are not new. Some 20 years ago, Dr Richard Laws, former director of the British Antarctic Survey and an expert on large mammals, was of the opinion that no species were threatened with extinction in Antarctica at that time (he was also an advocate of culling elephants in Kenya in the 1960s and '70s). Japan and her allies are determined to resume whaling, arguing that aside from cultural precepts whales consume huge quantities of fish – the same rationale often put forward to support the culling of seals. Meanwhile the killing continues apace. Norway intends killing 1,000 minke whales in 2007, with Japan taking 935 minke, sei, Bryde's and sperm whales, an increase on the previous year. Most worrying of all, Japan plans to take ten

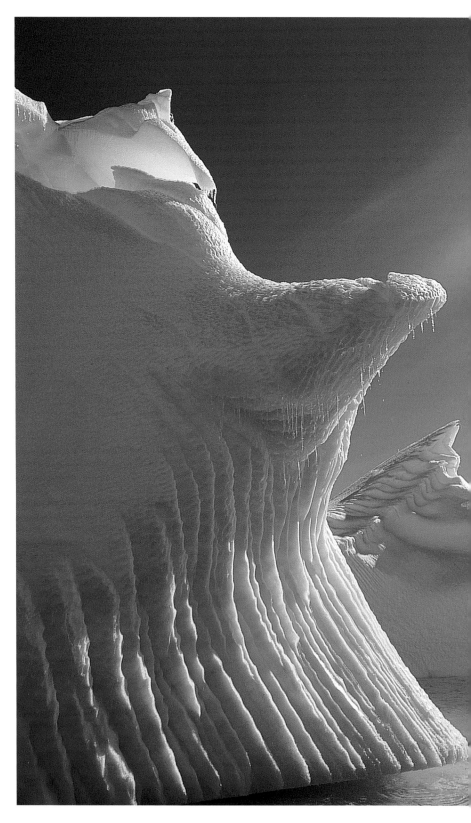

fin whales in 2007 in the Arctic and an additional 40 fin whales and 50 humpbacks in the next two years – both of which are listed as 'vulnerable' and on the Red List of endangered species of the World Conservation Union.

One solution would be for the IWC to set quotas based on advice from its scientific committee, but nobody knows exactly how many whales exist – they range so widely that it is difficult to estimate numbers accurately. And how do you ensure that sustainable quotas are not exceeded? If the past is anything to go by, then you need look no further than the example of Russia and its involvement in the whaling industry. Not so long ago the Russians finally admitted what had long been suspected: falsificatin of catch statistics from the 1950s onwards. The numbers are staggering – 100,000 more whales killed than had been reported, and of these 48,000 were humpbacks (the official figure for this species had been given as 2,710 killed).

Most of the world's whales and dolphins remain unprotected by international law, despite the fact that they are threatened by pollution, ozone depletion, climate change and the fishing industry. Humankind has always viewed the oceans as a bottomless pit, too vast and hidden from view for abuse to be registered easily, a dumping ground for all manner of waste from raw sewage to industrial chemicals that circulate from pole to pole on ocean and air currents. It is quite likely that such toxic substances compromise an animal's immune system, reducing its ability to resist disease, and all mammals are at risk from the transfer of toxins in their mother's milk, with toxicity increasing from one generation to the next. Apart from the role that toxic waste and radiation may play in incidences of mass stranding of whales, the main culprit is likely to be noise pollution caused by tankers, liners, warships and depth charges, all of which potentially have a disorientating effect on whales.

It is frustrating that the world cannot yet agree on issues such as this, but it is a warning too that nothing can be taken for granted, and that laws and conventions have substance only if they are enforceable. If the Southern Ocean is proving difficult to protect, one can only wonder what lies ahead as far as the continent itself is concerned. Early claims by Britain, New Zealand, Australia and Norway were a thinly disguised means of trying to protect their whaling interests. Industrialization has made the possibility of developing all forms of commercial interests in Antarctica that much more of a reality. The frigid conditions and huge distances involved are no longer an insurmountable barrier to development, though the fact that the continent is buried beneath a layer of ice 1.5 km (1 mile) deep has always seemed to be a powerful enough deterrent to mining in Antarctica. Add to this katabatic winds raging at 200 kph (125 mph), the hazards posed by icebergs and stormy seas, together with a short summer working season, and it is easy to see why Antarctica has managed to survive in a relatively pristine state thus far. But as mineral resources elsewhere become scarce and prices rise, mining in Antarctica will almost inevitably become commercially viable at some point, just another part of our world to be exploited – and then what? Far better, surely, that we leave Antarctica as the last great wilderness, a laboratory for science, a place of knowledge, a symbol of peace and goodwill to our planet and its other inhabitants.

OPPOSITE
Iceberg, Paradise Bay, Antarctic Peninsula. About four-fifths of an iceberg is (hidden) submerged beneath the surface. Above the surface of the water icebergs are sculpted by sun, wind, rain and wave action.

Preserving Antarctica's Resources

Although the thickness of the Antarctic ice sheet means that very little of the continent has been properly surveyed, mineral deposits undoubtedly exist in reasonable amounts. The Peninsula enjoys a common geological history with the mineral-rich Andes of South America and has yielded traces of gold, titanium, tin, copper, cobalt and uranium; the Transantarctic Mountains harbour considerable quantities of low-grade coal; substantial iron deposits have been found in the Prince Charles Mountains; and the Pensacola Mountains and Dufek Massif are also thought to have mineral reserves, with the latter possibly having sizeable quantities of platinum, cobalt and nickel, along with deposits of copper and iron. However, it would be impossible to undertake mining operations in Antarctica without causing permanent damage to the continent's fragile environment. Simply constructing the necessary infrastructure and transport systems would have major adverse consequences. If the Treaty nations wanted any reminding of the possible environmental hazards posed by mineral exploitation in Antarctica, they need look no further than the *Exxon Valdez* oil spill in Alaska in 1989, and the sinking of *Bahía Paraíso* near Palmer Station in the same year. Worryingly, oil biodegrades much more slowly in cold climates.

Thankfully, in 1991 the Treaty nations signed the Madrid Protocol, which came into force in 1998, stipulating a ban on all mining activity for at least 50 years, while allowing for scientific research into mineral resources. Who knows if this will prove sufficient to keep Antarctica safe; if the sanctity of North America's Arctic Reserve can be overruled by politicians, there is no reason to think that the same couldn't happen in Antarctica.

As far as living resources are concerned, the sealing industry has proved far easier to reach and implement agreement on than whaling, due to both economic and moral considerations – the fur industry began to experience strong resistance from the general public in the 1960s and '70s. The Convention for the Conservation of Antarctic Seals (CCAS) was agreed in 1972 and has been a triumph of international co-operation in Antarctica, providing complete protection for fur, elephant and Ross seals and establishing quotas for the other species. But it is telling that by the time the CCAS came into force in 1978 the sealing industry – unlike whaling – had long since collapsed, although 2,500 seals were said to have been killed in the 1960s by Russia, mostly for dog food.

In 1982, ten years after the implementation of CCAS, another landmark proposal came into being. The Convention on the Conservation of Antarctic Marine Living Resources (CCAMLR) is truly enlightened, defining its area of interest as everything within the Antarctic Convergence. This ecosystems approach acknowledges the vagaries of nature, and relates each species to its environment, reflecting more clearly the interdependency of all life and taking the position that Antarctica belongs to everyone. It also has the strength of having a permanent secretariat, demonstrating that the Antarctic Treaty can effectively govern affairs here. Even so, the fact that its name refers to 'resources' implies that Antarctica's abundant marine life is viewed as potentially exploitable for commercial purposes, albeit on a sustainable basis. The biggest weakness is that policing is left to the individual countries, and establishing quotas means conducting a proper assessment of resources and their place within the ecosystem – far from easy in the hostile conditions often encountered in this

OPPOSITE

Emperor penguins on fractured sea ice, off Cape Washington, Ross Sea.

part of the world.

With Antarctica custodian to 80 per cent of the world's fresh water, finding a way of harnessing water in icebergs has occupied the minds of scientists and entrepreneurs for many years. So far it has proved a dream, but towing icebergs within reach of countries thirsting for such a valuable resource is tempting and attractive, and has been pondered by desert nations as far afield as Saudi Arabia. However, even taking the rather less distant Australia as an example, the wide continental shelf makes it impossible to tow an iceberg with a draught of 200 m (650 ft) close to shore. The nearest location would be 35 km (22 miles) offshore of Rottnest Island near Perth, too far to be commercially viable – for the moment. But in years to come towing icebergs may prove cheaper than building desalination plants or pipelines from the tropical rainfall areas in northern West Australia, though the development of reverse osmosis methods has also

vastly decreased interest in exploiting icebergs.

And what of the effects of tourism, the other industry flourishing in Antarctica alongside science? There is no question that people need the opportunity to experience the southern continent, to marvel at the spectacle of its wildlife, the starkness and beauty of its landscape and purity of its whiteness – a priceless heritage. For the moment the privilege of visiting Antarctica is available to very few people – 26,245 ship- and land-based passengers visited in the 2005–06 season; as recently as 1992 it was only 6,704, a minuscule number compared with the 400,000 that annually visit the 1,500 sq. km (600 square-mile) Masai Mara Game Reserve in Kenya where we live. Antarctica though is fortunate in having a regulatory body – the International Association of Antarctic Tour Operators (IAATO) – that takes its role very seriously, and there are strict rules and guidelines governing the conduct of all visitors while ashore.

The Swede Lars Lindblad pioneered the concept of adventure tourism in Antarctica in 1969 with the unveiling of the first expeditionary tourist vessel, *Lindblad Explorer*, or 'little red ship', as she became known. Lindblad himself always believed that responsible tourism would have negligible long-term adverse effects here, reminding people that in Australia, which is smaller than Antarctica, you could count the ships in their thousands and the tourists in their millions. But this should not be taken as reason for a lack of caution. In Antarctica tourism is confined to relatively small parts of the continent – mainly the fringes of the Peninsula and its surrounding islands – with visitors arriving in the summer when seals, penguins and other seabirds are breeding, often in vast colonies. Not surprisingly the impact of people wandering around or through colonies has always been a cause for concern, and scientists are still debating

whether or not those are as negligible as some studies maintain. Unfortunately, a small number of tour operators belong to IAATO – it is not mandatory for those wishing to operate in Antarctica – so the potential for abuse is of very real concern.

One undoubted benefit of tourism is that it has helped to focus attention on the question of environmental pollution caused by the scientific bases, where refuse may be both unsightly and hazardous: a few years ago it was common to see rusting fuel drums scattered in the snow and garbage cans overflowing with litter. More recently a concerted effort has been made to resolve this issue with massive clean-up campaigns aimed at shipping out the tonnes of

ABOVE
Neko Harbour, Antarctic Peninsula. A visitor contemplates the honeycomb of pathways carved in the snow by gentoos moving to and fro between their breeding colonies and the sea.

waste products that have accumulated. Most visitors are there specifically because they are passionate about wildlife – and the environment – and are quick to co-operate in this way.

The remoteness of Antarctica is part of the attraction and potentially part of the danger. It is no coincidence that most people travel here by ship. In 1979 an Air New Zealand aeroplane with 257 people on board enjoying a one-day flight over the continent from Auckland crashed into the lower slopes of towering Mount Erebus, Antarctica's only active volcano whose summit is at almost 4,000 m (12,500 ft). In those days planes were flown using visual reference to the outside world rather than on a carefully defined flight path, and the pilots experienced a 'white-out', rendering the mountain invisible. There were no survivors, making this one of the worst peacetime disasters in New Zealand's history and highlighting concerns voiced by Treaty members: Antarctica is a seriously hazardous environment and there was no contingency plan for disasters of this magnitude, requiring search and rescue, evacuation and accommodation. The governments that run the various bases in Antarctica have little appetite for acting as nursemaids for tourists and make a point of reiterating their stance of not taking responsibility for the tourism industry. Not surprisingly talk of building hotels on the continent has been given a chilly reception, despite pledges to burn human waste or return it. But Australia now offers flights over the ice and apparently Argentina, Chile, Uruguay and Russia have all used some of their facilities on the continent as accommodation for 'paying guests'. Once tourists are able routinely to fly in directly and then take a cruise by ship, their numbers are likely to increase markedly.

The inability of the international community to reach agreement on the utilization of global resources such as those symbolized by Antarctica and the Southern Ocean is salutary. The world's poorer nations feel marginalized from the decision-making process in Antarctica and are demanding their voices be heard by the larger industrialized nations that are party to the Treaty. This is evident in the lobbying of the UN by the Group of 77 Third World Nations, led by Malaysia, who wish to establish a New International Economic Order and would like to see the UN, rather than the nations that undertake scientific research here, administer Antarctica. The Group of 77 resent the fact that international affairs are still biased by decisions made prior to their emergence as independent states. There is now a growing lobby from poorer nations for Antarctica to be considered as a 'common heritage of mankind'. This sounds wonderfully inclusive, akin to the ancient practice of allowing all people the use of common land, but could lead to an even greater demand for utilization.

It is imperative that Antarctica doesn't succumb to a greed-fuelled drive to exploit its resources – whatever those might be. In this respect there are lessons to be learned from the UN Law of the Sea Conference of 1967. The host nation, Malta, tabled a proposal to try to protect the ocean floor from being unnecessarily denuded of its wealth with the technologically advanced nations profiting unfairly. The idea of a common heritage of humankind found expression in a speech by Arvid Pardo, Malta's UN representative at the conference, in which he argued that the seabed should be exploited and its wealth distributed equitably for the benefit of humankind– not just for the developed nations who had the resources to get there first.

Pardo's utopian view was thwarted by the enemy of good intentions – greed. The coastal nations at the conference seized on the opportunity to extend their territorial rights to exploit the sea, voting to increase the limit of 12 nautical miles to a 200-nautical-mile Economic Exclusion Zone (EEZ) – a triumph for national self-regard over international interests. While the conference did endorse the concept of an international law of the sea, it lost a dramatic chunk of potential territory in the process.

Lessons from the Heroic Age

The world has changed in the last hundred years – it is a smaller place, a known world of limited resources. But Antarctica offers us the chance of a new beginning embracing all nations and providing for the destiny of our children. To safeguard places like this will need mutually agreed forms of regulation, whereby the exploiters – not the conservationists – have to justify their reasons to the rest of the world and where preservation of the environment is the priority, the starting point rather than just part of a plan.

Culture is embryonic in Antarctica. Among the oldest habitations are the historic huts left by Borchgrevink, Scott and Shackleton (Amundsen's hut was built on the ice and has long since found a grave in the Ross Sea) that along with the graphic images created by expedition photographers Ponting and Hurley – and painters like Edward Wilson – provide a window into the world these men embraced – their pain, their joy and their suffering. Those images somehow manage to capture what we all struggle with words to express – the whiteness, the ice, the stark beauty of Antarctica, the cold the men had to endure, the simple pleasures of smoking a pipe

**Ice cave created by wave
action, Antarctic
Peninsula. Images such
as this remind us of the
vulnerability of the polar
regions – which are
powerful indicators of
the health of our planet,
and the effects of global
warming.**

or hugging a sledge dog.

A visit to the huts is for many a highlight of the journey to the southern continent, a final chapter in their book of memories. Flying in by helicopter you gaze across the black and white landscape, bare rock exposed starkly against the snow and ice, the weather set fair if you are fortunate, the sky blue – Antarctica in summer. Today's visitors have the luxury of feeling safe. But when Shackleton, Scott and Amundsen journeyed here they were entering a world of uncertainty. As Shackleton's advertisement when he was looking for men to accompany him said,

there was no guarantee of returning home. All of us who visit the huts find a quiet moment to reflect on the conditions these men faced, and all of us question how we would have coped with the rigours of a winter that even the emperor penguins find testing. On the day we visit the temperature is –6°C (21°F), with a wind chill of –15°C (27°F) – cold enough to hint at what lay in store for those men as summer days turned wintry.

Scott's *Terra Nova* hut is irresistible theatre, brought to life by the encyclopedic knowledge and quirky Englishness of Bob Headland (former Curator of the Scott Polar Institute in

BELOW

Captain Scott at his desk at the *Terra Nova* hut, Cape Evans. Scott was a meticulous diarist, leaving a powerful testimony to his endeavours, hopes and aspirations. Cherry-Garrard later wrote: 'Scott was the strongest combination of a strong mind in a strong body that I have ever met.'

Cambridge); a magic lantern show of the polar party's lives nearly a hundred years ago, the dark interior illuminated by Bob's deftly wielded torches. A beam of light picks out the details. The neatly stocked kitchen with its rows of cups waiting to be filled with steaming hot tea or cocoa to coax the feeling back into frozen fingers and aching chests. A table covered with the paraphernalia of science – instruments, crucibles and flasks. The hut is sparsely functional – the only thing missing is the laughter and banter of the men themselves, something so richly captured in Ponting's photographs. To them the hut represented far more than just temporary living quarters; it was an extension of Naval tradition and the southernmost outpost of Empire.

There is a sense of orderliness – Scott expected things to be just right, no shoddiness. Everything had its place and so did each member of the party – scientists, officers, able seamen, photographer. A wall of provision boxes partitioned the wardroom where the 16 officers and scientists gathered from the mess deck housing the nine seamen – Navy standards, the way Scott liked it. To help them survive the experience each man would naturally have gravitated towards those with whom he felt the most affinity, due perhaps to a shared interest or position in the social hierarchy of those days. These were after all ordinary men – ordinary men who had been asked to live extraordinary lives in one of the most remote and treacherous places on Earth.

Britain was a very different place a hundred years ago – colder, with a greater degree of privation for many, difficulty in finding employment, a terrible war in the offing. Each of the men in Scott's party had his own reasons for wanting to experience life in Antarctica – ambition, money, status, an escape from a less exciting life, a desire to bring honour and glory to king and country. Once here in Antarctica the

men were welded together by a common purpose; they all needed to perform to the peak of their ability with no room for shirkers or freeloaders. When tensions developed, or already existed, they must have had their own means of exorcising their demons, of letting off steam when tempers frayed. There were always the dogs and the ponies to confide in, while some chose their diaries to express their feelings, soaking up the emotions like blotting paper, taking the sting out of the anger and irritation they must have felt at times.

For Angie and me, standing in Scott's hut at Cape Evans brought our journey full circle. The huts are all that are left here of that era, decaying monuments to our heroes. One of the reasons they have withstood the test of time so well is the cold, dry environment, allied to the fact that not many visitors come here (most of those who visit the Ross Sea make a pilgrimage to the huts, but that is only 2,000 people a year). Even so, time and the weather have taken their toll, and the fabric of the buildings is fragile. Ice is bubbling up under the floor while mould fingers its way over the food. Grit and dirt from visitors' boots abrade the floor, and sea-ice crystals corrode any metal they come into contact with, hence the rigorous cleaning of boots before you enter. Restoration work under the auspices of the New Zealand-based Antarctic Heritage Trust is currently underway on Shackleton's Nimrod hut at Cape Royds; next on the agenda is the Terra Nova hut (where 30 cm (12 in) of water swamped the floor of the hut in 2005 and again in 2006), followed by Carsten Borchgrevink's hut at Cape Adare, the oldest of them all, built in 1899 during the Southern Cross expedition that was the first deliberately to winter on the Antarctic continent. This is a multi-million-dollar project and some question why it should be done at all. For them the huts represent something too abstract, too far removed from the modern world.

Others insist that these fragile dwelling places symbolize the best of humanity, and as Sir David Attenborough said when visiting Scott's hut: 'It would be a scandal if Britain allowed this remarkable place to simply crumble to dust.' This is a sentiment echoed by Sir Edmund Hillary on visiting the huts recently to mark the fiftieth anniversary of New Zealand's Scott Base: 'To find these relics of a heroic age are barely supported by Britain is just a little disappointing.' Knowing Hillary's penchant for understatement, those words could not be more emphatic.

While Captain Scott lay dying in the tent with his two remaining companions, he wrote a letter to his wife Kathleen expressing the wish that she encourage their son Peter to study natural history, saying that 'It is better than games'. Little could he have realized how prophetic his words would be. Peter Scott determined from an early age to make his own way in life and avoid at all costs trading on his father's name as a famous explorer. When he eventually visited Antarctica he was 57 and a man of enormous accomplishment: wildlife artist, Olympic sportsman – excelling as an ice skater, yachtsman and glider pilot – and a conservationist of global significance. He took a typically unsentimental view of life in Antarctica. Of course he was greatly moved by the experience of visiting the Terra Nova hut, sitting for a while at his father's desk, mirroring the image that Ponting had captured of Captain Scott before he set off for the Pole, intent, writing his diary, pipe in hand – a picture that Peter Scott had lived with from childhood. Certainly he gained a measure of satisfaction from absorbing the aura left by the explorers of his father's generation, but more than anything he was concerned about what people were doing in Antarctica now, noting that 'isolation has been a poor defence against

contamination from the world. Adélie penguin eggs have been found with traces of DDT, and plastic rubbish is often washed ashore'.

Peter Scott felt sure that his father would have been delighted that Antarctica had become a place of science, an endeavour to which Scott of the Antarctic had always remained true. He may not have been first to the Pole, but if his memory can help us to preserve Antarctica for science – and science alone – then his tragic ending will have been worthwhile.

• • • ● • • •

Cherry-Garrard summed up the attributes of the explorers whose names live on in Antarctic history: 'For a joint scientific and geographical piece of organisation, give me Scott; for a Winter Journey, Wilson; for a dash to the Pole and nothing else Amundsen; and if I am in the devil of a hole and want to get out of it, give me Shackleton every time...' Each of these men gave his all and we reflect on them as the helicopter speeds us back to the deck of Kapitan Khlebnikov. Almost before we touch down the icebreaker is underway again, anxious to keep on schedule. Thoughts are shared – people seem drained by the experience of visiting the huts – most would have liked more time to sit quietly and absorb the feel of the place, but in today's world time is precious. Soon enough we are lost once again in the all-pervading whiteness of this beguiling and fragile Eden.

RIGHT

Adélie penguin on the pack ice, its natural home. The effects of global warming on the pack ice have caused a dramatic decline in some Adélie populations.

Bibliography

It would have been impossible to write this book without leaning heavily on the work of other authors. The aim has been to give an overview of Antarctica: the explorers, science and travel, to whet the reader's appetite for the wealth of writings by scientists, journalists and explorers on this extraordinary region.

Our most immediate source of information has been the lecture staff on board the various ships with which we have sailed to Antarctica these past 15 years. This unique and learned company of men and women comes equipped with a wealth of knowledge backed up by first-hand experience of the region. They provide both an education and an immensely powerful 'voice' to each and every trip south, capturing the essence of Antarctica through their talks on such varied topics as geology, glaciology, ornithology, mammology and Antarctic history. Visits to the scientific bases also proved highly informative, particularly at Palmer Station, where Dr Bill Fraser shared some of his findings on the effects of climate change on the biology of the Adelie penguin. It was this powerful combination of travel and education that inspired us to complete this book.

For those wishing to know more about penguins two books stand out: *Penguins* by Davis and Renner, and *The Penguins* by Williams; and for general information the Reader's Digest's Antarctica, and the encyclopedia by Mary Trewby both proved outstanding reference works. Cherry-Garrard's *The Worst Journey in the World* is a classic for those wishing to step back in time and immerse themselves in the world of the explorers of the 'heroic age', as is Caroline Alexander's *The Endurance: Shackleton's Legendary Antarctic Expedition*. While *The Falkland Islands* by Ian Strange provides a diverse and detailed account of those windswept islands.

We are only too well aware of the dangers of interpreting and simplifying the work of others, particularly when trying to summarize information gleaned from scientific papers. Accordingly, while we are indebted to the following authors, and particularly Bob Headland who very kindly trawled through the text for factual errors (and helped identify photographic locations), they remain blameless for any inaccuracies in our text, and we apologise for the inevitable simplifications.

Alexander, C. *The Endurance: Shackleton's Legendary Antarctic Expedition*. Alfred A. Knopf: New York 1998

Andrews, J. *Birds and their World*. Hamlyn: London, New York, Sydney & Toronto 1976

Antarctica: The Extraordinary History of Man's Conquest of the Frozen Continent. Reader's Digest: Sydney, London, New York, Montreal & Cape Town 1990

Austin Jr, O. L. *Birds of the World*. Paul Hamlyn: London 1961

Bainbridge, B. *The Birthday Boys*. Duckworth: London 1991

Beeley, F., Colwell, M., & Stevens, J. *Planet Earth: The Future*. BBC Books: London, England 2006

Berrill, J. *Wonders of the Antarctic*. The World's Work (1913): Kingswood, Tadworth, Surrey 1968

Bond, C., & Siegfried, R. *Antarctica: No Single Country, No Single Sea*. New Holland Publishers: London 1990

Bredeson, C. *After the Last Dog Died: The True-life, Hair-raising Adventure of Douglas Mawson and his 1911–1914 Antarctic Expedition*. National Geographic: Washington, DC 2003

Chester, S. R. *Antarctic Birds and Seals*. Wandering Albatross: San Mateo, California 1993

Cook, G. (ed). *The Future of Antarctica: Exploitation versus Preservation*. Manchester University Press: Manchester & New York 1990

Davis, L. S., & Renner, M. *Penguins*. T. & A. D. Poyser: London 2003

De-la-Noy, M. *Scott of the Antarctic*. Sutton: Stroud, Gloucestershire 1997

De Rohan, A. July 2003. 'Dolphins: Ocean Masters', *BBC Wildlife*, Vol. 21 No 7

Discovery: The World's Great Explorers – Their Triumphs and Tragedies. Readers

Digest, Australia: 1978

Diski, J. *Skating to Antarctica*. Granta: London 1997

Estensen, M. *Discovery: The Quest for the Great South Land*. Conway Maritime Press: London 1999

Ehrlich, G. 2006. 'Living on Thin Ice', *National Geographic*, January 2006 – Vol. 209 No. 1

Eliot, T. S. *The Waste Land and other Poems*. Faber & Faber: London 1940

Campbell, D. G. *The Crystal Desert: Summers in Antarctica*. A Mariners Book, Houghton Mifflin: Boston & New York 2002

Carr, T & Carr, P. *Antarctic Oasis: Under the spell of South Georgia*. Norton: New York & London 1998

Chadwick, D. H. 2005. 'Orcas Unmasked', *National Geographic*, April 2006 – Vol. 207 No. 4

Cherry-Garrard, A. *The Worst Journey in the World: Antarctic 1910–13*. Picador: London 1994

Clapham, P. *Humpback Whales*. Colin Baxter Photography: Grantown-on-Spey, Scotland 1996

Couve, E, & Vidal, C. F. *Albatrosses of the Southern Ocean*. Editorial Fantástico Sur: Punta Arenas, Chile 2005

Crane, D. *Scott of the Antarctic: A Life of Courage and Tragedy in the Extreme South*. HarperCollins: London 2005

De Bruin, N., & Tosh, C. 2006. 'Head Hunting in the Southern Ocean', *Africa Geographic*, November 2006 – Vol. 14 No. 10

Dodds, K. *Geopolitics in Antarctica: Views from the Southern Oceanic Rim*. John Wiley: Chichester, New York,

Weinheim, Brisbane, Singapore & Toronto 1997

Fiennes, R. *Captain Scott*. Coronet: London 2004

Fothergill. A. *Life in the Freezer: A Natural History of the Antarctic*. BBC Books: London 1993

Fox, R. *Antarctica and the South Atlantic: Discovery, Development and Dispute*. BBC: London 1985

Grenfell Price, A. (ed). *The Explorations of Captain James Cook in the Pacific – As Told by Selections of His Own Journals 1768–1779*. Dover: New York 1971

Heacock, K. *Shackleton: The Antarctic Challenge*. National Geographic: Washington, DC 1999

Heacock, K. 'Deadly Beauty: A photographer falls under the spell of Antarctica's leopard seals', *National Geographic*, November 2006 – Vol. 210 No. 5

Herbert, W. *A World of Men: Exploration in Antarctica*. Putnam: New York 1969

Holland, J. S. 'Icy Underworld', *National Geographic*, December 2006 – Vol. 210 No. 6

Honnywill, E. *The Challenge of Antarctica*. Anthony Nelson: Oswestry, Shropshire 1984

Hooper, M. *A for Antarctica: Facts and Stories from the frozen South*. Pan: London 1991

Huntford, R. *The Last Place on Earth*. Hodder & Stoughton: London 1979

Huntford, R. *Shackleton*. Hodder & Stoughton: London 1985

Hurley, F., & Laserson, C. F. *Antarctic Eyewitness: Charles F. Laserson's South With Mawson and Frank Hurley's*

Shackleton's Argonauts. Birlinn: Edinburgh 2002

Huxley, E. *Scott of the Antarctic*. Bison: University of Nebraska Press: Lincoln 1977

Imbert, B. *North Pole, South Pole: Journeys to the Ends of the Earth*. New Horizons: London 1992

Johnson, D. *New Zealand's Maritime Heritage*. William Collins: Auckland 1987

Lambert, K. 'Hell With A Capital H': An Epic Story of Antarctic Survival. Pimlico: London 2002

Laws, R. M. *Antarctica: The Last Frontier*. Boxtree: London 1989

Limb, S., & Cordingley, P. *Captain Oates: Soldier and Explorer*. Leo Cooper: London 1995

Love, J. A. *Penguins*. Whittet: London 1994

Love, J. A. *Penguins*. Colin Baxter Photography: Grantown-on-Spey, Scotland 1997

Mason, M., Greenhill, B., & Craig, R. *The British Seafarer*. Hutchinson: London 1980

Matthiessen, P. *End of the Earth: Voyages to Antarctica*. National Geographic: Washington, DC 2003

May, J. *The Greenpeace Book of Antarctica*. Dorling Kindersley: London 1988

McGonigal, D., & Woodworth, L. *Antarctica: The Blue Continent*. Frances Lincoln: London 2003

Messner, R. *Antarctica: Both Heaven and Hell*. The Mountaineers: Seattle 1991

Morrell, M., & Capparell, S. *Shackleton's Way: Leadership Lessons from The Great Antarctic Explorer*. Nicholas Brealey:

London 2001

Moss, S. *Natural History of the Antarctic Peninsula*. Columbia University Press: New York 1988

Murphy, G. *Christ Church Cathedral, the Falkland Islands: Its life and times 1892 to 1992.*

Naveen, R. *Waiting to Fly: My Escapades with the Penguins of Antarctica*. Quill: New York 1999

Naveen, R., Monteath, C., de Roy, T., & Jones, M. *Wild Ice: Antarctic Journeys*. Smithsonian Institution Press: Washington & London 1990

Peat, N. *Subantarctic New Zealand: A Rare Heritage*. Department of Conservation (Southland Conservancy, New Zealand): Invercargill 2003

Piggott, J (ed.). *Shackleton: The Antarctic and Endurance*. Dulwich College: London 2000

Pinnock, D. *Blue Ice: Travels in Antarctica*. Double Story Books: Cape Town 2005

Preston, D. *A First Rate Tragedy: Captain Scott's Antarctic Expeditions*. Constable: London 1997

Pyne, S. J. *The Ice: A Journey to Antarctica*. University of Iowa Press: Iowa City 1988

Ralling, C. *Shackleton*. BBC: London 1983

Rothenberg, D. March 2004. 'The Nature of Song', *BBC Wildlife*, Vol. 22 No. 3

Rubin, J. *Antarctica: A Lonely Planet Travel Survival Kit*. Lonely Planet: Hawthorn, Australia 1996

Sale, R. *To The Ends of the Earth: The History of Polar Exploration*. HarperCollins: London 2002

Scott, P. *Travel Diaries of a Naturalist*, Vol. 1. William Collins: London 1983

Seaver, G. *'Birdie' Bowers of the Antarctic*. John Murray: London 1938

Seaver, G. *Edward Wilson of the Antarctic: Naturalist and Friend*. John Murray: London 1933

Schillat, M. *First Antarctic Reader*. Editorial Fuegia: Ushuaia, Argentina 2001

Simpson-Housley, P. *Antarctica: Exploration, Perception and Metaphor*. Routledge: London, USA & Canada 1992

Smith, M. *I Am Just Going Outside: Captain Oates – Antarctic Tragedy*. Spellmount: Stroud, Gloucestershire 2006

Snyder, J., & Shackleton, K. *Ship in the Wilderness: Voyages of the MS "Lindblad Explorer" through the last wild places on Earth*. Dent: London & Melbourne 1986

Soper, T. *Antarctica: A Guide to the Wildlife*. Bradt: Chalfont, Buckinghamshire 1994

Spufford, F. *I May Be Some Time: Ice and the English Imagination*. Faber & Faber: London & Boston 1996

Strange, I. J. *The Falkland Islands*. David & Charles: Newton Abbot, London & North Pomfret (Vermont) 1972

Strange, F. I. *Albatross Alley*. Natural History (published by the American Museum of Natural History) July 1989

Suter, K. *Antarctica: Private Property or Public Heritage?* Zed Books: London & Atlantic Highlands, New Jersey 1991

Thomas, D. N. *Frozen Oceans: The Floating World of Pack Ice*. Natural History Museum: London 2004

Trewby, M. *Antarctica: An Encyclopedia from Abbott Ice Shelf to Zooplankton*. Firefly Books: Toronto & Ontario in Canada, Buffalo & New York in the US 2002

Vickers-Rich, P, & Hewitt-Rich, T. 'Dinosaurs of the Antarctica', *Scientific American*, Vol. 14 No. 2 2004

War on Whales. 'November 2003 News', *BBC Wildlife*, Vol. 21, No. 11

Wheeler, S. *Terra Incognita: Travels in Antarctica*. Jonathan Cape: London 1996

Wheeler, S. *Antarctica, the Falklands and South Georgia*. Cadogan: London 1997

Wheeler, S. *Cherry: A Life of Apsley Cherry-Garrard*. Modern Library: New York, 2003

Williams, H. *Whale Nation*. Jonathan Cape: London 1988

Williams, T. D. *The Penguins: Spheniscidae*. Oxford University Press: Oxford, New York & Tokyo 1995

Wilson, E. (ed. Roberts, B.). *Birds of the Antarctic*. New Orchard Editions: Poole, Dorset 1978

Wong, K. 'The Mammals That Conquered the Seas', *Scientific American*. Vol. 14 No. 2 2004

Worsley, F. A. *Shackleton's Boat Journey*. Norton: New York & London 1998

Acknowledgements

We have received such generous support from so many individuals and companies that it is possible to mention only a few of them here.

In the first instance Geoff and Jorie Kent of Abercrombie and Kent (AK) made it possible for us to travel to Antarctica on board MS Explorer – the 'little red ship' made famous in the 1970s by Lars Lindblad and his pioneering travel company Lindblad Travel. Alistair Ballantine, the President of AK at the time we travelled on Explorer in the 1990s, was unfailingly generous and supportive in facilitating our journeys to Antarctica, even organizing for our son David to join us on trips to South Georgia and the Peninsula – journeys he will remember for a lifetime. David Webber in his capacity as Financial Controller at AK was also extremely helpful. We all realized that we were sharing very special times on board Explorer and we were indeed fortunate to be able to spend time in the company of some exceptional individuals – the expedition staff. Words fail us when we attempt to describe just how outstanding our expedition leaders on those trips were: Matt Drennan, Michael Messick, Kim Crosbie and Kim Robertson.

The expedition leaders were ably assisted by their staff and team of lecturers: Marsha Green, Hans Iluk, Dennis Gillet, Megan McOsker, Helen Frichot, Jerry Webers, Lou Sanson, Larry Hobs, Sharon Chester, Anne Rowe, Victoria Underwood, Kristy Royce, Tony Chater, Brent Houston, Ashton Palmer, John Splettstoesser, Charley Wheatley, Ralph Eshelman, Dale Carolin, Dr Martin Albert, Henry Pollack, Kevin Clement, Moritz Odermatt, Alesandro Bonfanti, Rogerio Guillerimo, Gary Colt, Lorenz Ruppen, John Hammond, Alistair Burnett, Tim Baughman, Trip Dennis, Dr Bernhard Goodhead, Steve Emslie, Sir Wally Herbert, Marie Herbert, Geoff Renner, Dr Brooks Martin, Geraldine Massan, Robert Ulrich, Dr Carlos Camargo, Bill Romey, Doris Martin, Dr Cathy Grellet, Charles Swithinbank, Commander Angus Erskine, Dr Kelli Lewis, Brent Stewart, Peter Graham, Ingrid Nixon, Bob Burton, Robert Hoffman, Barbara Jones, Chris Cutler, Dr Peter Knoll, Peter Harrison, Michael Messick, Arnold Small, Richard Webster, Alison Burke, Therese Kapaun, Wolfgang Kaehler, Rod Allen. Our captains Uli Demel, Leif Scog and Peter Skog, their officers and all the ship's staff made sailing the Southern Ocean both exciting, a culinary feast of epic proportions and the greatest of pleasures. AK retired the 'little red ship' in 2003 after 33 years at sea, but to our delight there she was on our most recent visit, docked at Ushuaia waiting to board passengers under new owners.

In more recent times Paul Goldstein of Kicheche Mara Camp and Exodus Travels (First Choice group of companies) has made it possible for us to travel to Antarctica aboard Peregrine Travel's sister ships *Akademik Sergey Vavilov/Peregrine Voyager* and *Akademik Sergey Ioffe/Peregrine Voyager*. Paul is an irrepressible adventurer and has been a great supporter of our work over the years, and Andrew Prossin, manager of polar programs at Peregrine Travel was also extremely helpful in facilitating our visits to Antarctica. The expedition leader on all but one of these trips – on which occasion it was the excellent Dutch Wilmott – was David McGonigal, travel writer, photographer and co-author with Lynn Woodworth of the immense work *Antarctica: The Blue Continent*. David proved to be another exceptional expedition leader and was generous in helping us to maximize the photographic opportunities at landings. Both ships boast a fine array of staff and lecturers, all of whom helped to make these journeys a richly rewarding experience for travellers: Annie Inglis, Lynn Woodworth, Dr Colin Lee, Tanja Plasil, Kara Tring, Geoff Carpentier, Graham Charles, John Tully, Matthew Depko, Scott MacPhail, David 'Woody' Wood, Alistair Gunn, Kara Tring, Beth Anne Masselink, Martin Gray, Jacques

Sirois, Ray McMahon, Jack Sayers, Carolina Mantella, Shrek Johnson, Cameron Webb, John Rodsted, Phil Rouget and Sean Stephen.

Our most recent trip to Antarctica exceeded all expectations. Visits to the Peninsula have always been magical experiences, but our journey through the pack ice to the Ross Sea and beyond was simply surreal – another world that we feel incredibly privileged to have enjoyed. Our thanks for this start with Chris Breen and his assistant Isabel Gaitskell at Wildlife Worldwide, with whom we now offer Signature Trips to our favourite destinations worldwide. Helen Brocklehurst, our Editor at HarperCollins, wisely reminded us that it would be impossible to tell this story without our visiting the historic huts at Cape Evans and going in search of emperor penguins. Chris contacted Quark Expeditions in the knowledge that they were the operator of choice for a trip such as this on board their icebreaker *Kapitan Khlebnikov*. The results of that journey are included in this book, and we want to thank everyone at Quark for their help in making it possible, particularly Lars and Erica Wikander, owners of Quark, who exact the highest standards from their operation – it is no coincidence that Lars was part of Lindblad Travel in the early days of the 'little red ship'. Francesco Contini, VP Marketing and Groups for Quark, could not have been more helpful in making this trip a reality for us. On board, expedition leader Shane Evoy headed a very professional team of staff and lecturers: Jaye Martin and John Palmer, Robert Headland (an encyclopedic source of information on all things Antarctic), Rod and Jeannie Ledingham, Norman Lasca, Delphine Aures, Tony Dorr, Heather and Stuart Thorne, David McEown and Daisy Gilardini.

Closer to home Frank and Dolcie Howitt continue to be the best of neighbours, and are an inspiration to all of us living in Nairobi.

Both Angie and I have family living overseas who have been an unfailing source of help and encouragement: Jonathan's sister Caroline, his brother Clive and his wife Judith, and Angie's mother Joy, brother David and his wife Mishi. Our children Alia and David and his wife Tara have been incredibly generous with their time and support in helping us with our work, as has Alia by looking after our house in Nairobi during our many absences.

During our visits to England many people have nurtured us: Brian and Annabelle Jackman, Peter and Jennie Hughes – and for many years Pippa and Iain Hunter, and Pam Savage and Mike Skinner generously made their homes in London available to us during the time they lived there. Cissy and David Walker continue to provide us with the same generous support at their home in London that they have offered to us on so many occasions in the past. In Bristol, Robin and Elin Hellier, Keith and Liz Scholey, and Andy Chastney and Mandy Knight, have all been wonderfully hospitable over the years, as have Dr Michael and Sue Budden in Buckinghamshire, and Charles and Lindsay Dewhurst in West Sussex. Paul and Donna Goldstein not only helped to keep Antarctica alive for us, but provided us with a roof over our heads at a moment's notice and cooked fine food as well – what would we do without friends like these?

Neil and Joyce Silverman have been great friends to our family over many years and we have enjoyed safaris together in Africa and Antarctica. Whenever we have visited them in America Neil and Joyce have made their home our home, as well as sharing their wonderful collection of Antarctic books, diaries and memorabilia with us. This book is dedicated to them.

Carole Wyman is one of Angie's closest friends and has been unbelievably generous to all our family – and is godmother to our son David. One of these days we are determined to persuade Carole and her husband Kama to journey to Antarctica with us, or even the Masai Mara so they can see for themselves the cause of our addiction.

Brian Hall of Experience Seminars (UK) has been the most helpful of friends in ferrying our camera gear to and from Canon (UK) Camera Division. We would also like to thank Robin Rata, David Brockett and David Miller at York Cameras, the Canon Camera Specialists in Bury Street, Holborn, and David Leung, the Canon Camera Specialist in Ilford – all of whom have helped us to stay equipped wherever we are photographing in the world. Kishor

Dhayatker and everyone at CPS and the Canon Service Unit at Centennial Park in Elstree, and Robert Scott of EOS *Magazine* have all provided us with a highly professional service.

Kenya Airways have been incredibly helpful whenever we have travelled with them, and operate a first-class international service. They have been generous in sponsoring us during fund-raising events at the Royal Geographical Society in London and Hong Kong for the conservation and humanitarian projects we support, and in helping us transport our camera gear all over the world. Thank you to all Kenya Airways staff and in particular to David Granville, Hazel Smith, Sally Peters and Lea Valaris in the UK; and to Hugh Fraser, Catherine Mwangi and Peter Woodrow in Kenya.

John Brinkley and Christine Percy at Swarovski UK Ltd generously provided us with binoculars of unrivalled quality for our work both in Antarctica and Africa.

Pankaj Patel of Fuji Kenya kept us well stocked with slide film prior to our converting to digital, and our old friends at Spectrum Colour Lab (Nairobi), Mehmood and Shaun Quraishy, always did a first-class job of processing our films.

Nigel Pavitt, a loyal friend and fellow photographer living here in Nairobi, has been a wonderful support to Angie during the testing transition to digital – and particularly with learning the intricacies of working up digital files into high-quality images. Nigel has

been incredibly generous with his time and patience in helping us to get the digital pictures for this book ready for publication.

Caroline Taggart has edited all but one of our books over the past 25 years, and has once again transformed 80,000 scruffy and disorderly words into a text that is barely recognizable from the original draft. Caroline has lived through years of Africa's big cats and the wildebeest migration to finally help our Antarctic work see the light of day, all with the utmost professionalism and sensitivity. Caroline, we salute you once again for transforming our dreams into reality. The same could be said of our commissioning editor at HarperCollins, Helen Brocklehurst, who has to be the most patient and understanding editor we could ever hope for; working with professionals of this calibre makes the whole process of undertaking projects such as this so worthwhile. Thank you, Helen, for your trust and loyalty through many a long day – or was it years?

Also at HarperCollins our thanks go to Liz Woabank for her excellent help with picture research, Julia Koppitz for guidance in the latter stages of production, Emma Jern for her stunning jacket design, Mark Thomson for inspirational art direction and Nikki Sims for her punctilious proofreading. Once again, designer Liz Sephton translated it all into the book we had hoped for, and Keeley Everitt oversaw the repro and printing stage of the book with extreme skill and reliable attention to detail.

Our literary agent at Curtis Brown, Jonny Pegg, and his assistant Shaheeda Sabir have acted for us with great dexterity and effectiveness, and have let us use their offices whenever we have been in London, as well as acting as a poste restante for correspondence. It is greatly appreciated.

Our photographic images are held by three agencies: Getty, NHPA and ImageState, where Ross Walker and Peter Bennet, Tim Harris and Lee Dalton, and Diana Leppard respectively have been incredibly helpful and generous with their time and in providing us with access to our images for projects such as this at a moment's notice. Richard Newstead at Getty provided invaluable advice on all things digital in preparing the images.

Our heartfelt thanks to you all.

Index